1970

This book may be kept

THE GAYETY OF VISION

Books by Robert Langbaum

THE POETRY OF EXPERIENCE

THE GAYETY OF VISION

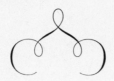

THE GAYETY OF VISION

A Study of Isak Dinesen's Art

ROBERT LANGBAUM

RANDOM HOUSE · NEW YORK

To My Parents

"Freud . . . will, I make no doubt at all, be honoured as the path-finder towards a humanism of the future, which we dimly divine and which will have experienced much that the earlier humanism knew not of. It will be a humanism standing in a different relation to the powers of the lower world, the unconscious, the id: a relation bolder, freer, blither, productive of a riper art than any possible in our neurotic, fear-ridden, hate-ridden world."

(Thomas Mann, " Freud and the Future ")

ACKNOWLEDGMENTS

In the making of this book I have incurred many happy debts. For permission to quote from the works of Isak Dinesen, I am indebted in the United States to Random House, and in Britain to Putnam (for *Seven Gothic Tales, Out of Africa, Winter's Tales, Last Tales and Ehrengard*) and Michael Joseph (for *Anecdotes of Destiny* and *Shadows on the Grass*). Thanks to the following: Alfred Knopf for permission to quote from Thomas Mann's *Essays of Three Decades*, translated by H. T. Lowe-Porter; Merle Armitage for permission to quote from Don Gifford's translation of Kleist's "The Marionette Theatre", in Armitage's edition of *Five Essays on Klee*, published by Duell, Sloane and Pearce; Princeton University Press for permission to quote from Kierkegaard's *Either/Or*, Vol. I, translated by David F. and Lillian Marvin Swenson, and *Fear and Trembling*, translated by Walter Lowrie; Hill and Wang for permission to quote from *Tales of Hoffmann*, edited by Christopher Lazare. Thanks also to Robert Haas for permission to quote from his correspondence with Isak Dinesen; and to the Rungstedlund Foundation for permission to quote from Isak Dinesen's unpublished documents.

Part of Chapter 4 appeared in Danish translation in *Karen Blixen*, the memorial anthology published by Gyldendal, and in English in *The Virginia Quarterly Review*. Part of Chapter 7 appeared in *The American Scholar*. Thanks to the editors for permission to reprint these sections.

I am grateful for much generous financial support. While I taught at Cornell University, the Faculty Research Grants Committee helped with incidental expenses, and the English Department Grant-in-Aid Fund made possible my first trip to Denmark in the summer of 1959. A Grant-in-Aid from the American Council of Learned Societies made possible my second trip to Denmark in the summer of 1961. The main support came from the Center for Advanced Study in the Behavioral Sciences, Stanford, California, where during 1961-62 this book was mainly

written amid the ideal working conditions provided by Ralph
W. Tyler and his staff. The University of Virginia Research
Committee has, since my return from the Center, taken care of
incidental expenses.

Not the least of the advantages of the Center was the learned
company of the other Fellows. I shall never forget conversations
about literature with Reuben Brower and about the anthropology
of Africa with Victor Turner. Franklin Ford answered questions
about European history; Kenneth Colby about psychoanalysis;
Marija Gimbutas, Rodney Needham and McKim Marriott about
their areas of anthropological study. Friends elsewhere who
helped are John B. Cobb, Jr., who answered questions about theology, Stanford Drew, who answered questions about history,
Walter Heilbronner and Christopher Middleton, who answered
questions about German literature, Robert Kellogg, who answered questions about Icelandic literature, my uncle Marco
Treves, who answered questions about the divine law of proportion. Stanley Loomis and Robert Scholes read the book in
typescript and offered valuable suggestions. I received much help
from the staffs of the Royal Library of Copenhagen and the
University of Virginia's Alderman Library, especially from Helen
a Koiner of Alderman.

Finally, my very special thanks to Jørn Christiansen, who did
most of the Danish translation; to Clara Svendsen, Isak Dinesen's
secretary, who answered questions, looked up information and
sent me material with an assiduity I can never repay; and to my
wife, Francesca, who acted all along as my research assistant and
best critic. My little girl, Donata Emily, put up with much travelling but had her recompense when, at the age of three, she
took tea at Tivoli with Isak Dinesen.

R.L.

Charlottesville, Virginia, April 1964.

CONTENTS

THE GAYETY OF VISION

Chapter 1

THE OLD ORDER AND THE NEW

I AM writing about Karen Blixen, whom English-speaking readers know as Isak Dinesen, because I want to express my admiration for her work and make connection with her other admirers. I want to find the reasons why we like her—for one admires before one knows why—and to suggest that Isak Dinesen is an important writer, that her work is literature. It belongs miraculously to English as well as Danish literature, for with only a few exceptions she wrote in English first and translated into Danish afterwards. Since I naturally hope to win her a few new admirers as well, I have given fairly complete accounts of her works so that readers not acquainted with her can follow my argument.

I have done this also as a way of demonstrating the high quality of her stories by explaining them. For there is a suspicion, even among her admirers, that her stories are brilliant mystifications and nothing more. I have heard and read certain of her admirers who praise *Out of Africa* and then either admit that they don't make much of the stories, or else praise the stories for the wrong reasons—because they recapture the magic of fairy tales and the old oral narratives and thus take us on an enthralling flight away from the sordid realities of the modern world. It is true of course that Isak Dinesen has restored a magical quality to fiction, and this is no small part of her achievement. But this makes her, if it is all that can be said, a master of *pastiche* and of sensational effects, a fine entertainer certainly, but not a writer worthy of serious critical attention. The point is that the quality we recognize as magical is a quality of literary intelligence; it is the quality of all great imaginative thought that lights up from within and brings to life the things it talks about.

My purpose in describing the stories will be to show their coherence and their relevance to modern life. My purpose will be further to show the coherence of Isak Dinesen's entire work, her imaginative vision. My judgment of her rests on the assumption that such coherence is a good thing in a writer. My judgment of

Isak Dinesen rests on another assumption as well—that a good writer thoroughly understands the literary tradition in which he works and takes in his writing the inevitable next step required by that tradition. Isak Dinesen's coherence derives from her fidelity to the romantic idea; and it is because she shows herself in her work such an excellent critic of the romantic tradition, because she sums it up and carries it a step forward, that she is in the main stream of modern literature.

That she is in the main stream of literature generally will, I hope, appear through the comparisons I shall make of her with certain writers whose greatness is acknowledged. The immediate purpose of these comparisons will be to clarify a point in her work by showing how some other writer said the same sort of thing. But the long-range purpose will be to let the reader test for himself the adequacy of her vision against that of the admittedly great writer. The point will be not to rank her with the great writer—it is too early to decide how important a writer she is—but simply to suggest that she is important, that her work will be with us for a while. Where the writer in question is a modern writer, it will be apparent enough that she is dealing with the same distinctively modern themes that he is.

Implicitly, the book is directed to still another question—that of fiction today. At a time when so many people are saying that the novel, and especially the psychological novel, is played out, it seems worth while to examine a writer who works in direct and self-conscious opposition to the novel and yet gives us the modern subject-matter, the characteristically modern historical and psychological view of the world which we had supposed to be the special province of the novel. I am not in the least recommending that young writers imitate Isak Dinesen; I don't think she can be imitated. But her work does remind us that the novel is only one form of fiction and that certain of the other forms may dramatize better than the novel a psychology even deeper than that which the novel has made its province.

Her stories show us how psychology may be dealt with in terms that are purely literary. They show us the point at which psychology makes contact with literature, and they thus make us realize that the old literary forms—tragedy, comedy, romance, pastoral —are names for clusters of concepts that we would nowadays call psychological insights. By revivifying the old forms as cultural externalizations of psychic life, Isak Dinesen is able to talk at once about psychology and culture; she is able to be psychological without being analytic and reductive. For the old forms carry assertions of value; while psychological analysis has, in the modern novel, separated our internal from our external life in order to discredit the external life. Psychological analysis has thus tended to dissolve the outlines of character and dissipate the magic or glory of the life dealt with. Isak Dinesen's method is a way of reconciling the knowledge of life with the praise of it.

Although Isak Dinesen scored her first success in the United States, she only began to receive critical attention here in the last few years.[1] She used to complain that the Americans liked her better than her own countrymen did, but the truth is that if the Danes discovered her a year later than we did and had more reservations about her, they also took her from the beginning far more seriously than we did. In Denmark, there have been those who liked her work and those who didn't; and those who didn't took the trouble to say so in print. Articles for and against her began to appear soon after the Danish edition of *Seven Gothic Tales* came out in 1935; and by 1949 one of Denmark's leading critics, Professor Hans Brix, had in a big book on her work hailed her in effect as Denmark's most important living writer.[2] In this country, instead, there have been only those who liked her work and those who were indifferent to it.

Isak Dinesen did not even offer her first book, *Seven Gothic Tales*, to a Danish publisher, so sure was she of a refusal at a time when the Danish literary scene was given over to sociological realism. After an English publisher—Constant Huntington of Putnam whom she met in England at Lady Islington's — declined to look at the book, she sent it to a friend of the family, the American novelist Dorothy Canfield, who passed it on to her friend, Robert Haas. *Seven Gothic Tales* was published here in 1934 by the firm of Robert Haas and Harrison Smith, which later merged with Random House. When the book came out in America, Putman liked it and bought the British rights from Haas. *Seven Gothic Tales* was well reviewed here, was a Book-of-the-Month Club selection and a best-seller, and the same is

---

[1] In 1961, there appeared the first book-length study of her in English, Eric O. Johannesson's *The World of Isak Dinesen* (Seattle: University of Washington Press).

[2] *Karen Blixens Eventyr* (*Karen Blixen's Tales*) (Copenhagen: Gyldendal).

true of Isak Dinesen's next two books—*Out of Africa* (1937) and *Winter's Tales* (1942). Yet there was nothing to distinguish these books from all the other well-reviewed best-sellers that disappear into the night—except the fact that after the first flurry was over the books were somehow still there, still being read, and still being recommended and talked about at least privately.

She received her first important public recognition in the English-speaking world from Ernest Hemingway, who when he won the Nobel Prize in 1954 said he would have liked to see the prize go "to that beautiful writer, Isak Dinesen".[1] I remember how pleasantly surprised I was by Hemingway's praise. I was surprised because I was not used to seeing her rated so high in public, and because I would not myself have connected so aristocratic and civilized, so even over-civilized a writer as Isak Dinesen with a primitivist like Hemingway. But then I realized that *Out of Africa*, Isak Dinesen's memoir of her African years, is pastoral and aristocratic in a manner very like Hemingway's, that both writers appreciate and connect primitive and aristocratic virtues.

Take as an example the passage from *Out of Africa* in which Isak Dinesen and the Englishman she loved, Denys Finch-Hatton, return on a motor trip to a place where Denys on the way out had shot a lioness who was feeding on a dead giraffe. Now they find on the giraffe the lioness's mate who, darkly magnificent against the flaming sky of sunrise, looks like a lion in heraldry. Denys hands her his rifle. Her shot she calls "a declaration of love", and the scene of carnage—the two lions dead on the dead giraffe whose belly they had torn open—reminds her of "the fifth act of a classic tragedy". After Denys and his boy had skinned the lions,

we had a bottle of claret, and raisins and almonds, from the car; I had brought them with us to eat on the road, because it was New Year's Day. We sat on the short grass and ate and drank. The dead lions, close by, looked magnificent in their nakedness, there was not a particle of superfluous fat on them, each muscle was a bold controlled curve, they needed no cloak, they were, all through, what they ought to be.[2]

[1] In an interview, *New York Times Book Review*, November 7, 1954, p. 1.
[2] New York: Modern Library, 1952, pp. 230-31; London: Putnam, 1937, p. 247.

Those last words sound like Hemingway and sum up an aristocratic ideal shared by both writers. The difference is that Hemingway would consider the passage spoiled by the cultured references to medieval heraldry and classical tragedy. For he is interested in a natural aristocracy which exists outside culture and in spite of culture. Hemingway, in his African stories, sees in Africa a state of nature we have lost. But Isak Dinesen, who has a sharper sense of the past than Hemingway, sees in Africa also a kind of civilization we have lost. She links the natural aristocracy with the official aristocracy of European tradition. Both see the aristocrat as out of place in modern life; Hemingway, because modern life is cut off from nature. But Isak Dinesen sees modern life as cut off from a traditional civilization that had its roots in nature. "Perhaps the white men of the past, indeed of any past," she says in *Out of Africa*, "would have been in better understanding and sympathy with the coloured races than we, of our Industrial Age, shall ever be. When the first steam engine was constructed, the roads of the races of the world parted, and we have never found one another since."[1] Her sympathy for the past makes her at once more civilized and more primitive than Hemingway.

The sense in which this is possible is beautifully explained in "Copenhagen Season" (*Last Tales*), where an old artist holds forth wittily on the abundance of large noses he sees around him at an aristocratic reception. He is being complimentary, for

the five senses—and among them the sense of smell surely holds a high rank—make up the *savoir vivre* of wild animals and primitive people. When, in the course of progress, these innocents are blessed with a bit of security and comfort, and with a bit of education, nosing out things becomes an extravagant undertaking, noses will deteriorate and grow blunt, and with them good manners. Our domestic animals, which are used in the progress of civilization and so are procured for and somewhat educated, have lost the keenness of their senses, and our pigsties and duck yards display but little manners. The middle classes of our civilization have obtained security and a bit of education— and where, my dears, are now their noses? With them the word of smell, even, has become an unseemly word. It is only when one gets up to your own lofty social level that one will again meet with keenness of the senses as with *savoir vivre*. For what is the end of all higher education? Regained naïveté.

He goes on to associate large noses with the capacity for tragedy.

[1] New York, pp. 215-16; London, pp. 230-31.

5

They will pass together into extinction; for as the senses shrivel, so does the emotional and spiritual life. Tragedy combines what is highest in man with what is most primitive.

Isak Dinesen began writing her tales in Africa; and though none of them is really set there, one understands after reading *Out of Africa* that they derive their special quality from the violent contrast in her life of Europe and Africa. The love of Nordics for the South, she says, is like the love of men for women—the love of one's opposite. Africa gave her the chance to achieve that enormous expansion of sympathy, that ability to love and reconcile opposites,[1] which makes her work remarkable.

It is because her sympathy is so thorough that she does not use Africa as simply an escape from civilization to nature. Her very immersion in the high culture of Europe enables her to learn from Africa the essential style of all civilizations. She never lets you forget Africa's sad tie to civilization through slavery. Her description of Somali women makes you realize how miraculously civilization transforms females into mannered and mysterious works of art.[2] She speaks of Masai warriors as having "that particular form of intelligence which we call *chic*;—daring and wildly fantastical as they seem, they are still unswervingly true to their own nature, and to an immanent ideal. Their style is not an assumed manner, nor an imitation of a foreign perfection; it has grown from the inside, and is an expression of the race and its history, and their weapons and finery are as much part of their being as are a stag's antlers."[3]

Compare this to her description in "The Roads Round Pisa" (*Seven Gothic Tales*) of the epicene old Prince Potenziani, who in the Italy of 1823 maintains the daring and fantastic style of the *ancien régime*. He is seen through the eyes of a young Danish nobleman, Count Augustus von Schimmelmann, who in the manner of the new romantic generation of the North worries about truth and sincerity.

The one who attracted Augustus's attention, as he would always attract the attention of anybody near him, was a man of about fifty, very tall and broad, and enormously fat. He was dressed very elegantly in black, his white linen shining, and wore some heavy rings and in his

---

[1] New York, p. 17; London, pp. 17-19.
[2] Part III, Chap. 3.
[3] New York, p. 135; London, p. 145.

large stock a brilliantly sparkling diamond. His hair was dyed jet black, and his face was painted and powdered. In spite of his fatness and his stays, he moved with a peculiar grace, as if he had in him a rhythm of his own. Altogether, Augustus thought, if one could get quite away from the conventional idea of how a human being ought to look, he would be a very handsome object and a fine ornament in any place, and would have made, for instance, a most powerful and impressive idol. It was he who spoke, in a high and piercing, and at the same time strangely pleasing, voice.

Prince Potenziani tells a tale by way of which he accuses his friend, the handsome young Prince Giovanni, of treachery. A man of style himself, Prince Nino, as he is sometimes called, remarks that the tale lacks an end, and to make an end of it tosses a glass of wine into the old man's face. The way in which Prince Potenziani masters the situation shows Augustus the potency (the word is imbedded in the impotent old Prince's name)[1] of style.

Augustus now saw who he was really like: he had the soft fullness, and the great power behind it, of the ancient statues of Bacchus. The atmosphere of the room became resplendent with his rays, as if the old god had suddenly revealed himself, vine-crowned, to mortals. He took up a handkerchief and carefully dabbed his mouth with it, then, looking at it, he spoke in a low and sweet voice, such as a god would use in speaking to human beings, aware that his natural strength is too much for them.

"It is a tradition of your family, Nino, I know," he said, "this exquisite *savoir-mourir*." He sipped a little of his lemonade to take away the taste of the wine which had touched his mouth. "What an excellent critic you are," he went on, "not only of your own Tuscan songs, but of modern prose as well. That exactly was the fault of my story: that it had no end. A charming thing, an end. Will you come tomorrow at sunrise to the terrace at the back of this house? I know the place; it is a very good spot."

Prince Potenziani is godlike because he has at his command the absolute wisdom of an ancient civilization—manner, style, form being the language in which such wisdom manifests itself to mortals.

This little scene takes us a long way into Isak Dinesen's special quality. But then "The Roads Round Pisa" is, in its surface and its depth, an extreme instance of that quality. The surface is

[1] Isak Dinesen originally called him Pozentiani, but quite properly changed the name to Potenziani for the British and Danish editions.

mannered to the point of seeming pseudo-aristocratic, pseudo-heroic, operatic; and it is this surface which first attracts those who like Isak Dinesen and which no doubt first repels those who do not. Isak Dinesen's real admirers take to the manner as thirsty men take to water. For the manner gives us all the things of which modern fiction deprives us, while talking about the things modern fiction talks about. The manner is relevant to modern life as an instrument of defiance; it snaps its fingers at modern dreariness and timidity. That is why we want the manner so exaggerated, and why Isak Dinesen's most extravagant volume, *Seven Gothic Tales*, remains her best. That is also why her admirers are, I observe, admirers of the modern literary movement.

But where, the reader may well ask, is the modern subject-matter to be found in a story about Italian princes fighting duels in 1823? This brings us to the substance of "The Roads Round Pisa", which announces its theme as modern in the opening scene, where we find Count Augustus von Schimmel-mann strolling down a highroad near Pisa worrying about the relativity of truth and personal identity. His habit as a student of looking at himself in mirrors was not, he reflects, due to vanity. "I looked into the glasses to see what I was like. A glass tells you the truth about yourself."

We see the sexual consequences of Augustus's plight when we learn that he has come to Italy to escape an unsuccessful marriage. His wife is jealous, not of another woman for she knows he does not care much about women. She is jealous because she does not possess *him* and he does not really see or care for *her*. She wants a genuine touching of identities, and there is just a hint that on his side at least there may be no fixed sexual identity to touch, when the theme of sexual ambiguity is brought to the fore by what happens next.

A coach pulled by runaway horses comes rushing down the road, is upset, and a bald old gentleman is thrown out. When the gentleman recovers his bonnet and fixes it on his bald head, the bonnet has fastened inside it an abundance of silvery curls and the gentleman turns into a fine old lady, the Countess Carlotta de Gampocorta. The lady is put to bed in Augustus's inn, and tells him her story in that celestial style of old-regime wit that distin-guishes Isak Dinesen's work. Carlotta wants Augustus to bring to her bedside her step-granddaughter, Rosina. Carlotta, who never had it in her really to care for any male, had a terror of childbearing. To make sure that Rosina would not die in child-birth like her mother and grandmother before her, Carlotta arranged for Rosina to marry Carlotta's old friend and admirer, Prince Potenziani, who had the advantage that " 'a caprice of nature had made him, although an admirer of our sex, incapable of being a lover or a husband' ". The Prince went to great lengths not to have this known.

After the betrothal Rosina announced that she had fallen in love with her cousin Mario. Carlotta argued the irrelevancy of this but to no avail. A friend of Rosina's, Agnese della Gherard-esci,[1] "a real child of the age", who admired Lord Byron and dressed like a man, helped Rosina to escape with Mario, but Carlotta overtook them and forced Rosina to go through with the marriage. A month after the marriage, Rosina petitioned the Pope for an annulment on the ground that the marriage had not been consummated. Prince Potenziani was publicly humiliated, Rosina got the annulment,[2] married her Mario, and has since become pregnant. In despair, Carlotta was rushing to her side when the accident occurred. Now she expects to die and wants only to see Rosina first.

So Augustus sets out for Pisa to find Rosina. At an inn just outside Pisa, he falls into conversation with a graceful boy who is trying to escape from " 'the recollection of one single hour of my life' ". The boy reveals that he is really a young lady. At that point Prince Potenziani and Prince Giovanni make the entrance which has already been described. Upon seeing them, the young lady leaves and Augustus overhears their conversation.

In a style, the choicest part of which is its blandness, Prince Potenziani tells the story of a rich nobleman of his grandfather's time who, having been insulted and publicly humiliated by a young friend upon whom he had bestowed every benefaction, realizes that this matter would " 'spoil his sleep' " unless he had revenge. He hired for this purpose a young bravo who was heavily in his debt, and thought the job done. He slept soundly and enjoyed a rebirth of innocence when he thought his enemy

[1] An ungrammatical modification of della Gherardesca, the family name of Dante's Count Ugolino, a Pisan.

[2] The story of the annulment was suggested by Zola's novel *Rome*. See Isak Dinesen's letter to Hans Brix, published in his *Analyser og Problemer* VI (Copenhagen: Gyldendal, 1950), p. 301.

was dead, and only felt himself in hell when he learned later that his enemy was alive and flourishing in Rome. Remembering "how kindly he had thought of his young enemy during that short period when he believed him to have been killed, . . . he thought hell is very likely filled with people who have not carried out what they had meant to do."

Until now the mystery has thickened. But now we see that Prince Potenziani's story connects with Carlotta's. Rosina, we are to understand, is the young friend upon whom revenge was to be taken. Prince Giovanni is the bravo who did not do the job he was paid for; and Prince Potenziani is, by way of the story, telling Prince Giovanni that he will again feel kindly toward him after he has killed him.

Prince Potenziani is inviting Prince Giovanni to precipitate a duel so that he may kill the young man. But Prince Potenziani is also making of the invitation a brilliant occasion. We must be constantly alive to the spirit of play in the discourse of Prince Potenziani and to a lesser degree everyone else. The best conversation is always in Isak Dinesen an artistic enterprise which, partly comic and partly lyric, is carried on in a spirit of pure intellectual freedom, of a self-consciousness verging on self-parody. The participants co-operate by opposing each other. Ideas are put forward and responded to in order to make delightful configurations—as though they were musical notes or movements in a dance. Neither the characters nor we are fully engaged by the dramatic situation and the result is a curiously metaphysical effect.

It is because we see the story as a kind of dance that Prince Potenziani, who ought to be the villain of the story is, instead, as its most skilful dancer, not its hero (Augustus is that) but something more, its presiding deity. *Out of Africa* helps us to understand the sense in which Prince Potenziani appears as at least a surrogate-god. Because the Negro is "adjusted for the unforeseen and accustomed to the unexpected", because he is "on friendly terms with destiny", imagination, Isak Dinesen tells us, ranks high among the qualities he looks for "in a master or a doctor or in God". "It may be on the strength of such a taste, that the Caliph Haroun al Raschid maintains, to the hearts of Africa and Arabia, his position as an ideal ruler; with him nobody knew what to expect next, and you did not know where you had him.

When the Africans speak of the personality of God they speak like the Arabian Nights or like the last chapters of the Book of Job; it is the same quality, the infinite power of imagination, with which they are impressed."[1]

It is Prince Potenziani's imagination that makes Giovanni adore him. The Prince is " 'a child compared to any of us' ", Giovanni tells Augustus.

"It will be as natural to him to live for two hundred years as for us to live sixty. The things that wear us down do not touch him. He is very wonderful".... The low and clear cry of a bird sounded from the garden, like the voice of the night itself. "Do you hear the aziola [i.e. assiolo] cry?" asked Giovanni. "That used to mean that something fortunate was going to happen to me. I do not know," he added after a while, "what it would be now, unless God has very much more power of imagination than I myself have—that is, unless he is very much more like my friend the Prince than he is like me. But that, of course, I trust him to be."

The significance of imagination, both as accounting for the structure of the story and as answering Augustus's original questions, becomes clear when Augustus and the young lady in man's clothes go that evening to a marionette comedy called *Revenge of Truth*.[2] Augustus has told her about the duel and the conversation which led to the challenge; and she, after making him repeat the old Prince's story of the bravo, says that she knew something fortunate was going to happen to her. When Augustus hears her repeat Prince Giovanni's words and learns that she once saw Prince Giovanni, he is pleased that he has "come upon a vein of events in life". He is pleased to have come upon a story, a chain of coincidence which reveals an artist's hand on life.

The marionette comedy teaches him why he should be pleased. It is about a witch who curses a house by making all the lies told within it come true. Thus the woman who tries to catch a rich husband by pretending to love him, really does fall in love with him; the braggart becomes a hero; the hypocrites become virtu-

---

[1] New York, p. 23; London, p. 25.

[2] Isak Dinesen refers to "the immortal *Revenge of Truth*, that most charming of marionette comedies. Everybody will remember how. . . ." This is a private joke, for she wrote the comedy herself as a girl. Although she published it in the Danish literary magazine, *Tilskueren*, May 1926, the readers of "Roads" would not have been aware of it.

ous; and the miser, who pretends to be poor, loses all his money. When in the end the witch is asked what is really the truth, she answers: " 'The truth, my children, is that we are, all of us, acting in a marionette comedy. What is important more than anything else in a marionette comedy, is keeping the ideas of the author clear. This is the real happiness of life, and now that I have at last come into a marionette play, I will never go out of it again. But you, my fellow actors, keep the ideas of the author clear. Aye, drive them to their utmost consequences.' "

Life is to be understood on the analogy of art in which everything, even the pain and the evil, is esthetically necessary. That is part of the meaning of all Isak Dinesen's stories—which is why she refers so often to the Book of Job as answering the enigma of life and art. God answers Job not logically but lyrically, in a series of lyrical exaltations of His Creation. It is the artist's justification of his work. Our duty is to play our roles to the hilt, to love, as Isak Dinesen says in *Out of Africa*, our destiny and the "pride" or destiny of our adversaries and of all people and animals[1]—to see them with the artist's, which is to say God's eye as co-operating in the marionette comedy, the divinely appointed dance.

Why then should lies come true? Because our purpose, as we see it, is one thing, and as the artist or God sees it quite another. To be in a marionette play is to know that your purpose is part of a grand design. It is for reflecting creatures to know what your purpose is, to be as sure of it as are the wild animals who act on instinct. This is the sense in which art restores us to the connection with the absolute that we had in a state of nature, the sense in which " 'regained naïveté " is, as the artist says in "Copenhagen Season", the end of our highest education.

If we understand why it is well to "come upon a vein of events in life", or to "come into a marionette play", we can begin to understand why Isak Dinesen writes *stories*. We can understand what is meant by the old storyteller in "The Blank Page" (*LT*) when she tells us that her grandmother, who taught her the art, warned, " 'Be loyal to the story. . . . Where the story-teller is loyal, eternally and unswervingly loyal to the story, there, in the end, silence will speak.' " Silence is the absolute. The story transforms human purposes into the divine purpose. It is the

[1] New York, p. 261; London, pp. 279-80.

means by which the artist can show both the limited points of view of the characters and the abiding view of God: just as in certain Italian paintings the martyr seems in the very midst of his martyrdom to be absorbed already in the enjoyment of his heavenly throne.

Hence the elegant disengagement of Prince Potenziani and Prince Giovanni in the matter of their duel. They are not only acting out their own purposes, they are also "keeping the ideas of the author clear". To subordinate the characters' motives to the needs of the plot, this is to be loyal to the story. To betray the story is to be, one gathers, naturalistic; it is to allow some theory of the way people are or the way things happen to interfere with that magical movement of events which is symbolic of the absolute. It is to seek a merely relative explanation where there ought to be mystery. " 'It is not a bad thing in a tale,' " says the teller of the story in "The Dreamers" (*SGT*), " 'that you understand only half of it' ".

It is with the assurance of well-rehearsed actors that Giovanni and the old Prince meet at dawn for their duel. Augustus, Giovanni's second, feels Giovanni "clinging to the fatefulness of the coming hour with a passionate tenderness, so that he would not have allowed anything in the world to take it away from him". And the old Prince is "deeply moved". He plays his role with that combination of art and simplicity which marks the great virtuoso who on his violin runs up and down the scales as if it were child's play. Whereas the others are disguising their real feelings, "he showed his distress with the simplicity of an unspoiled child, perfectly confident of the sympathy of his surroundings. His dark eyes were moist, but frank and gentle, as if everything in life were natural and sweet to him." That touch, after all that has been said about Prince Potenziani's hard artificial surface, shows a remarkable writer; and the combination of hardness and ineffable sweetness, of a humanity which gains outline and authenticity through the formality of its surface, is the quality of Isak Dinesen's art at its best.

Prince Potenziani's naturalness is the last triumph of art. By the unhurried punctiliousness of his movements he gives the occasion its rhythm; he transforms it into an artwork. "It was clear, from the moment when he came in, that everything would proceed with the measure and grace of a perfectly performed minuet."

Now the plot unwinds. For the mysterious girl in youth's clothing, who is Prince Potenziani's second, stops the duel to tell the old Prince a tale. She tells him that a year ago his wife, Rosina, stole out in the middle of the night to meet her cousin, Mario, and left in her place in bed her friend, a virgin like herself. She is that friend, Agnese della Gherardesci.

When the old Prince says after a time that he might then have found Rosina and Mario together and had them in his hand, Agnese says, " 'But they would not have minded being killed by you if they had died together.' "

"No, no, no," said the old Prince, "by no means. How can you imagine that I would have killed either of them? But I would have taken their clothes away and told them that I was going to have them killed in a terrible way, in the morning, and I would have had them shut up together alone over the night. When she was frightened or angry her face, her whole body, blushed like an oleander flower". . . . Suddenly a great wave of high color spread over his old face.

"And," he exclaimed with deep emotion, "I should have had her, my lovely child, to play with still!"

There was a long silence; nobody dared to speak in the presence of so great a pain.

Suddenly he smiled at them all, a very gentle and sweet smile. "Always," he said in a high and clear voice, "we fail because we are too small. I grudged the boy Mario that, in a petty grudge. And in my vanity I thought that I should prefer an heir to my name, if it was to be, out of a ducal house. Too small I have been, too small for the ways of God."

"Nino," he said after a minute, "Nino, my friend, forgive me. Give me your hand." Deeply moved, Giovanni put away his pistol and took the hand of his old friend.

Now we can see, remembering the story of the bravo that Prince Potenziani directed at Giovanni, that the thing Giovanni was to have done for the Prince was to sleep with Rosina so that she would not be able to prove her marriage unconsummated and would not therefore be able to get the annulment. When Rosina did get the annulment, the old Prince thought Giovanni had betrayed him—which is why he now apologizes. Giovanni slept in Rosina's bed, but with Agnese.

The scene is remarkable not only for its fantastic morality or immorality, but also for its combination of opposite effects. For the Prince's regret, his repentance really, at not having adopted an even grosser expedient than he did, is certainly comic; it reverses the direction which a properly Christian repentance would take. And yet this is the moment of his greatest sincerity, sweetness and moral insight. " 'Always we fail because we are too small.' " Outrageous as his scheme was, it was still not outrageous enough. He had been too timid, too conventional to play the vicarious husband precisely through his wife's lover. His was a failure of imagination. The sign of this is that events have passed out of his hands, that he could not keep pace with the imagination of God.

This is also the moment of the Prince's greatest passion. His passion comes through as intense, tragic, beautiful. The effect is remarkable when you consider that the passion is stirred up by the mere thought of a vicarious pleasure, and that the heartfelt " 'I should have had her, my lovely child, to play with still!' " means that Rosina would not, had the Prince allowed her Mario, have been able to get the annulment. There is a grossness here, a heartlessness even, which the Prince's manner both acknowledges and does not quite allow to come to the surface. And yet that manner—which by its bland irony shows such awareness of all that is being flouted—becomes at this point the very instrument for revealing not only the Prince's sincerity but also his passion.

So intense is his passion that at the next moment the Prince literally dies of love. But the name which issues from his mouth, "slightly open, as if he were going to sing", is not Rosina's but that of Rosina's step-grandmother, the bald old lady whom Augustus rescued. " 'Carlotta,' " he says, and rolls off his chair to the ground. "At that moment his pistol, which he was still holding in his hand, went off, the bullet, taking a wild line up in the air, passed so close to Augustus's head that he heard its whistle as it passed, like a bird's singing. It stunned him for a second, and brought back the image of his wife."

The moment is astounding. It forces us to recapitulate and reassess all the events of the story. We now understand that the Prince was not merely playing the vicarious husband to Rosina but that the marriage itself was the vicarious realization of his unconsummated love for Carlotta. The theme of vicariousness appears over and over in Isak Dinesen. She uses it to illustrate the difference between conception and execution, imagination and reality—to talk not only about the nature of the artist and the difference between art and life, but to talk also about the nature of God and the enigma of His ways.

We can see from this story that the imaginative faculty is linked with—indeed its intensity derives from—the lack of ability for physical consummation. It is because the artist does not "live", is physically impotent and sterile, that he lives so strongly in the imagination as to give life to other people through an overflow of imaginative energy. The artist is in this sense like God who does not share in the warm flesh-and-blood life He creates. But when the artist is, like Carlotta or Prince Potenziani, an artist in life, the events he sets in motion get out of hand and make a design better than the one he intended. That is because "God has"—as Isak Dinesen was fond of saying, it was the lesson her own life had taught her—"a greater and finer power of imagination than we have."

It is the Prince's unfulfilled desire which, after his death, infuses life into the other characters. Expressed as the almost sung " 'Carlotta' ", the Prince's desire continues by way of the bullet which, "like a bird's singing", reminds Augustus of his wife and points an answer (though we do not yet know what it is) to his problem. The passage is so densely written that the reader, bewildered by the shocking movement of events, may not even notice the reference to Augustus's problem. The reference is, I think, too brief. Here and elsewhere Augustus's story is inadequately told. So for that matter is Carlotta's, and yet we see from Prince Potenziani's death scene how crucial she is. The inadequate treatment of Augustus and Carlotta keeps Isak Dinesen's boldest and most powerful conception from being the masterpiece it ought to have been.

The next passage, the climax, is the boldest stroke of a bold writer; it is bolder even than the ending of "The Monkey" (*SGT*), where the venerable Prioress turns into a monkey. Here the author attempts nothing less than the apotheosis of Prince Potenziani and the comparison of his passionate death to the Passion of Christ. "They remained", we are told, "quite still" around the Prince's body. "The figure of the old Prince, lying immovably on the ground, still held the center of the picture as much as if he had been slowly ascending to heaven, and they his disciples, left behind, gazing up toward him."

"The Monkey" merely challenges our credulity, and we are

used to suspending disbelief for the sake of a tale. But this passage challenges our taste, our sense of fitness. The passage stretches as far as it will go the tension we have noted between an almost grotesque content and the surface elegance by which it is curiously suppressed and transformed. The surface is strengthened at this point by the comparison with what one imagines to be a baroque painting. If we remember that baroque is the style which meets the challenge of deformity and absurdity, we can understand the style of this passage and of the whole story.

The passage does not succeed in making us feel all that about the Prince. But it remains a *tour de force* if we do not balk (and the reader who has enjoyed the story this far does not, I think, balk) but pass over it or rather up it to the pitch of ecstasy at which the next chapter takes place. The next chapter is called "The Freed Captive", and is about Giovanni and Agnese who, after the Prince's body has been removed, find themselves "face to face on the deserted terrace".

An allusion to Peter's denial of Christ expresses the intensity of Agnese's unspoken accusation against Giovanni for having denied her his love after taking her favors. When Giovanni asks her to stay, she says he cannot have anything to say to her, and indeed he cannot until he breaks out with the lines in which Dante sees Beatrice again in the Earthly Paradise at the top of the mountain of Purgatory. They were brought together physically when they acted out the old comic tale of the substitute bride. Now, by stepping into a more exalted artwork, they are brought together spiritually. By calling himself Dante and her Beatrice, Giovanni can say things he could never say "sincerely", in his own person; he can give voice to his deepest desire. He recites the lines in which Dante repents after Beatrice has chided him for his faithlessness to her. And she answers with Beatrice's words of forgiveness and her assurance (as Isak Dinesen apparently interprets Dante's meaning) that God's vengeance can be softened.[1]

In the end, Agnese reveals to Augustus that she is no more shut up within the one hour of which she told him at their first meeting. She is "the freed captive" of the chapter's title. She has been freed from an experience which was traumatic because unconsummated emotionally. And she now realizes that Prince Poten-

[1] *Purgatorio* xxx, 34-39; xxxi, 85-89; xxxiii, 31-36.

ziani, whom she hated, was responsible for the action that freed her.

The Prince is justified as the artist, the maker of the story would be justified. It is he who has brought the two sets of lovers together and has taught Augustus the lesson he set out to learn. The impotent old Prince has even in a sense vicariously fathered Rosina's baby. When Augustus in the last chapter visits the old Countess, Rosina and the baby, he finds the old lady changed by her love of the baby, the first male creature she has ever loved. She has apparently become more womanly. Remembering Prince Potenziani's love of her, we can infer that that love, too, has had a vicarious fruition in the baby.

" 'When I was a little girl,' " Carlotta says to Augustus, pointing the moral of the story,

"I was told never to show a fool a thing half finished. But what else does the Lord himself do to us during all our lives? If I had been shown this child from the beginning I . . . would have understood the pattern, and would not have shaken it all to pieces so many times, and given the good Lord so much trouble in putting it together again."

Augustus now has the answer to the question about truth with which he started. Truth is in "the vein of events", and the vein even works itself out for Augustus when, as a token of gratitude, Carlotta gives him a small heartshaped smelling-bottle which she received from the first of the three women (the other two are Rosina's mother and Rosina), who are the only people she has until now loved. Augustus sees painted on the bottle his own house in Denmark. The bottle is the counterpart of a bottle which Augustus received from a maiden aunt of his father's. This bottle, which has been talismanic in Augustus's life and played a part in bringing him to Italy, has painted on it what we now recognize to be Carlotta's villa. On both bottles are the words *Amitié sincère*. The two women exchanged these bottles on parting, and their love has borne fruit for Augustus.

Augustus has his answer, but it does him no good. The sign of this is that he does not, by producing his own smelling-bottle, make a tale Carlotta "would forever have cherished and repeated", that "might even come to be her last thought on her deathbed". "He was held back by the feeling that there was, in this decision of fate, something which . . . he could not share with anybody else any more than he would be able to share his dreams." Handed by destiny an almost absurdly obvious story, he is unable to get out of himself sufficiently to step into it. As he leaves the villa, a rainbow, sign of God's providence, stands low in the sky. But he does not look at it either. Instead, he looks "thoughtfully" into a small mirror. The word *thoughtfully* is important, because Augustus's failure is the failure of the critical intellect. He now *knows* everything. He knows that the truth lies in significant action. But he still cannot break out of the circle of reflection. He is back to the mirror with which he started. He cannot, in the phrase of Kierkegaard (whose influence on Isak Dinesen is considerable), win his way through to existence.

Presumably, Augustus ought to have learned from Prince Potenziani's example that you do not find out who you are by introspection, by looking into a mirror, but by putting on a mask and engaging in an action with such intensity that you step from a human story into God's story, from your own relative to God's absolute purpose. I think we are intended to see the difference between Augustus and the two other epicene characters, Prince Potenziani and Carlotta. Prince Potenziani in pretending to be a man becomes one, and Carlotta in pretending to be a woman becomes one; this is the way in which, as in the marionette comedy, the lies of the story become truth. The lies become truth because they represent a truth deeper than the obvious one. In his imagination, Prince Potenziani always was very much a man. He has a strongly erotic imagination. One assumes that Carlotta's case is like Prince Potenziani's, but we do not know enough about her to be sure. Augustus, on the other hand, who makes no pretense, who is "sincere" and introspective, is nothing and becomes nothing. He is epicene because his imagination has not awakened to the erotic idea. He deceives his wife in the way reflective men always, in Kierkegaard's analysis of modern love,[1] deceive women—by not being really *there* with her.

In contrasting a romantic, Hamletlike Northerner, a nine-teenth-century type, with old-regime Italians, Isak Dinesen is exploring the nineteenth-century question of sincerity and

---

[1] See "Shadowgraphs" and "Diary of the Seducer", in *Either/Or*, Vol. I, translated by David F. and Lillian M. Swenson (London: Oxford University Press, 1944; with revisions and a foreword by Howard A. Johnson, Garden City, N.Y.: Anchor Books, 1959).

experience as against artifice and tradition. She comes out with a twentieth-century answer. The meaning of the story is, I think, in the title. The truth is in Pisa, the heart of life is there. But the story that reveals the truth is played on the roads round Pisa. After the story on the road, Augustus reaches Pisa where he goes in for "experience". He has a love affair with a Swedenborgian lady; he becomes interested in the attempts of two priests to convert him to the Church of Rome; he joins a revolutionary society. Clearly, nothing is *happening* to him in Pisa; and it is significant that the story of the smelling-bottles, which he has the chance to step into, occurs again outside Pisa. The point is that you don't get at the truth about the world or yourself by going straight to it. You get at it by seeming to move away to an esthetic distance. You get at it through artifice and tradition—by assimilating your particular event to a recurring pattern, your particular self to an archetype. Readers of Yeats will be reminded of his evolution from the nineteenth-century doctrine of sincerity to the twentieth-century doctrine of the mask.

To surmise all this about Augustus, however, I have had to use evidence from two other stories in which he appears. One, an amazing little dialogue with all the dramatic power of a story, is called "In the Menagerie" and appears in the "From an Immigrant's Notebook" section of *Out of Africa*. A Danish traveller to Hamburg, Count Augustus von Schimmelmann is irresistibly drawn to visit every day a small itinerant menagerie, where he finds in the mystery of the brute creation the antithesis of his Kantian, relativistic rationalism. " 'The wild animals,' " he says to the proprietor, " 'which run in a wild landscape, do not really exist,' " for no one sees them. " 'They see one another,' " says the showman. When Count Schimmelmann doubts this, since the giraffes do not know a square and cannot be said to see the square markings on each other's skins, the showman adds: " 'God sees them.' "

The showman, a bald, sickly little man with a fallen-in nose (a sign of syphilis), had to give up theological studies because of a scandal the nature of which was, one suspects, homosexual. He repeats the legendary idea that hyenas are hermaphrodites, and he wonders whether the hyena would, when shut up alone in a cage, " 'feel a double want, or is he, because he united in himself the complementary qualities of creation, satisfied in himself, and in harmony?' " The man who understands animals is the faintly repulsive man of double nature and double vision, who combines theology and debauchery. He is wondering whether it is better to be double or single in your nature and vision.

The showman is comparable to the hyena, in that you have to appreciate in him the union of "complementary qualities" to overcome an initial repulsion. It is the repulsion Count Schimmelmann feels at the story of the hyenas, and it is caused by the single vision, the need to separate good and evil, male and female, to which he and we are committed.[1] The Count is drawn to the animals by his own potentially double nature. But he is not true to his nature; for he had, we are told, "arranged his life according to the ideas of other people".

He is again repelled when the showman lets a snake wind itself around his arm. " 'The man who can caress a snake can do anything.' " He can do anything because he ignores moral and utilitarian distinctions. In the showman's beautifully repetitive reply, we have the point of "Roads" and many of the other stories.

The showman had stood for a little while in deep thoughts. "Your Excellency," he said at last, "you must needs love snakes.[2] There is no way round it. Out of my own experience in life, I can tell you so, and indeed it is the best advice that I can give you: You should love the snakes. Keep in your mind, your Excellency, how often,—keep in mind, your Excellency, that nearly every time that we ask the Lord for a fish, he will give us a serpent."

The fish, ancient symbol of salvation, comes in a form which looks as though it is from the devil but is really, when we understand the whole pattern, from God.

If this is optimism, it is the optimism of the Book of Job, in

[1] The terms *single vision* and its concomitant *double vision* come from Blake who says he hopes always to have at least "twofold" vision. "May God us keep/," he says, "From Single vision & Newton's sleep" (last lines of "With happiness stretched across the hills"). *Single vision* is the scientist's way of seeing facts as just facts, and the rationalist's way of accepting as real the relative world of categories. *Double vision* is the capacity to read facts symbolically and see through to an absolute realm where opposites merge. Although Isak Dinesen did not know Blake at all well and does not herself use these terms, I shall use them to describe a contrast which is central in her work and in the whole romantic tradition.

[2] Coleridge's ancient mariner has to overcome an initial repulsion to the water snakes and learn to love them before he can be "saved". Isak Dinesen described to me the overpowering effect "The Ancient Mariner" had on her when Denys Finch-Hatton first gave it to her to read in Africa.

which, as Isak Dinesen sees it, God answers Job's complaints about the evil in the world by pointing to His animal creation, making no distinction in it between what man calls good and evil. Early in *Out of Africa*, Isak Dinesen observes that the Natives are at home in life,

within their own element, such as we can never be, like fishes in deep water which for the life of them cannot understand our fear of drowning. This assurance, this art of swimming, they had, I thought, because they had preserved a knowledge that was lost to us by our first parents; Africa, amongst the continents, will teach it to you: that God and the Devil are one, the majesty coeternal, not two uncreated but one uncreated, and the Natives neither confounded the persons nor divided the substance.[1]

That might be Blake, for whom innocence consists of just such knowledge.

The other story in which Count Schimmelmann appears is "The Poet" (*SGT*), where he figures as the critic, the foil to the poet. He is now middle-aged, and has taken to living "upon the envy of the outside world", to pretending to consider himself fortunate for possessing the things the world envied him for—his estate, his wealth, his prestige. This is the end-product of his relativism which, after undermining all other basis for values, leaves him with only the basis of common consent.

Given the continuity of Count Schimmelmann's name, character and personal history, it seems fair to read across the three stories to understand him; and what one sees is how much more understandable he is, how much more the author understands about him, in the latter two stories than in "Roads" which is the earliest.[2] In "The Poet", her understanding goes farthest, and the Count is at his most interesting here, where he is a merely subordinate character; he is more interesting indeed than the hero, "the poet" himself. " 'As we live,' " he says in a style rather more like Prince Potenziani's than he has been wont to use, " 'we become aware of the humiliating fact that as we are dependent upon our subordinates—and without my barber I should be, within a week, socially, politically, and domestically a wreck—so are we, in the spiritual world, dependent upon people

[1] New York, pp. 19-20; London, p. 21.
[2] "Roads" is the first of her mature works, and apparently the only mature story that was completely written in Africa.

stupider than ourselves.' " A shrewd critic of art, he has

"learned that it is not possible to paint any definite object, say, a rose, so that I, or any other intelligent critic, shall not be able to decide, within twenty years, at what period it was painted, or, more or less, at what place on the earth. The artist has meant to create either a picture of a rose in the abstract, or the portrait of a particular rose; it is never in the least his intention to give us a Chinese, Persian, or Dutch, or, according to the period, a rococo or a pure Empire rose. . . . I am thus so far superior to the artist that I can mete him with a measure of which he himself knows nothing. At the same time I could not paint, and hardly see or conceive, a rose myself. I might imitate any of their creations. I might say: 'I will paint a rose in the Chinese or Dutch or in the rococo manner.' But I should never have the courage to paint a rose as it looks. For how does a rose look?"

It is the same with religion, he continues. It would hardly be an intelligent question to ask what God is like, for the Hebrews conceived their God in one way, the Aztecs in another. " 'At the same time I should be, for this superior view of mine, in debt to the naïve people who have believed in the possibility of obtaining a direct and absolutely truthful idea of God, and who were mis-taken.' " He tells a story about a sign, the point of which is that we can know only our own categories.

The story comes from Kierkegaard,[1] and suggests that Isak Dinesen is in substance an existentialist writer—though she did not consider herself an Existentialist and disclaimed any extensive understanding of Existentialist philosophy. It is safe to say that Isak Dinesen is an existentialist in the way that all romantic writers either are or are on their way to being existentialists. For it is a basic tenet of romanticism that existence precedes essence, that experience is more fundamental than idea.

The romanticist is the man who starts in the world of ideas and deals with the problem of how you break out of it to know yourself and the external world. His answer is that if you act with an *ad hoc* self upon the world, the action will reveal both your self and the world. To show this, the earlier romantic writers made their characters assume a role and embark upon a career of experience. A modern romantic writer like Isak Dinesen makes her characters don a mask and step into a fruitful fiction. One of the main differences between early and late romanticism is that late romanticism increases the emphasis on art as artifice and

[1] "Diapsalmata", *Either/Or*, Vol. 1, New York, p. 31; London, pp. 25-6.

gives increased importance to art as artifice in solving the romantic problem.

The interesting thing for us is the way Isak Dinesen offers the
form she is using, the story, as the solution to the problem posed
in the story. Her stories are often about people who play at being
God. This is to say that they are, like Prince Potenziani and
Carlotta, artists in life, who know the world by repeating God's
act of creation, by creating the world as a vein of events, a
fiction. Each character knows himself and the world through his
fiction, his construction of the world. When he finds that the
events he set in motion have got out of hand, that miraculously he
has stepped from his own story into God's, then he has arrived at
absolute knowledge.

It is this view of reality as a texture of fictions that accounts for
Isak Dinesen's most conspicuous narrative device. I mean her
frequent use of tales within the tale as a kind of dialogue that
advances the action. Inset tales are to be found within the stories
of *The Arabian Nights*; they are to be found in Ovid, Cervantes,
and the whole romance tradition—the tradition that presents the
story as story rather than as an imitation of reality. The inset
tales are usually digressions; sometimes they advance the narrative. In Isak Dinesen, they always advance the narrative. What
she does is to give us a philosophical and ironical awareness of
the device itself. Her inset stories have an ironic double reference;
for apart from their intrinsic interest, they are the symbolic
language through which the main story is told. Thus Prince
Potenziani's "Story of the Bravo" is his way of accusing Prince
Giovanni of treachery. We come to understand "The Story of
the Bravo", as the main story, with its subsequent inset tales,
unfolds; while at the same time, "The Story of the Bravo" helps
us understand what is unfolding.

One has always to be reading backwards and forwards in this
way. One has always to be weaving the pattern of the story,
asking how "The Story of the Bravo" or the marionette comedy
bear upon the rest of the story. The effect of so many strands is
to give us the sense of having a space to inhabit, of being in the
midst of details; they serve, in other words, the function of details
in the novel.

If the novel can be said to compose into an artwork raw bits
of life, then the elements of Isak Dinesen's stories are themselves

little artworks. Or if it is true, as Ortega y Gasset suggests in his "Notes on Novelists", that the novelist wants us to forget we are inhabiting an artwork, that he wants us to take the world of the novel for the real world,[1] then it might be said that Isak Dinesen does not for a minute want us to forget that we are inhabiting an artwork. She gives us within her frame enough intricacy of texture to create an illusion of, or perhaps a substitute for, depth; but she reminds us that the canvas is there by fabricating her inner world of tales that are *told*, even bringing us back at intervals to the teller when the tale is long.

Yet her stories cannot—in spite of her own claims to the contrary—really be classed with the sort of stories you can tell orally. The complexity of pattern, the need to read backwards and forwards, would make the stories impossible to take in by ear.[2] Nor would E. M. Forster's definition of story in the oral sense—"a narrative of events arranged in their time sequence . . . . *Qua* story, it can only have one merit: that of making the audience want to know what happens next"[3]—suit a story which exists really all at the same time. For the past appears not in sequence but through tales which advance the present situation, and we do not let go of one understood episode to move on to another but insert as it were the later episodes into the earlier in order to understand them. The main question in an Isak Dinesen story is not what will happen next, but what is happening or what is the meaning of what is happening now. Her method is a way of penetrating in depth. It is a way of penetrating, through a structure such as Kierkegaard often uses in his philosophical writing, a structure like that of Chinese boxes arranged one inside the other, to the heart of life.

Her method requires that she assume the character of a latter-day Scheherezade who has revived the lost art of the oral story. For her method requires that she call attention to the anachronistic nature of her art, that she make us aware of the naturalistic fiction she is taking off from. By making us aware of anachronism,

[1] *The Dehumanization of Art and Other Writings on Art and Culture* (Garden City, N.Y.: Anchor Books, 1956), p. 73.

[2] She admitted, when I questioned her characterization of herself as a latter-day Scheherezade, that she had never *told* the whole of any of her stories but only the inset tales from her stories.

[3] *Aspects of the Novel* (New York: Harcourt, Brace, 1927, p. 47; London: Arnold, 1927), p. 43.

she can assign philosophical significance to the formal elements of her art. She can make the story itself, as a form opposed to other forms, part of the thing her stories are about. She can make it her answer to Augustus's questions about truth and identity.

All this is explicitly dealt with in the first story of *Last Tales*. A superb story, "The Cardinal's First Tale" sums up in its plot and meaning the essence of all Isak Dinesen's work; and when, in the course of it, the Cardinal argues for the divine art of what, in opposition to the novel, he calls the story, we can only read this as Isak Dinesen's explicit defense of her own apparently anachronistic art.

" 'Who are you?' the lady in black asked Cardinal Salviati." That is the opening sentence. It strikes the characteristic Isak Dinesen note, for it states, in the question it asks, the theme of almost all her stories, and it establishes two immediately vivid figures as nothing more than pregnant mysteries. The black clothes, the name and title, touch off cultural recollections out of which these figures take shape, and the story develops by rendering the question and the figures even more mysterious.

The Cardinal answers with a story—which is to say an enigma, another question. He tells the story of a proud and selfish Prince Pompilio who to produce an heir marries a girl much younger than himself. When the girl gives birth to a son with one eye, the doctors suggest the couple wait a few years before having another child. In the interval, the Princess becomes interested in music; and at a performance in Venice of Metastasio's masterpiece, *Achilles in Scyros*, she hears the great *castrato* Marelli sing. "How describe the beatitude into which, in the course of a few hours, her whole being was transported. It was a birth, the pangs of which were sweet beyond words . . . in which, undergoing a total change, she triumphantly became her whole self." While the house is afoot and madly applauding, the two exchange across the pit "a long deep silent glance, the first and the last". When after the appointed term of waiting Prince Pompilio turned once more toward his spouse, "Princess Benedetta's lovely person", we are told, "was changed by more than time. By now she knew the nature and value of what she was giving into the arms of her husband, and in her second bridal night she shed tears different from those of her first."

Partly of course the references to Metastasio and the *castrato* are picturesque details of eighteenth-century Italy. But they are also the cultural allusions that give us the sense of Europe as a marvelous configuration of mind and spirit. That sense is the elevated material out of which Isak Dinesen shapes all her stories, as the sculptor shapes his statue out of precious stone. If Benedetta's love has an elevation beyond what one might have thought possible in modern prose fiction, it is partly owing to our sense of the musical experience through which she falls in love, and partly owing to the Cardinal's graceful reference, in describing her beatitude, to Saint Thomas Aquinas. "*Gratia*, Saint Thomas Aquinas himself says, *supponit et perficit naturam*—Grace presupposes Nature and brings it to perfection. Any person of soul and imagination will recognize the experience, every lover in the world is a disciple of the Angelic Doctor." "Smile not— not even in pity—" the Cardinal continues with a wit of remarkable delicacy that in no way detracts from the elevation of his account, "at the fact that the youth, who called to life a young woman's heart, was a being of Marelli's kind, a *soprano*, formed and prepared in the Conservatorio of Sant' Onofrio, and once and for all cut off—no, laugh not!—from real life. But bear in mind that this whole love affair was of a seraphic order and went to a tune."

The theological and musical setting helps turn what would otherwise be a merely playful and extravagant idea—that the *castrato* might through a woman's love be endowed with manhood and become the spiritual begetter of her child—into a poetic representation of the highest Western idealism, both as regards the dualism of body and soul and the possibility of spiritual love. Marelli's world-famous treble changed, we are told. "It had been a celestial instrument, carried from stage to stage by an exquisitely elegant and graceful doll. Now it was the voice of the human soul." When he sang in St Petersburg, "the Empress Catherine, who had never been known to weep, sobbed bitterly all through the programme and cried: '*Ah, que nous sommes punis pour avoir le coeur pur*'" Who can separate the comedy and poetry of that!

In the conflict that develops between the Prince and Princess over the naming of the second child, there is a clear representation of the split between the two sides of Western idealism—the Apollonian and the Dionysian. The Prince insists that the child, if a boy, is to be named Atanasio after St Athanasius, "the Father of Orthodoxy". But the Princess, faithful to the child's real father, insists that the child is to be named Dionysio, "in reminiscence of the God of inspired ecstasy, for a name is a reality, and a child is made known to himself by his name". She gives birth as it turns out to twin boys, so that each parent is able to appropriate a child and give it the name of his choice. But then there is a great fire, which only one of the twins survives. Since they are identical, there is no way of knowing which has survived. The Prince declares the survivor to be Atanasio. The Princess never argues the matter with her husband, but is secretly sure that the child is Dionysio. She calls him in their most intimate hours by the pet name of Pyrrha (the Greek word for *fiery red*, applied to wine and therefore another way of calling him Dionysus, god of wine).

So the boy is now officially Atanasio and only secretly Dionysio —a perfect fable of the union within the individual of a cultural polarity, with the Apollonian officially victorious over the Dionysian. It is psychologically appropriate that the secret Dionysian life is carried on with the mother, and that the days before the fire, before the fall from the innocence and perfect happiness of the fully gratified instinctual life, when the boy was openly Dionysio, were also the days when he was his mama's *"bambino* lover". But the passage in which those days are described draws not upon psychological knowledge but upon that traditional knowledge of the relation between a mother and her baby boy which is embodied in the most famous icon of Mediterranean civilization—the Madonna and Child.

As "a woman of the South, Madame", the Cardinal says,

you will know that to watch our Southern mothers playing with and fondling their infants is to see the hearts aflame, and that an infant son, while still in swaddling clothes, may well be his mama's lover. It will be so, most of all, in the cases in which a divine power has condescended to take human form, and where the young mother feels that she is fondling or playing with a saint or a great artist. . . . I am not blaspheming, Madame, when I express the idea that any young mother of a saint or great artist may feel herself to be the spouse of the Holy Ghost.

The mother in love with her son may feel herself to be the mother of a god and therefore the spouse of one. The theme of spiritual impregnation, of in other words the Holy Ghost, recurs throughout Isak Dinesen. The finely comic detail of the *castrato* lover merges here with mythological lore about heroes begotten by gods upon mortal women to suggest—if we take into account what we know of the Oedipus complex, whereby the son rejects his biological father to seek his real or spiritual father—the point where psychology and anthropology turn into mythology. But all this is accomplished without any loss of lightness and without the remotest reference to psychology and anthropology. Isak Dinesen seems to contain and avoid our knowledge, to have access to it through some older source.

The fable of the double nature continues as we are told that the boy was trained both as a priest and a worldling; and that the older brother dies, leaving Atanasio to become a Prince temporal and spiritual. The point is that you cannot distinguish in the Cardinal the artist from the priest. " 'Pity him not, this man,' " says the Cardinal, for he knows the Lord did not " 'create a pretty and neat world' " but a " 'sublime' "one, and he knows that from him must be withheld " 'certain spiritual benefits, granted to other human beings . . . the benefit of remorse' ". In endowing the artist with both priestly and Dionysian or demonic elements, Isak Dinesen is romantic. But she moves to a late phase of romanticism, the phase, say, of Flaubert and Nietzsche, when she denies the artist the benefit of remorse and of our pity—when she denies him a personality, preferring that the artist and his work be superhuman. She repeats, to bring her esthetic thinking up to date, Yeats's voyage to Byzantium—his voyage from a naturalistic and human, to an autonomous and superhuman, art.

Isak Dinesen now undertakes the defense of her own art; and we see that her art is modern because it is deliberately anachronistic, deliberately pitted against the prevailing art of the novel. The lady sees the hero of the Cardinal's story very clearly, " 'as if luminous even, and on a higher plane. But my teacher and adviser—and my friend—is farther away than before. He no more looks to me quite human, and alas, I am not sure that I am not afraid of him.' " " 'Madame,' " says the Cardinal,

"I have been telling you a story. Stories have been told as long as speech has existed, and *sans* stories the human race would have perished, as it would have perished *sans* water. You will see the characters of the true story clearly, as if luminous and on a higher plane, and at the same time they may look not quite human, and you may

29

well be a little afraid of them. That is all in the order of things. But I see, Madame," he went on, "I see, today, a new art of narration . . . it has gained great favor amongst the readers of our time. And this new art and literature—for the sake of the individual characters in the story, and in order to keep close to them and not be afraid—will be ready to sacrifice the story itself. The individuals of the new books and novels—one by one—are so close to the reader that he will feel a bodily warmth flowing from them, and that he will take them to his bosom and make them, in all situations of his life, his companions, friends and advisers. And while this interchange of sympathy goes on, the story itself loses ground and weight and in the end evaporates, like the bouquet of a noble wine, the bottle of which has been left uncorked."

To the lady's protest, the Cardinal replies that the novel " 'is a human product. The divine art is the story. In the beginning was the story,' " he says reminding her of Genesis. " 'But you will remember . . . that the human characters in the book do come forth on the sixth day only—by that time they were bound to come, for where the story is, the characters will gather!' "

The novel wants to look as though it was made by human beings, its characters. The events are the occasion for the characters to manifest themselves—which is why we do not want uncaused events, and why our sympathy for the characters exceeds anything called for by the events and may even at times contradict the events. In the story, instead, the more magical the events the better. For the story wants to look as though it was made by God, or by the author who speaks with the voice of God in that he uses traditional plots the meaning of which he as a person may not understand. The story is a manifestation of the divine order, and the characters are called into being to act out the story.

The Cardinal's remarks are perceptive as literary and cultural history. For the story celebrates communal values and treats values as transcendent or ordained by God; whereas the novel takes a critical and relativistic attitude toward communal values, it treats values as man-made and declares its right to dissolve communal values in favor of the individual case. " 'A story,' " says the Cardinal, " 'has a hero' "; it also

"has a heroine—a young woman who by the sole virtue of being so becomes the prize of the hero, and the reward for his every exploit and every vicissitude. But by the time when you have no more stories, your young women will be the prize and reward of nobody and nothing. . . . A poor and sad lover . . . will stand by to see his lady disrobed of her story or her epos and, all naked, turned into an individual."

The novel undertakes to tell us who the individuals are who are playing the roles of hero and heroine; and they turn out to be human beings with whom we can identify ourselves, but no longer in the magical sense heroes and heroines. The Cardinal foresees the ultimate paradox of the novel—that in dissolving communal values in favor of the individual, the novel has in its latest phase dissolved away the individual himself. It has dissolved the lines of class, manners and moral degree which give the individual external configuration; it has reduced the individual to his chemical and psychic elements—leaving us for characters streams of response, which are distinguishable from each other only abstractly.

It is this condition which has caused certain weary novel readers to turn for relief to Isak Dinesen. For she establishes value as a magical presence, though she arrives at traditional values only through the most strikingly modern transvaluations. And she gives us, in spite of her proclaimed preference for the wood over the trees, precisely individuals—characters with strong markings and firm outlines, who yet contain the divided modern consciousness. Her stories, in other words, are both like and unlike their archaic models. The difference is beautifully illustrated by the Cardinal, who has a thoroughly modern consciousness in that he makes himself the hero of an old tale of mistaken identities, and understands, as the hero of the old tale would not, that he has both twins within himself, that he is divided between Apollo and Dionysus.

In "Sorrow-acre" (*Winter's Tales*), considered by many her masterpiece and ranked by all among her best stories, Isak Dinesen pits against each other the archaic and modern modes of feeling and thinking. "Sorrow-acre" is based on a folk tale of Jutland about a peasant woman who, in order to save her son from execution, is required by the local lord to reap between sunrise and sunset a field of rye which it would normally require four men to reap in a day. The woman does it and drops dead; her superhuman feat is commemorated by the name "sorrow-acre" which thereafter attaches to the field.

Isak Dinesen told me[1] that she read while in Africa a modern rendition of this tale by the Danish writer, Paul la Cour.[2] She felt la Cour had made a mistake in establishing the boy's innocence, that the point ought to have remained ambiguous. The occasion for attempting her own version occurred many years later, after she had returned to Denmark. In the course of arguing with a socialist friend, she asked him whether there really was such a thing as an *arbejderkultur*, a proletarian culture distinct from the middle-class culture that seemed to give the workers all their values. He asked her in return whether there was such a thing as an *herregaardskultur*, a distinctively manorial culture. She wrote "Sorrow-acre" to show what such a manorial culture was like and how different its values were from ours—to suggest, one gathers from the story, that you cannot speak of the past as evil since our ideas of good and evil have changed.

By establishing the boy's innocence, la Cour follows the folk tale in making the mother's feat an imitation of Christ, the meaning of which is single and enduring. Isak Dinesen, instead, makes the question of the justice of the task as enigmatic as reality itself. She then subjects the task to the contrasting judgments of the old order and the new. To do this, she moves the story up from its vaguely medieval setting to the late eighteenth century, the period just before the liberation of the serfs in Denmark (1787) and the Revolution in France. The late eighteenth century operates here like the early nineteenth-century setting in "Roads" and in so many other of Isak Dinesen's stories —to bring the old order into conjunction with the new.

The story is seen through the eyes of the old lord's nephew Adam, who, on the day of the peasant woman's ordeal, returns from England where he has encountered the great new humanitarian ideas of the age. In contrast to the old lord, who wears powdered wig and brocade, Adam dresses simply, wears no wig, and displays the new romantic taste in landscape, literature and mythology. To the Greek and Latin gods he prefers, he tells his uncle, the gods of Nordic mythology because they were more moral. " 'Ah, it was easier to them,' " for

---

[1] My interviews with Isak Dinesen took place in New York in February 1959, and during the summers of 1959 and 1961 in Denmark—mainly at her estate, Rungsted-lund.

[2] "Danske Sagaer" ("Danish Sagas"), *Tilskueren*, March 1931, pp. 231-40; la Cour also transcribes the original folk tale.

"They were not as powerful," said his uncle. "And does power," Adam again asked, "stand in the way of virtue?" "Nay," said his uncle gravely. "Nay, power is in itself the supreme virtue. But the gods of which you speak were never all-powerful. They had, at all times, by their side those darker powers which they named the Jotuns, and who worked the suffering, the disasters, the ruin of our world. They might safely give themselves up to temperance and kindness. The omnipotent gods," he went on, "have no such facilitation. With their omnipotence they take over the woe of the universe."

The lord's statement is our guide for judging his conduct toward the peasant woman.

As the day wears on, Adam finds the peasant woman's suffering unendurable to behold. Sensing impending disaster for the arrogant aristocratic order, Adam threatens to leave the estate forever, to go to America, if his uncle does not release the woman, Anne-Marie, from their cruel bargain. The lord will not yield. To release Anne-Marie now, " 'at the eleventh hour' ", would be to make " 'light of her exploit' ", to turn her into " 'a figure of unseemly fun' " by pulling out from under her grand gesture the external necessity which gives it tragic substance. " 'I gave Anne-Marie my word,' " he says. " 'In the beginning was the word. . . . My own humble word has been the principle of the land on which we stand, for an age of man. My father's word was the same, before my day.' "

In Adam's reply, that the word does not remain the same but " 'is creative—it is imagination, daring, passion' ", and that " 'a life is a greater thing even than a word' ", we see the opposition of the two world-views. The new one, in which the word changes, is concerned with the individual and is therefore humanitarian. But the old one, in which the word is always the same, is concerned not with the individual but with the idea. We are told that it hardly mattered to the nobility which individual "out of a long row of fathers and sons, at the moment in his person incarnated the fields and woods, the peasants, cattle and game of the estate". The old lord and the young noblewoman, who married just to perpetuate the lord's name, are as hard on themselves as the lord is on Anne-Marie. It is significant that the lord is never named and that his young wife has the name of the Dowager Queen, which was bestowed upon her by the old Queen as a mark of her favor.

Since for Adam value is problematic and only the individual

is real, his main concern is to minimize Anne-Marie's suffering. But since for the lord value is the only enduring reality, his main concern is to allow Anne-Marie to transcend herself through suffering. Tragedy, he says, is man's highest, his unique privilege, for God Himself cannot experience it. Comedy is the mode of the gods, as of the aristocrat who, to the extent that he is freed from necessity, plays at being a god.

Like a god, the lord looks down from a pavilion of his garden upon the rye field where the peasants of the manor watch and suffer with Anne-Marie. The lord wears a brocade dressing-gown, two footmen take him morning chocolate on large silver trays. Late in the afternoon, after the debate with Adam and as if to answer Adam, he very deliberately has himself changed, there in the pavilion, into full court regalia; he dines there ceremoniously, and finally, wearing all the signs of his rank and privilege, he descends to the rye field to watch the dénouement of the suffering he has ordained. The contrast is as cruel as Isak Dinesen can make it. The story is cruel, perhaps her cruelest, that is its genius. For she does not sentimentalize the old order, or gloss over the hardness of the reality she is out to justify.

The justification is in the double judgment she maintains throughout—Adam's and the lord's, the relative and the absolute. The absolute judgment is manifested through what can only be called beauty. The story begins with a lovely description of the pyramidal pattern of all Danish manors, seen in the ideal summer light of the hour before sunrise. The point is that the hierarchical order of the manors is an emblem of civilization, the right kind of civilization that arises from the soil and is the mark man's thoughts and longings make upon the soil. The manor is beautiful because it fits into and enhances the Danish landscape. Adam's response at the outset to the beauty of the manor, as well as his deeply irrational attachment to it as the place where he grew up, contains already the answer to his anxious doubts— the answer he will learn to formulate in the course of the story.

The lord's cruelty, too, is beautiful, because authentic (the old regime was cruel and beautiful) and because the lord's solemnity, his all-day vigil in the pavilion, suggests so much awareness of pain. (The story is like a knife-stab just because it conveys an acute sense of everyone's pain, including the lord's.) Because the lord's cruelty seems to contain and transcend the ordinary human compassion for Anne-Marie, it becomes emblematic of a truth which operates by laws other than ours. His adherence to ceremony does her honor, since ceremony is the visible sign of the law by which they both transcend themselves. In asserting his rank, in playing to the full his punitory role, he does not compete for her tragic role but allows her the unqualified glory of transcending a substantial necessity.

This is all part of what Adam, the new or innocent man, the man who as a reformer wants to start over again as though the past had never happened, this is all part of what he learns. Impressed by the beauty of his uncle's manor, Adam compares it to the Garden of Eden. But he learns from Anne-Marie's story, and his uncle's part in it, that evil has gone into the making of this beauty and that an omnipotent God is responsible for the evil as well as the good. The lesson reconciles him to ceremony and to a society based on ceremony. He decides not to go to America after all, but to stay with his uncle. For he realizes that the absolute to be found in nature can be found also in the forms of civilization.

A low thunder develops on the horizon, and "the tragic and cruel tale" of Anne-Marie re-echoes in Adam's head "like the recurrent, hollow throbbing of a muffled drum". The tale is the counterpart of the thunder. When Adam decides to stay on the manor, there is a loud roll of thunder. The thunder announces itself as part of the beauty of the landscape, as part of Eden. Adam feels the landscape has spoken, that it has answered the question he asked at the beginning of the story—the question as to whether his revolutionary ideas could be brought into line with the manor, or whether the manor and the feudal past must be definitively broken with. The answer is that the present can be made continuous with the past by means of the romantic idea of the organic unity of nature with consciousness and civilization.

The absorption of the thunder in the landscape prepares us for the scene in which Anne-Marie, as a triumph of nature and civilization, transcends tragedy to move into an Eden-like state of comic bliss. The transcendence is brought off literally before our eyes in the remarkable description of Anne-Marie's final moments. Through the steadiness of its rhythm, Anne-Marie's labor turns in the gold and silver sunset hour into a gorgeous ritual the movements of which, having transcended the necessity which gave them their occasion, are now ends in themselves, expressive of an absolute judgment reinforced, orchestrated as it were, by nature in its splendor and by the past, by the lord and the peasants in their splendor.

Now we see that the lord is justified—as are by analogy the ways of God to man—in having saved Anne-Marie from the merely human settlement, the mere avoidance of pain. But the conclusion is not so simple as that; it rarely is in Isak Dinesen, in whom any statement is likely to contain its own ironic counter-statement. The old lord is not after all a god. In his public capacity, the aristocrat is godlike and in touch with the absolute, and he can therefore take a comic view of his inferiors. But the human being inside the aristocratic role is as much a tragic victim of necessity as is Anne-Marie in her role. Adam has a sympathetic vision of his uncle as "a thin black anchorite upon his own land", as himself the servant to an idea of continuity. And when we see him in the end as the pathetic victim of a vast historical joke, then it is we who take a comic view of him. We see the dance of nobleman and peasant, that he and Anne-Marie have executed so beautifully together, as the last dance of a dying order.

It is significant that Adam is not there to watch the climax of the dance. He is in the house with the lord's young wife. "He felt that he was, in the rooms of the manor, and even by the harpsi-chord on which he accompanied his aunt to her air from *Alceste*, as much in the centre of things as if he had stood in the rye field itself, and as near to those human beings whose fate was now decided there. Anne-Marie and he were both in the hands of destiny, and destiny would by different ways, bring each to his designated end." It is the destiny of Anne-Marie and the old lord to die, and it is the destiny of Adam to inherit the lord's estate and marry his young wife—to serve the lord's idea of continuity. The air from Gluck's *Alceste* contains two lines the aunt sings throughout the story: "There is no sweeter effort / Than to die for one you love." The song connects Anne-Marie with the young people by connecting the dying for a son, on the one side, with the birth, on the other, of the sexual love that produces children. The song suggests that they all fulfill their destiny by fulfilling their deepest desire.

The aunt is innocent in a way opposite to Adam's. He is all

nature, individuality, sincerity; she is all form. Brought up at Court, she is a doll "exquisitely and innocently drilled to the stately measure of a palace". She was supposed to have married the old lord's son, but when the son died she married the father without a demur; for it was a rank and a name she was marrying. She awakens in the story, however, to her own desire for love, for the right man within the rank and name. She moves toward the nineteenth century, while Adam reaches back to make connection with the old order. They start with opposite ideas of the absolute, but arrive at the same reconciliation of absolute and relative.

How does the old lord fulfill his destiny? In the same way as the writer of a story, by making the other characters fulfill theirs. It is his social function to do this; for he stands in the same relation to his manor as God does to the world. It is even clearer in "Sorrow-acre" than in "Roads" that civilization assigns us roles analagous to the roles of the characters in a story—roles that make our limited and relative purposes serve a grand design. The aristocrat, the artist and God are therefore analagous figures.

The old lord is in his relation to Anne-Marie like that " 'cruel' " storyteller, described in "The Cardinal's First Tale", who moves his characters through the paces required by the story in order that they may transcend their ordinary selves and yield the story's absolute meaning. The Cardinal's kind of story has passed out of fashion, because the absolute has become obsolete. The apparently cruel storyteller is the mouthpiece of an apparently cruel God who thinks greatness more important than absence of pain. But there has been, the Legitimist Cardinal tells us in "Deluge at Norderney" (*SGT*), " 'a fall of the divinity. . . . There has taken place, in heaven, a tremendous overturning, equal to the French Revolution upon earth, and its after-effects. The world of today is, like the France of today, in the hands of a Louis-Philippe.' " God is now a constitutional monarch, who conforms to our relative ideas of right and wrong and never requires us to do anything that transcends those ideas. That is why our civilization is no longer like a story, no longer connected with imagination and therefore no longer connected with nature. That is why we no longer have stories but, instead, novels.

Chapter 2

TRAGICOMEDY AS ULTIMATE VISION

KAREN CHRISTENTZE DINESEN was born on April 17, 1885, in Rungstedlund, her father's estate that stands on the Sound, looking across to Sweden, midway between Copenhagen and Elsinore. She lived there, after her return from Africa, until her death—in the big, low, rambling, five-hundred-year-old house that in the seventeenth and eighteenth centuries served as an inn. Johannes Ewald, the Danish poet whose name appears so often in her work, lodged there from 1773 to 1776; one of his poems is called "The Beatitudes of Rungsted". Isak Dinesen used Ewald's room as her study; there is a plaque to him on the house; and a pleasant little hill on the grounds is called Ewald's Hill.

She was the second of five children; her older sister died in 1922, she had two younger brothers, and a younger sister who died in 1959. On her father's side she came of an old military and landowning family with noble connections but not themselves titled. Her mother's father, Regnar Westenholz, made a fortune as a grain merchant in London, then returned to Denmark, bought an estate in Jutland, and became for a short time Minister of Finance in the Danish government. Her maternal grandmother was half-English and a Unitarian; her mother's side of the family remained Unitarian, an unusual thing to be in Denmark. Although baptized in the Danish Church, Karen, whose upbringing after her father's death was influenced by her maternal grandmother, was raised as a Unitarian—a fact which one Danish critic considers significant for understanding her work.[1]

Her half-English grandmother, Mary Hansen (whose mother's family, Grut, came from Guernsey), had a hand in teaching the girl English and may in part explain an affinity for English so strong that Karen was to become a writer in both English and Danish. She made it clear to me, however, that she was out of

[1] Johannes Rosendahl, *Karen Blixen: Fire Foredrag (Four Lectures)* (Copenhagen: Gyldendal, 1957).

38

sympathy with her mother's family and associated herself instead with her father and his family. She evolved her own view of life largely in reaction to the overly rationalistic and moralistic Unitarian view; "it hardly seems", she said to me of Unitarianism, "a religion at all". The conflict in her work between the bourgeois-moralistic and the aristocratic-esthetic attitudes reflects the difference she discerned early in life between her mother's family and her father's. Like others who have written well about the aristocracy, Isak Dinesen was close enough to the aristocracy to know it but sufficiently on the periphery to be able to *see* it.

Her father committed suicide when she was ten. This was the terrible event of her childhood. "I had", she told me, "to live with my mother's family. I was not like them. I was like my father's family. My grandmother did not understand me. She liked my sisters better. I was very unhappy as a child." One can understand how she would have idealized her dead father and modelled her career on his in combining adventurous action with literary accomplishment.[1]

Adolph Wilhelm Dinesen was a remarkable man who seems to have modelled his own career on that of his father, also Adolph Wilhelm, who was an officer (he served in Denmark's wars against Prussia and later in the French army), a writer on military subjects, and owner of the beautiful castle Katholm in Jutland. A second son, the younger Wilhelm fought as a Lieutenant in the Prusso-Danish War of 1864. This was the second war over Schleswig-Holstein, a war disastrous for Denmark because her defeat in it marked the end of Denmark as a power of consequence in Europe. The defeat left Wilhelm, who was nineteen at the time, in a state of great depression. He quit the Danish army and joined the French to fight the Prussians again in 1870. Like his father, he received the order of the Legion of Honor. He was in Paris at the time of the Commune and later wrote a book on the subject (*Paris Under the Commune*, 1872), in which he sympathized with the Communards. He seems to have had the affinity for lost causes that characterizes his daughter's writing.

---

[1] Her brother, Thomas Dinesen, has followed the same pattern. He won the Victoria Cross for extraordinary valor with the Canadian Army in World War I, and has since written books and articles as an avocation. Her younger sister, Mrs Ellen Dahl, published a volume of essays under the pseudonym of Paracelsus.

He went to the United States in 1872. In an article of 1887, he describes his feelings at that time: "I was sick in my soul. I had fought in the Franco-Prussian War and had seen the hope for revenge of 1864 crushed. I had witnessed afterwards the civil war in Paris and got fed up with both sides. I was living partly in Denmark and partly in France. I was feeling unsatisfied, restless, tired, and I doubted my own ability to do anything. Then came personal troubles and I gave everything up and went to America."[1]

He spent two years as a hunter among the Pawnee and Chippewa Indians in Nebraska and Wisconsin, and he identified himself with the Indians, whom he characterizes as a dying race, in opposition to the white Americans. He returned to Denmark in 1874 to help his sick father manage his farm, then fought on the Turkish (again the losing) side in the Turkish-Russian War of 1877-78, then returned, bought Rungstedlund and another farm Folehave, married and settled down to that gentlemanly combination of pursuits—farming, politics and writing. He became a Leftist[2] member of parliament in 1892 and, after several books on his military experiences, published in 1889 and 1892 two volumes of *Jagtbreve* or *Hunting Letters* which are still widely read in Denmark. Published under the pseudonym of Boganis—a name the Indians gave him, meaning wild nuts—Wilhelm Dinesen's *Hunting Letters* seem, with their feeling for nature, the model for *Out of Africa*. His sympathy for the Indians, in the article on America, resembles his daughter's sympathy for the Africans; he says of the injustice done the Indians what she is to say of the injustice done the Africans. "What we have needed thousands and thousands of years to reach," he writes, "we only give him [the Indian] days to catch up with."[3]

Young Karen was educated at home by governesses. "I never was properly educated," she liked to say, "I just read what I pleased." But her brother Thomas tells us, in his memoir of her in the American edition of the Isak Dinesen memorial anthology, that she was at fourteen fluent in English and French, and had a good knowledge of literature, art and history—though she com-

[1] "Fra et Ophold i de Forenede Stater" ("From a Stay in the United States"), *Tilskueren* 1887, p. 778.

[2] The Venstre party was, however, to the right of the then emerging Social Democrats.

[3] *Tilskueren*, 1887, p. 792.

plained in later life of her complete ignorance of science and mathematics.[1] As a girl she loved to tell stories, but she wanted to study painting. She studied English at Oxford in 1904 and painting, first at the Danish Academy of Art, then in Paris in 1910. The painter's eye is apparent in all her writing, especially in her landscapes. All this time she was writing; she published her first two stories in 1907, when she was twenty-two, and a third in 1909, all under the Indian pseudonym of Osceola. The posthumous volume of her uncollected Danish stories and poems is appropriately called *Osceola*.[2]

In 1912, she stayed in Rome with a cousin who was wife to the Danish Minister there, and Italy seems to have made the impact on her which figures in the lives of so many sensitive Nordics. Everything she says in *Out of Africa* about the Nordic "susceptibility to the Southern countries and races"[3] would have applied, before she went to Africa, to Italy. Indeed, Italy remained the *other* country of her fiction. When she didn't set her stories in Denmark or Norway, the countries she really knew, she generally chose Italy which seemed to her, she told me, "the natural setting for stories. Shakespeare used it that way even though he had never been there."

When I asked her why she had never written any stories about Africa, she replied with a surprising rush of emotion, "No, no, I never wanted to, I never could. It is too close." But when I asked her the same question two years later, she gave me a more reasonable answer. "What would I write about? A native king and a native princess? I might write about the natives if I were to write poetry. But I couldn't write stories about them, they are too different. And I couldn't write about the white settlers." "Why not?" I asked. "Think of the people in 'The Roads Round Pisa', they are hardly"—she smiled—"the white-settler type." The general run of white settlers were too crude to interest her. And as for the natives, she could only have written about them as you write about nature, as the *other* thing against which you define yourself. That is why she might have written poetry about them, nature poetry; but not fiction, for which you need

[1] (New York: Random House, 1964.) This is an abbreviated and slightly changed version of the Danish edition that came out in 1962 under the title *Karen Blixen*, ed. Clara Svendsen and Ole Wivel (Copenhagen: Gyldendal).

[2] Ed. Clara Svendsen (Copenhagen: Gyldendal, 1962).

[3] New York, pp. 16-17; London, p. 17.

41

to know people from inside. The statement tells us about her fiction and about her treatment of the Africans in *Out of Africa*.

The decision to go to Africa was made in 1913 when Karen Dinesen—Tanne, as she was called by family and friends[1]— became engaged to her cousin, the Swedish Baron Bror von Blixen-Finecke, on whose estate in a provincial section of South Sweden she was determined not to live. An uncle of theirs, Count Mogens Frijs, came back at that time from big-game hunting in East Africa and told such wonderful tales of the place and of the money to be made there that the young couple decided to emigrate to Kenya. A company was established, in which her family bought shares (in 1916, it came to be called the Karen Coffee Company). Blixen-Finecke went out first, and bought a 6,000-acre coffee farm above Nairobi. She followed in January 1914; they were married in Mombasa on the 14th. Their divorce in 1921 initiates the period when she was alone, managing the farm on her own, that is mainly described in *Out of Africa*.[2] The site of the farm is now a suburb of Nairobi called Karen. The house, called Karen House, was bought by Denmark in 1963 and given, to be a girls' school of Home Economics, to the new state of Kenya on its Independence Day, December 12, 1963.

Although she published in *Tilskueren* a poem "Ex-Africa" in April 1925, and in 1926 the marionette comedy referred to in "Roads", she did not during her early years in Africa think of becoming a writer. She did not, she liked to say, want to become "a piece of printed matter"; she "wanted to ride, to shoot, to live". In *Out of Africa*, she says that she began writing again in order to forget her worries about the farm. "I began in the evenings to write stories, fairy-tales and romances, that would take my mind a long way off, to other countries and times. I had

[1] Later, her foreign friends called her Tania. Her books have been published in Germany under the name Tania Blixen.

[2] She mentions her husband only once, (New York, pp. 265-266; London, p. 285-286) to say that, when World War I broke out, he volunteered his services to the British and left her alone. Baron Blixen-Finecke was himself a dashing figure. Related to the Danish royal family, he became after the divorce one of the best known white (professional) hunters of East Africa. In this capacity, he knew Hemingway, the Prince of Wales and other celebrated big-game hunters of the period. He married again two times and was killed in an automobile accident in 1946. See his memoirs, *African Hunter* (translated from the Swedish by F. H. Lyon, London: Cassell, 1937; New York: Knopf, 1938), in which he tells the story about Isak Dinesen (New York, pp. 91-92; London, p. 84) that she herself tells, with much modesty one realizes, in *Out of Africa* (New York, p. 269; London, p. 289).

been telling some of the stories to a friend [Denys Finch-Hatton] when he came to stay on the farm."[1]

It has become apparent since her death that she took her early stories and notebooks with her to Africa; and we can infer from the dates in one notebook that she returned to work on her notes no later than the summer of 1926. Writing occupied her increasingly. And when years later, because of the Depression and the collapse of world coffee prices, it became clear that she really was going to lose the farm, writing remained her refuge; as it did during the terrible year of 1931 when, having lost every cent, all her dowry, which had been tied up in the farm, she returned brokenhearted to Denmark to begin life again at forty-six.

She liked to tell how she asked her brother Thomas to finance her for two years while she found something to do. There were only three things, she told him, she could do better than average. She could cook (during her first visit back to Europe—she returned every four years, with stops in Paris to buy clothes—she had taken lessons from a French chef and now thought she might study cooking for two years in Paris, then open a small restaurant in Copenhagen); she could take care of mad people; she could write. They settled on writing, and she produced *Seven Gothic Tales* two years later.

The story is amusing, but it cannot be taken seriously when we consider how much writing she had already done in Africa. Notebooks of the African period—four softcovered notebooks apparently bought in Nairobi—contain first jottings, largely in English, of all the stories of *Seven Gothic Tales*, except for "Deluge at Norderney"; while another kind of notebook—hardcovered, bought in Copenhagen probably before she came to Africa since it contains pages of an unfinished story that seems to belong to the Osceola period—contains opening pages, in Danish, of two stories of *Winter's Tales*: "The Fish", called by its present Danish title, and "Peter and Rosa", called "Elskovs Gækkeri" or "Love's Frolics". "Roads Round Pisa" is the only story she remembered having completed in Africa, but she was always vague about what she had written in Africa and what in Denmark. Her vagueness suggests little break in her literary activities between her last years in Africa and her first years back in Denmark. The sign of this is that she continued writing in English—the language

[1] Pp. 44-45.

that had become natural to her in Kenya—even after she returned to Denmark.

Her literary career falls into three distinct periods. There is the first, spectacular period, represented by her first three books— *Seven Gothic Tales* (1934), *Out of Africa* (1937), *Winter's Tales* (1942)—in which she appeared as a fully matured artist and made the reputation she has today, for her reputation still rests on her first three books. There is the long hiatus of fifteen years during which her only book was the novel, *The Angelic Avengers*, a thriller which she published in 1946 under the name of Pierre Andrézel, and which she was not for many years willing to acknowledge. There is the third period of recrudescence, remarkable for a writer in her seventies, which saw in rapid succession two volumes of stories, *Last Tales* in 1957 and *Anecdotes of Destiny* in 1958, a collection in 1961 of four more African reminiscences, *Shadows on the Grass*, and the posthumously published story *Ehrengard* in 1963. The first seven stories of *Last Tales* come from *Albondocani*, a long, complicated novel which she was working on during the last twelve years of her life; it was to have been made up of 100 stories, each a separate unit yet all related.

The books of 1957 to 1961 do not make any advance in thought or technique on her first three—development is not to be expected of a writer who published her first book at forty-nine—but they do perfect and complete the thought and technique of the earlier books. The amazing thing is that the last books do in so many places come up to the best of her earlier achievements. They have not to be sure the bite and passion, the shocking extravagance of the never-equalled *Seven Gothic Tales*, but she did not want to reproduce the quality of that book. She spoke of it with embarrassment as "too elaborate" and as having "too much of the author" in it. She revealed her aims by preferring *Winter's Tales*, because it is "simpler, more sober", and has "not so much of the author" in it. The reader does not find more of the author in her first than in her other collections of stories. It was, I think, the audacity, the estheticism, the "decadence" if you like of *Seven Gothic Tales*, especially its treatment of sexual perversion, that embarrassed her—that and her own awareness of how deeply personal the book is.

The extravagance of *Seven Gothic Tales* is the literary equivalent I think, of the first shock after her return from Africa, when she

44

was very ill with headaches: when, we may surmise, all the conflicts that in her life are summed up by the opposition between Africa and Europe must have struck her again with an impact that would have shattered whatever organization she had achieved to contain them. In *Seven Gothic Tales* these conflicts are set forth as irreconcilable through gestures so fantastic that they border on madness. Yet the book seems to have helped her solve the problem it posed, not only by bringing her success but also by showing that the fantastic gestures were themselves the means of containing the conflicts. She continued to explore the same conflicts in her subsequent work, but with increasing serenity.

She showed after *Winter's Tales* a decline in compulsive energy that explains, I think, the hiatus from 1942 to 1957. To be sure, the Nazi occupation deflected her from serious work, and ill health slowed her down. In 1955 an operation on her spine made it impossible for her to sit at the typewriter. She had to learn to dictate her stories; she dictated *Last Tales* lying on her back, much of the time on the floor. In the best of health she was an extraordinarily slow writer, capable of doing a story fifteen times over. She wrote, she told me, the way the Boers ploughed new land; she went forward, then went back again in order to go forward a little more. It is also true that her last books collect work that had been appearing in magazines or as separate books since World War II. Nevertheless, her first three books seem to have been written out of a single motivating force that ends with *Winter's Tales*. In the last books she reworks insights stemming from the experience that lies behind the first three.

The experience is of Africa, but of Africa experienced as one side of that antinomy in the modern European soul, which we call romanticism—that antinomy between the modern European and the pre-scientific, pre-industrial past from which he has been cut off, a past rooted in nature and human nature. Isak Dinesen has been able to reinvigorate the romantic tradition because she rediscovered in Africa the validity of all the romantic myths, myths that locate spirit in the elemental—in nature, in the life of primitive people, in instinct and passion, in aristocratic, feudal and tribal societies that have their roots in nature. She could not, however, have seen Africa as she did had she not brought to it eyes prepared by European romanticism, had she not discovered Europe in Africa. The stories she wrote before she went to Africa show the influence of romanticism as a literary inheritance.

The posthumous volume, *Osceola*, opens with an unfinished and hitherto unpublished story that Isak Dinesen wrote around 1905 when she was about twenty. Entitled "Grjotgard Ålvesøn og Aud" ("Grjotgard Ålvesøn and Aud"), it is based on Snorri Sturlason's Norse King sagas that, along with the other Icelandic sagas, Mrs Dinesen used to read to the children. An amazingly powerful piece of work, "Grjotgard" is romantic in its reconstruction of archaic modes of feeling and thinking, in the sense it conveys that the people of the story are different from us. The people of the story are at a point of transition between paganism and Christianity that is analogous to the point at which Isak Dinesen was to find her Africans.

The two stories published in 1907, "The Hermits" and "The Ploughman",[1] deal with nature and the supernatural and seem to be companion pieces. Both deal with the old theme of the demon lover, but the thing that makes them romantic is the meaning they give to the supernatural theme. The lovers are demonic because their energies are associated with the energies of nature, so that our sympathy is with them. "The Hermits" is about the sea; the lover is a ghost who wins the heroine over to his element, the sea, and she dies. "The Ploughman" is about the earth; the lover's mother is a witch and his energies, amoral as the untamed earth's, are rendered evil by their clash with society. He recalls the highly moral heroine to her proper element, the earth, but she redeems him by harnessing his energies—she sets him to plough the earth.

The talent exhibited in these two early efforts is less that of a storyteller than of a lyric poet, a romantic nature poet. The author's interest does not seem to be in the story but rather in evoking a sense of nature; the story rises as a kind of emanation from the scene. Like other beginning writers of romantic sensibility, Isak Dinesen had to learn what to do with the characters that materialize all too easily out of a mood or a landscape. Yet to the end she most often started with, as she put it, an atmosphere, a place, an "air", and she let the story grow from that.

[1] "Eneboerne" in *Tilskueren*, 1907, pp. 609-35; "Pløjeren" in *Gad's Danske Magasin*, October 1907, pp. 50-59. Both by Osceola, reprinted in *Osceola*.

Of the four elements, she liked to say, air was her element. Air was what she considered a work of art, whether a painting or a story, ought to have; the thing she remembered about a painting or a story was its air. "Supper at Elsinore" (*SGT*) grew out of an attempt to render the air of that harbor town; "The Invincible Slave-owners" (*WT*) grew out of a visit to Baden Baden and an attempt to render its faded charm; and in writing "Sorrow-acre", she began by rendering the air of an old Danish manor at sunrise, then she put a figure into the landscape and went on. Her two rather crude stories of 1907 have, therefore, greater bearing on her future development than has the far more successful "Family de Cats", an incisive little satire of the bourgeoisie, which appeared two years later and which is in its quite different vein a finished piece of work.[1]

Although "The Family de Cats" is Isak Dinesen's only straight satire, the satirical element is never absent from her later work as it is absent from the stories of 1907. One might say that she achieved a fusion of the styles of 1907 and 1909, and that the later stories are more or less successful just to the extent that both styles are present. On the one hand, the later stories show the sort of ironical awareness of their own extravagance which is absent from the stories of 1907; on the other hand, the irony of the later stories does not dispel their imaginative quality. In her best stories, Isak Dinesen achieves the peculiarly romantic kind of satire that feeds and is fed by imaginative activity.

Different as are the styles of 1907 and 1909, the moral ideas are the same. "The Family de Cats" continues the morality of nature of the first two stories, for it treats good and evil as problematical abstractions from an original moral unity identical with the oneness and vitality of nature. The point of the satire is that the two poles of what Blake calls "the cloven fiction" cannot exist without each other, and that it is relative and problematical which name, good or evil, can be applied to any person. All three stories look ahead to Isak Dinesen's rediscovery in Africa of the romantic morality of nature she brought there.

Her first attempt to bring together fantasy and satire, the styles of 1907 and 1909, is to be found in "Revenge of Truth",

[1] "Familien de Cats", under the heading, "Sandsynlige Historier" ("Probable Stories") by Osceola in *Tilskueren*, 1909, pp. 1-19. This was one of a series of stories she wrote around 1905; she never published the others. Reprinted in *Osceola*.

the marionette comedy which she wrote as a girl of sixteen or seventeen, then rewrote in 1915 when she was thirty, and finally revised and published under the name of Karen Blixen-Finecke in 1926.[1] It is significant that she first combined the two styles by means of marionettes, for marionettes and the Book of Job are the references that recur most often in her work. They are both used to answer the same question—how to find the ideal in the real, the absolute in the relative. They would seem to offer opposite answers—the Lord's lyrical celebration of the life of nature as against lifeless dolls. Yet to understand Isak Dinesen is to understand the sense in which the two answers can be reconciled. For she likes the extremely natural and the extremely artificial; she is a nature writer and a writer about styles of art and civilization. Her references to Job tell about one aspect of her art—the intensification of the natural to yield the ideal. But her references to marionettes tell about the twin aspects of her art— the imaginative intensity with which she bodies forth the ideal and the satire which invokes the ideal to criticize the real. The marionettes also illustrate her use of characters as both natural- istic representatives of their own relative viewpoints and stylized agents of the plot, representatives of the absolute.

In using marionettes, Isak Dinesen for the first time calls attention to the art form itself as part of what she is saying. Marionettes offer a simplified diagram of the double vision that makes art art; for we play along with the pretense that they are not marionettes, that they have purposes of their own, while perfectly aware that someone is pulling the strings. The latter awareness is in the case of marionettes so exaggerated as to make every marionette play a comedy no matter how painful the material.[2] Although Isak Dinesen was never again to use marionettes, the marionette comedy helps us understand some of her most characteristic qualities—the deliberate emphasis on

[1] "Sandhedens Hævn", *Tilskueren*, May 1926, pp. 329-44. The play was given as a special midnight performance at the Danish Royal Theater in Copenhagen on March 28, 1936, and it was performed on the Danish television on October 3, 1960. It was published as a booklet in 1960 (Copenhagen: Gyldendal). At the time of her death, Isak Dinesen was translating it into English for possible performance in the United States. The play was never actually given with marionettes, but always with live actors.

[2] One thinks of Bergson's definition of the comic as "a momentary anesthesia of the heart" that occurs when we see life as mechanical and therefore withdraw our sympathy (*Laughter*).

artifice and the imposition on painful material of a comic awareness, the awareness that someone is pulling the strings, as an answer to the story's problems.

Comedy has always made a certain self-parodying use of the form to solve the problem of the play. Events reach an impasse, and the playwright with a smile and a flick of the wrist pulls a god down from the machine or turns up somebody's long-lost daughter. In self-consciously modern literature, the comic solution takes on a metaphysical significance as a way of dealing with the materials of modern disorder. The writer points up the chaos of life by reminding us that his solution is a mere trick of art—as in Brecht's *Threepenny Opera* where, after the hero has been saved from hanging by an unexpected pardon, the cast reminds us in a sardonic song, "Happy Ending", that in life it would not work this way.

But there is also in modern literature an even more complex use of the comic solution which goes a step farther and says that what looks like a trick of art is symbolic of some ultimate order in life, which uses the artifice to project a vision of order upon the naturalistic vision of disorder. This is the understanding of artifice behind the highly "esthetic" nineteenth- and twentieth-century literary talk about marionettes, dolls, masks and the stylized movements of the dance. Since this talk is directed against scientific naturalism, it is more belligerent—it conceives artifice as more artificial—than the traditional understanding which takes the formal aspects of art rather more for granted. The Aristotelian idea is that the order in art corresponds to the order in nature. The modern theorist says that the order in art symbolizes an order in nature which we cannot perceive, hence the more artificial the symbol, the more it sets our ordinary perceptions at nought, the better; but if we could understand nature completely, we would understand it as we understand a work of art—we would understand it, in Coleridge's phrase, as "the art of God".[1] We need the whole of this concept to understand Isak Dinesen's references to both the Book of Job and marionettes, to understand the sense in which she is a nature writer and a writer about styles of art and civilization.

In two perceptive radio talks, published as *Karen Blixen og Marionetterne* (*Karen Blixen and the Marionettes*), the Danish critic,

[1] " On Poesy or Art "

Aage Henriksen, says that Isak Dinesen uses the marionettes as symbols in the myth which is central to her work, the myth of the fall.[1] The point is that the self-consciousness that came with the fall made man imperfect, because it gave him the possibility of separating his own will from God's. Since the fall, perfection has consisted either in having no consciousness, like marionettes, or in having unlimited consciousness, like God. The mechanical doll, the most inhuman possible image, becomes therefore a symbol of divinity.

Henriksen applies the ideas of the most complete discussion we have of the esthetic significance of marionettes, the brilliant "Dialogue on the Marionette Theater", written at the turn of the nineteenth century by the German playwright Heinrich von Kleist,[2] who also wrote tales that combine, like Isak Dinesen's imaginative intensity with satire. A famous dancer remarks in the dialogue that "the puppets could be very effective teachers of the dance". When the author asks how the puppeteer manages "the confusion of strings" necessary "to direct the small limbs in the intricate rhythms of the dance", the dancer replies that the limbs are not separately controlled. " 'Each puppet', he said, 'has a focal point in movement, a center of gravity, and when this center is moved, the limbs follow without any additional handling. After all, the limbs are pendula, echoing automatically the movement of the center.' "

The esthetic principle is that the artist does not consciously govern a multitude of details which it would be beyond anyone's capacity to govern. His conscious intention is simple, but if it is esthetically right, if it is at "the center of gravity", the ramifications will automatically follow. It is the automatism that transforms nature into art.

The dancer admits that the marionette's dance is not entirely mechanical; it is to some degree expressive of the puppeteer. Yet he goes on to speculate that " 'this last vestige of human spirit can be eliminated from the marionettes; and then their dance would be completely mechanized' "—it would be perfect. If an artisan would build him a marionette according to his directions, that marionette could " 'perform a dance which neither I nor any

---

[1] ([Copenhagen:] Wivel, 1952.)

[2] Trans. Don Gifford in *Five Essays on Klee*, ed. Merle Armitage (New York: Duell, Sloan and Pearce, 1950), pp. 63-81.

other capable dancer of this era could duplicate' ". The marionette would be perfect because the placement of its center of
gravity would be, paradoxically, " 'more true to nature than in
the common marionette' ". The completely mechanical artwork
would meet, in other words, the natural ideal; for if the center of
gravity were just where it ought to be, then all intentions would
be subsumed, the right intention would be built in and there
would be no need or possibility for conscious intention to inter-
vene between nature and art. Since the puppeteer could no
longer exercise choice, the completely mechanical marionette
would never, like human dancers, slip into affectation.

"Great blunders," he added, "are inevitable. We have eaten from
the tree of knowledge; the paradise of Eden is locked up; and the
Cherubim is behind us. We must wander about the world and see if,
perhaps, we can find an unguarded back door."

Art is the back door to Eden—art that delivers us from self-
consciousness through ritual or, in Yeats's phrase, dying into a
dance. " 'We see,' " says the dancer, " 'that in the natural world,
as the power of reflection darkens and weakens, grace comes
forward more radiant, more dominating.' " Art, however, gives
knowledge too, so that it restores

"a purity that has either no consciousness or consciousness without
limit: either the jointed doll or the god."
"Therefore," I said, a little distracted, "we must eat from the tree
of knowledge again and fall back into a state of innocence."
"By all means," he replied, "that is the last chapter in the history
of the world."

We have here the central myth of romantic literature; it is the
secularized and psychologized version of the central myth of
Christianity—the myth of the fall and redemption. Concerned
less with sin than with the question whether sin was possible at
all, whether values had any objective reality and the self any
relation to the outside world, the romanticists interpreted the
fall as a fall in perception—a fall into the analytic fragmentation
of a world which was once perceived singly, a world in which
subject and object, fact and value, and the values themselves,
beauty, truth and goodness, had no separate names. All this is
in English literature most explicitly set forth by Blake, who takes
off from the theological paradox of the Fortunate Fall—the

paradox that man, in regaining Eden through moral choice and an awareness of God's grace and love, will have gained a greater Eden than that unconscious state of innocence which he lost. In the romantic version, the paradox is interpreted to mean that art recaptures for consciousness the data of unconscious knowledge and thus regains for us our lost unity of perception through an expansion of consciousness. That is the meaning of Kleist's conclusion.

In Isak Dinesen's stories, we have already seen how an artist in life sets in motion events that take over of themselves, producing a pattern and meaning beyond the character's intention. The artist-character is like Kleist's puppeteer; the events are like the dead limbs of the marionettes; the point where the human turns into the divine artwork is the point of transcendence where art and nature meet. At the point of transcendence, Isak Dinesen's characters lose the naturalistic identities they have had in the story and become automatons of some higher artwork. Sometimes they are compared to marionettes; sometimes they take on the mythical identities required by some other form of art.

When he suggests in the end that the cure for consciousness is more consciousness, Kleist's dancer uses as an example a concave mirror where " 'the image vanishes into infinity and appears again close before us' ". This follows the author's story about a young man who " ' "lost his innocence" ' " because he became aware of his own beauty in a mirror. Isak Dinesen uses mirrors in her stories—in "Roads", for example—with just the meaning Kleist assigns them. In Milton's *Paradise Lost*, Eve's first act after she has been created is to gaze longingly at her own reflection in water; and the suggestion is that the fall began at that moment. In Isak Dinesen, there are many scenes in which young women, like so many Eves, first discover their womanhood by falling in love with their own nakedness in a mirror.

The theme symbolized by the mirror—a theme I would call the mysteries of identity—emerges from the romantic interpretation of the fall. Since the romanticists interpreted the fall as a fall in perception, they saw the main problem left by it as a problem of epistemology or psychology. The problem was how to regain a connection with the outside world, how to find a basis for action or an action adequate to one's awareness of one's own potentiality. The question was at what level of behavior—and in literature through what kind of plot—a person manifests his true self.

Isak Dinesen is an important writer because she has understood the tradition behind her and has taken the next step required by that tradition. Like the other, more massive writers of her generation—Rilke, Kafka, Mann, Joyce, Eliot, Yeats, too, though he is older—she takes off from a sense of individuality developed in the course of the nineteenth century to the point of morbidity, and leads that individuality where it wants to go. She leads it back to a universal principle and a connection with the external world. The universal principle is the unconscious life of man and nature, which, welling up in the human consciousness as myth, is the source of civilization, individual consciousness, and our concept of God's unlimited consciousness. It seems to have been the function of the literary generation born in and around the decade 1875-1885—the generation after that of Nietzsche, Frazer and Freud, the great explorers of myth and the unconscious—to effect a transition from the individual to the archetypal character: from the novel, with its separation of psychological and external data, to the myth which speaks with one voice of both.

Thomas Mann, in an essay of 1936 called "Freud and the Future", speaks of the transition in his own fiction from the psychological and naturalistic *Buddenbrooks* to the mythical *Joseph and His Brothers*.[1] Speaking of the "point at which the psychological interest passes over into the mythical", Mann says: "It is plain to me that when as a novelist I took the step in my subject-matter from the bourgeois and individual to the mythical and typical my personal connection with the [psycho]analytic field passed into its acute stage." The connection lies in the answer, which is "the innermost core of psychoanalytic theory", to "the mystery of the unity of the ego and the world". The answer lies in the perception to which psychoanalysis leads us that "the apparently objective and accidental" is "a matter of the soul's own contriving", that "the giver of all given conditions resides in ourselves". When we remember, Mann explains, all Freud has revealed about "error, the retreat into illness, the psychology of

---

[1] *Essays of Three Decades*, trans. H. T. Lowe-Porter (New York: Knopf, 1947; London: Secker & Warburg, 1947).

accidents, the self-punishment compulsion", we realize that it is through our deepest desires that we make connection with external events.

The psychological interest passes over into the mythical at that psychological depth where we desire to repeat mythical patterns. Life at its intensest is repetition. Mann tells us that the ego of antiquity became conscious of itself by taking on the identity of a hero or a god. Caesar trod in the footsteps of Alexander, and Cleopatra made herself into the earthly embodiment of Ishtar, Hathor and Isis. She manifested in dying her mythical ego, for there exists a statuette of Ishtar holding a snake to her bosom. Jesus quoted on the Cross the Twenty-second Psalm, " 'Eli, Eli, lama sabachtani' ", to say in effect, " 'Yes, it is I!' " of whom the Psalm speaks. "Precisely thus", says Mann in a ravishing comparison, "did Cleopatra quote when she took the asp to her breast to die; and again the quotation meant: 'Yes, it is I!' "

These examples from Mann help us understand the style of so many characters and scenes in Isak Dinesen—the godlike qualities of Prince Potenziani in "Roads", and the lovers quoting Dante at each other. They help us understand, as we shall see, the big moment in "The Deluge at Norderney" (*SGT*) when Miss Nat-og-Dag says to Kasparson, " '*Fils de St Louis, montez au ciel!*' " Isak Dinesen's characters are, like Mann's antique figures, artists of their own personalities in that they know what powers they draw upon.

Mann also helps us understand the comic element in this view of life as repetition. For he describes the characters of his *Joseph* as puppets who know they are puppets reeling off, in the hoaxing of Esau the Red for example, "a plot abiding from past time and now again present in a jest". The effect is actually, as Mann makes clear, tragicomic; for Mann's characters feel the emotions they know they are representing. They are like and unlike puppets in a way which helps us understand the quality of *Seven Gothic Tales*, the way in which it is like and unlike "Revenge of Truth". The word of Mann's which best describes the quality of *Seven Gothic Tales* is "blithe"; for the word implies in Mann's context the triumph over difficulties, the triumph of comedy over tragedy. It is this blitheness—"a blithe skepticism . . . a mistrust that unmasks all the schemes and subterfuges of our own souls"— that Mann sees as Freud's contribution to the art and humanism of the future. The mythical view, says Mann, although it came early in the life of the race, is in the life of the individual "a late and mature" view.[1]

In describing the mythoi of tragedy and comedy, Northrop Frye tells us that we reconcile ourselves to tragedy, which is the myth of autumn or death, because it leads by implication to comedy, which is the myth of spring or rebirth.[2] If Frye is right, then tragicomedy ought to be the vehicle of the complete or ultimate vision—which may be why Greek tragedy finished with the tragicomedies of Euripides, and why Shakespeare finished by writing those curious last plays that illustrate better than anything else in literature the ripeness or blitheness of which Mann speaks. If the seventeenth and eighteenth centuries liked best among Shakespeare's works his early comedies, and if the nineteenth century liked the tragedies best, it is possible that the last tragicomedies may in the future have most to say to us. Shakespeare's career might be interpreted according to the romantic myth of the fall from innocence (the pastoral comedies) into experience (the tragedies) back to a regained innocence (the tragicomedies) that comes from completion of the tragic knowledge.

One recalls in connection with the last plays Sidney's remark that old writers love the marvelous.[3] One recalls, too, the tragic gayety which is the hard-won achievement of the aged Yeats in his last poems. Isak Dinesen, who published her first volume at forty-nine, must be understood as starting at the stage of vision appropriate to old writers. In taking the pseudonym Isak—which means laughter—she must have remembered Sarah, who laughed when she bore Isaac because she thought it a fine jest of the Lord's to give her, after a lifetime of barrenness, a child in her old age. "And Sarah said, God hath made me to laugh, so that all that hear will laugh with me" (Genesis 21: 6). *Seven Gothic Tales* was both Isak Dinesen's late-born child and the vehicle of the laughter she wanted everyone to hear. Her laughter is the laughter of rebirth—of wonder at the power of the divine imagination that, having given her happiness in so unexpected a

[1] Isak Dinesen did not know this essay of Mann's, but she knew "by heart" the *Joseph* novels (1934 on) where she would have found the same ideas. She loved the novels, she said, because they were comic and charming.

[2] *Anatomy of Criticism* (Princeton: Princeton University Press, 1957), p. 215.

[3] " In Apology for Poetry ".

place as Africa, took it all away and then allowed her to recover what she had lost through imagination.

When we were talking once about the sense in which she used the word *tale*, Isak Dinesen said that she did not intend the word in the sense of the Danish *eventyr* (which Danes translate as *fairy tale* and associate with Hans Christian Andersen), but in the sense of Shakespeare's *Winter's Tale*. Her second volume of stories takes its title from Shakespeare's play, and the Danish title, *Vinter-Eventyr*, is a translation from the English. For the Danish titles of *Seven Gothic Tales* and *Last Tales*, she uses the word *fortællinger* which does not carry the connotation of fairy tale. If, following her hint, we assimilate her use of the word *tale* or *story* to Shakespeare's last plays, we may understand her to mean romance, but romance used to achieve tragicomedy—to subsume the opposition between the tragic and comic, that is discussed throughout her work, in the naive view of a child or primitive who sees a story as neither tragic or comic but as marvelous.

We have already seen how in "Roads" the events take over of themselves to turn the tragedy set in motion by Carlotta and Prince Potenziani into a divine marionette comedy. In the last story of *Seven Gothic Tales*, "The Poet", the man who tries to manipulate the other characters as though they were marionettes in a comedy of his own devising, finds that he has created instead a tragedy of which he is himself the tragic hero. (But even here he realizes, at the moment of his death, that in playing out his tragedy he has stepped into a divine artwork that is itself comic.) It is because the two stories make such a nice pair of opposites—showing, respectively, that comedy is the divine art and tragedy the human art—that in the author's arrangement, which is to be found in the British and Danish editions, they open and close the volume and, in their final effect, subsume tragedy and comedy in tragicomedy.

Only in the American edition does "Deluge at Norderney" come first, presumably because the publisher felt it would draw readers into the volume. The American editors were not wrong to place "Deluge" first, for it is among Isak Dinesen's very best stories. I think it is her best because it is her wittiest. It combines the greatest number of her characteristic themes, and the most widely opposite effects. The wit fuses all these things into a story

56

that manages at every point to be both tragic and comic. "Deluge" is Isak Dinesen's supreme achievement in tragicomedy.

Take, for example, the brilliant opening paragraph, which so lightly sketches out for us the cultural history of Europe.

> During the first quarter of the last century, seaside resorts became the fashion, even in those countries of Northern Europe within the minds of whose people the sea had hitherto held the rôle of the devil, the cold and voracious hereditary foe of humanity. The romantic spirit of the age, which delighted in ruins, ghosts, and lunatics, and counted a stormy night on the heath and a deep conflict of the passions a finer treat for the connoisseur than the ease of the salon and the harmony of a philosophic system, reconciled even the most refined individuals to the eternal wildness of the coast scenery and of the open seas. Ladies and gentlemen of fashion abandoned the shade of their parks to come and walk upon the bleak shores and watch the untameable waves. The neighborhood of a shipwreck, where, in low tide, the wreck was still in sight, like a hardened, black, and salted skeleton, became a favorite picnic place, where fair artists put up their easels.

The style is built on the contrast of comic and tragic implications —the frivolousness of the romantic spirit and the ladies with their easels play against the hereditary role of the sea and the skeleton of the shipwreck. The contrast becomes even more violent when we learn that "the peasants and fishermen of Norderney[1] themselves learned to look upon the terrible and faithless gray monster westward of them as upon some kind *maître de plaisir*". It is a sign of the *embourgeoisement* of the peasants and fishermen as of the aristocracy that they have begun to flirt with "the dangerous powers of existence". The changed attitude toward the sea marks the end of the *ancien régime.*

When the sea shows itself in its full power, most of the guests depart. This happens in the late summer of 1835, when after a three days' storm the sea breaks through the dikes and floods the land. We hear of the stricken farmers, and of the already half-mythical figure of the 73-year-old Cardinal Hamilcar von Sehestedt, who is giving them miraculous support in their despair. Like the Cardinal of *Last Tales*, Cardinal von Sehestedt is Isak Dinesen's ideal figure in that he combines aristocratic lineage with spirituality. He also combines wit and imagination.

---

[1] Norderney, on the west coast of Holstein, may have been suggested by Heine— Isak Dinesen herself was never there—who writes of it in *The North Sea* Part III. Heine's visit to the bath is mentioned in the story.

The old man was spending the summer in a fisherman's cottage, collecting into a book his writings on the Holy Ghost. For he held with the medieval divine, Joachim de Flora, that the testament of the Third Person of the Trinity remained to be written.[1] He had with him "only a sort of valet or secretary, a man by the name of Kasparson . . a former actor and adventurer". In the collapse of the Cardinal's cottage at the start of the flood, Kasparson was killed and the Cardinal badly wounded so that he now wears during his rescue work "a long, blood-stained bandage wound about his head".

It is late afternoon when the last rescue boat of the day starts back with the remaining survivors from the bath. The miracle-working Cardinal is in charge There is a rich, crazy old maiden lady, Miss Malin Nat-og-Dag, "the last of the old illustrious race which carried arms two-parted in black and white, and whose name meant 'Night and Day' ". She has with her the sixteen-year-old Countess Calypso von Platen-Hallermund; the two ladies gave "that impression of wildness which, within a peaceful age and society, only the vanishing and decaying aristocracy can afford to maintain". On the way back, a peasant family signal them from the hayloft of a sinking farmhouse. Since the boat cannot hold more people, it is necessary for some of the passengers to change places with the family of the farmhouse. The Cardinal rises first, followed by Miss Malin, the Countess Calypso and a young man, Jonathan Mærsk. Since it is now dark, they will have to wait until dawn for a boat to return. The question is whether the boat will return before the farmhouse sinks.

The symbolism is perfect. These four choice souls are to spend the night in a sinking loft. There is nothing for them to *do*; they can only show what they *are*. There is a preliminary pause, like that marked by the tapping of the conductor's baton before the orchestra starts, then the story moves upward to a new level of imaginative intensity. The transition occurs in the following sentence: "As if they had been four marionettes, pulled by the

---

[1] Joachim de Fiore (c. 1145-1203) held that in the coming Age of the Holy Ghost, there would be no need of the discipline of the Church. The doctrine seems to reinforce the romantic idea that in modern times the source of true religion is the imagination. "The next era is the era of the Holy Ghost," writes D. H. Lawrence (*Studies in Classic American Literature*, Chap. 6; Garden City, N.Y.: Anchor Books, 1953, p. 89; London: Martin Secker, 1933, p. 82).

same wire, the four people turned their faces to one another."
The two couples, one old, one young, wait to begin the dance of
wit.

At the Cardinal's suggestion, Miss Malin gets the dance going
by playing the role of hostess, as though the hayloft were her
salon and she had "death itself, like some lion of the season,
some fine Italian tenor, out of the reach of rival hostesses, waiting
outside the door to appear and create the sensation of the night".
We are told her story—that if she appears a bit off her head, it
may be from choice. As a girl, she was a fanatical virgin who took
too literally the Bible's words against lust. To Malin, a man's
desire for her was "a deadly impertinence", like an "attempted
rape". The man whom she finally picked out to marry, Prince
Ernest Theodore of Anhalt, the most sought after young man of
his time, could have found in Miss Malin "nothing striking but
the price. That this thin, big-nosed, penniless girl, two years
older than he, would demand not only his princely name and a
full share in his brilliant future, but also his prostrate adoration,
life-long fidelity, and subjection in life and death and could be
had for nothing less,—this impressed the young Prince." He was
so nervous about this first risk of refusal that he did not propose
until the evening before his departure for war. He was killed at
Jena. Miss Malin renounced all further thought of marriage,
thus completing an old-fashioned story of monumental frustration. Her kind of sexual deficiency, which Isak Dinesen treats
in several stories, comes from too high an idealism.

At fifty she came into a large fortune, but she was changed by
"what changes all women at fifty: the transfer from the active
service of life . . . to the mere passive state of a looker-on. . . . In
her laughter of liberation there certainly was a little madness."
The description of her madness is high comedy. "She believed
herself to have been the grand courtesan of her time, if not the
great whore of the Revelation. She took her fortune, her house,
and her jewels as the wages of sin, collected in her long career of
falls." If in young men she had taken the pursuit of adultery for
the deed, she now took for the deed the acts of compliance she
had not committed. By acknowledging her participation in that
fall which she had already incurred through imagining it, she
has, in Kleist's phrase, fallen back into the state of innocence
that her fierce virginity had lost her. It is in this state of innocence

regained, "this glow of milk madness and second youth", that we now find her.

The Cardinal introduces a new subject with one of those fantastic opening sentences that in Isak Dinesen sound like an orchestra striking up its first chords. " 'When, as a boy, I stayed for some time at Coblentz, at the court of the emigrant Duke of Chartres, I knew the great painter Abildgaard.' " The Danish painter, Abildgaard, used to tell the court ladies who came to have their portraits painted to wash off their powder and rouge, for if they would paint their faces themselves he could not paint them. The Cardinal reflects that this is what the Lord is continually telling us: " ' "Wash your faces. For if you will do the painting of them yourselves, laying on humility and renunciation, charity and chastity one inch thick, I can do nothing about them." ' " Such antinomian morality hardly suits a Cardinal, but it is part of the story's point and prepares us for a surprising revelation about the Cardinal; as does the reference to the Duke of Chartres who would have been, according to the chronology of the situation, Philippe-Egalité before he became in 1785 Duke of Orléans.[1]

" 'Where in all the world did you get the idea that the Lord wants the truth from us?' " Miss Malin asks. " 'It is a strange, a most original idea of yours, My Lord. Why, he knows it already, and may even have found it a little bit dull. Truth is for tailors and shoemakers, My Lord. I, on the contrary, have always held that the Lord has a penchant for masquerades.' " She is talking about the difference between the quantitative truth, which is important only for people who have to take measurements, and the qualitative truth which gives life its value. The latter operates through concealment and even deception, through the symbolic mode of art. It is because the symbolic mode is enigmatic that its truth is not information but an evocation of life as having depths and extensions, connections with some infinite resource of power the consciousness of which gives us the courage to live life as though it were something grander than the utilitarian business of seeking pleasure and avoiding pain. The idea is at the heart of Isak Dinesen's defense of the old European order, which operated by symbols rather than facts.

[1] The term "emigrant" would apply better to his son Louis-Philippe were it not for the chronology. I find no evidence that either of them held court at Coblentz.

They are " 'really of one mind' ", the Cardinal says gently. " 'This world of ours is like the children's game of bread and cheese; there is always something underneath—truth, deceit; truth, deceit!' " His point is that the mask reveals some deeper truth than the facts can, so the mask is after all true. " 'So speaketh the Arbiter of the masquerade: "By thy mask I shall know thee." ' " God is the Arbiter, and when at the day of judgment He lets fall His mask—it will be the supreme comic moment.

The Cardinal proposes that they let fall their masks. " 'Tell me who you are, and recount to me your stories without restraint.' " The Cardinal turns first to Jonathan Mærsk, whose story is comic, a little joke really, though it is about his fall into self-consciousness when he learned that he was the illegitimate son of a great nobleman, that he was in spite of himself a man of fashion. To escape this fact, he became a misanthrope; he was known in Copenhagen as Timon of Assens, after the seaport town on the island of Funen where he was born. But his very misanthropy became the fashion.

" 'What a story, Monsieur Timon,' " exclaims Miss Malin, " 'What a place this is! What people we are!' " They all share the qualities which make Jonathan so right. He has noble blood, the more he disdains his nobility the more he demonstrates it. He is a true wit; they are all true wits, which is why Miss Malin exults. She wants him for Calypso. He is the man to *see* Calypso; for if his problem is that he was seen only in his worldly or external aspect and therefore not in himself, Calypso's problem is that nobody could or would see her in her external aspect, her beauty, and nobody therefore could see her in herself.

Miss Malin's story about Calypso is in a comic vein far wilder, far more fantastic than Jonathan's story. She is more imaginative than Jonathan, and "Deluge" is designed to increase steadily in imaginative intensity. Miss Malin begins her story by naming the German romantic poet, Count August von Platen-Hallermund.[1] " 'As he is not a man, but an angel,' " she says slyly, " 'we shall call him the Count Seraphina.' " He is Calypso's uncle; and she

---

[1] Isak Dinesen follows Heine's "The Baths of Lucca", in which Platen is satirized for his estheticism and homosexuality as well as for his humorless pomposity. Since she probably recognized the recollections of Platen in Mann's "Death in Venice", she would have chosen Platen as a significantly modern European case.

was raised, after her parents died, in his ivory tower, the castle of Angelshorn. Now the Count Seraphina, as the neuter name suggests, is not a man in two senses—he is not a human being and not a male. He " 'disliked and mistrusted everything female; it gave him goose flesh,' " Miss Malin continues. " 'His idea of paradise was, then, a long row of lovely young boys, in transparent robes of white, walking two by two, singing his poems to his music . . . or otherwise discussing his philosophy, or absorbed in his books upon arithmetics.' " Count Seraphina dressed and educated Calypso as though she were a boy, until certain " 'signs' " made his " 'failure' " apparent. Then " 'he turned his eyes away from her forever' " and, we are told satirically, " 'annihilated her' ".

In figures like Counts Seraphina and Schimmelmann, and Jonathan Mærsk's father Baron Gersdorff, Isak Dinesen is satirizing estheticism and rationalism. Isak Dinesen associates esthetes, rationalists and moralists as opponents of instinct and experience—of reality. In considering Calypso annihilated, Count Seraphina is like the Schimmelmann of "In the Menagerie" (*Out of Africa*), who thinks that " 'the wild animals which run in a wild landscape, do not really exist' ", because no one sees them. Schimmelmann implicitly shares Count Seraphina's feeling that " 'the existence of the brute creation was an enigma and a tragedy' "; for both follow Descartes in assuming that things exist only inasmuch as they are thought about, so that the forms of life that are not self-aware must be machinelike. The Schimmelmann of "Roads" shows like Count Seraphina the desexualizing consequences of rationalism. Isak Dinesen is deliberately vague about whether Schimmelmann's and even Count Seraphina's homosexuality is active or only latent. That is because she is interested in their kind of homosexuality as a mental condition—as the inability of a mind to love anything beyond its own diagrammatic imprint upon the external world. To love women and wild animals, you have to believe in the concrete reality of objects other than the self.[1] The esthete is not distinguished by his love of art but by his desire to organize all of life like a work of art; and he is, in his desire to see the imprint

---

[1] One recalls Yeats's characterization of aristocrats as "the lovers of women and of horses" ("The Gyres"), and the connection in Hemingway of hunting or bullfighting with heterosexuality and an aristocratic code.

of human will and consciousness on everything, as rationalistic as the engineer.

To fit into this rationalistic environment, Calypso decides to do physically what so many women have for the same reason done psychologically—she decides to cut off her long hair and chop off her breasts. Hatchet in hand, she steals one night to a room where there is a long looking-glass and, as she sweeps down her clothes to the waist in front of the glass, we are given one of those scenes of Isak Dinesen in which a young girl discovers her nakedness in a mirror. It is the beginning of the fall—a sweet triumph among people who, like Miss Malin in her youth, have sinned in their attempt to avert the fall. Determined to preserve her womanhood, Calypso escaped from the castle to Miss Malin, her godmother.

Miss Malin has the Cardinal marry the young couple with a new rite appropriate to a marriage which can be consummated only in spirit and must be lived out in one night. When the ceremony is over, the Cardinal remarks on " 'the tremendous courage of the Creator of this world' ". For the Cardinal, had he made the world, " 'would not have dared to arrange these matters of love and marriage as they are' ". We fail, in other words, to understand reality because we are not imaginative enough; our plans and expectations are always too rational. The Cardinal makes the point explicit in one of those fine cries which, like Prince Potenziani's " 'Always we fail because we are too small' ", gives us a direct glimpse into the depth of tragic sincerity which we otherwise only sense in the special complexity of the wit. " 'What an overwhelming lesson to all artists! Be not afraid of absurdity; do not shrink from the fantastic. Within a dilemma, choose the most unheard-of, the most dangerous, solution. Be brave, be brave!' "

This is just what Isak Dinesen does to bring "Deluge" to its climax. The Cardinal proceeds to tell his story, " 'The Wine of the Tetrarch' ", which is the best of the three inset stories, as by its position it should be. It is not comic in the manner of the first two, for it takes off from the Gospels in subject and manner and has all the solemn resonance of a Biblical parable when it is read aloud in church.

"As, then, upon the first Wednesday after Easter," the Cardinal began, "the Apostle Simon, called Peter, was walking down the

streets of Jerusalem, so deeply absorbed in the thought of the resurrection that he did not know whether he was walking upon the pave-
ment or was being carried along in the air, he noticed, in passing the
Temple, that a man was standing by a pillar waiting for him. As their
eyes met, the stranger stepped forward and addressed him. 'Wast thou
not also,' he asked, 'with Jesus of Nazareth?'
" 'Yes, yes, yes,' Peter replied quickly."

The great achievement of this story is its projection of inward-
ness. Each man seems to be wrapped in the aura of his own
thoughts; the dialogue is heard as traveling a long distance from
outside in. The effect is achieved through the stately diction and
pace, through the use of stillness as a form of action and the
management of pauses,[1] through the steady deepening of
implication that gives to every word and glance ultimate importance. The repeated play on *wine*, and *body* as it applies to wine,
develops the ironic contrast between Peter and the other man, a
robber whose concern with the events of Friday is that his friend
was crucified with Jesus.

After inviting Peter for a drink at an inn, the robber asks
whether his friend went to paradise on Friday as " ' "this Rabbi
of yours promised" ' ". When Peter assures him that it is so, the
man complains that the wine of Jerusalem has all turned bad
since the earthquake. " ' "And good wine is my great pleasure.
Now I do not know what to do." ' "

He tells how having heard of a shipment of priceless red Capri
which the Emperor of Rome was sending to the tetrarch Herodes,
he said to his friend, Phares, that he would give his heart to drink
that red wine of the tetrarch's, and Phares said that to show his
love for him he would kill the overseer of the transport and bury
the wine until they could drink it together. Phares did all this,
but was caught and condemned to be crucified. Disguised as a
beggar, the speaker broke the law and got himself imprisoned
with Phares in order to smuggle him a file and rope. The speaker
was caught in the act of escaping, and Phares, who had already
made good his escape, would not desert his friend, so the two
were returned to prison and Phares was crucified on Friday.
" ' "Since you are here, you got off somehow?" ' " Peter asks.

" 'Yes; I got off,' said the man, and gave Peter a strange deep

---

[1] "All Natives," says Isak Dinesen in *Out of Africa*, "are masters in the art of the
pause and thereby give perspective to a discussion" (New York, p. 48; London,
p. 52). She may have learned her own art of the pause from them.

glance. 'I meant, then, to revenge Phares's death. But since he is in paradise I do not see that I need to worry. And now I do not know what to do. Shall I dig up this hogshead of the tetrarch's wine and drink it? . . . If that wine also has gone bad and gives me no pleasure, what am I to do then?' "

We can see the ironic parallel between the priceless red wine of the tetrarch and the blood of Christ; between Phares's self-sacrifice and Christ's; between Phares's plan to bury and resurrect the wine and drink it together, and the Communion ritual; between the robber's sense of the new dispensation and Peter's. Peter, however, is emotionally involved in the disparity and similarity. On the one hand, he only half attends to what seems a trivial complaint about wine; on the other hand, this robber unknowingly establishes a community of guilt between them. The man's question, " ' "Wast thou not also with Jesus of Nazareth?" ' " is the question Peter was asked when he denied Jesus three times, which is why Peter gives his affirmative answer three times quickly.

It is after sitting " 'a little while in his own thoughts' " that Peter says, " ' "there are other things in life to give you pleasure than the wine of the tetrarch" ' ". The man agrees that he might try his two lovely wives and a virgin of twelve he has just purchased, but he fears that they may also have been affected by the earthquake. What is for us an accumulating irony is for Peter an accumulating blasphemy which finally, when the man reveals what he is after, drives home to Peter his own far more serious blasphemy—for Peter knew what *he* was saying.

" 'I have been informed that your Rabbi, on the night before he died, gave a party to his followers, and that at that time a special wine was served, which was very rare and had some highly precious body in it. Have you, now, any more of this wine, and will you consent to sell it to me? I will give you your price.'

"Peter stared at the stranger. 'Oh, God, oh, God,' he cried, so highly affected that he upset his wine, which ran onto the floor, 'you do not know what you are saying. This wine which we drank on Thursday night, the Emperor of Rome cannot pay for one drop of it' His heart was so terribly wrung that he rocked to and fro in his seat.'

The upsetting of the wine brings back the Crucifixion.

Yet looking at the man, it came over Peter that he was " 'of all people in the world, . . . the one whom he could not help' ". We see why in the absolute opposition of their hopes. To Peter's

" ' "Take up your cross . . . He will help you to carry it" ' ", the man declared he would need no help to carry a cross. If, before, we saw through the man's ironic uncomprehension a despair corresponding to Peter's, we now see by the same means a strength of character equal to Peter's. The man bares his chest and shoulders to show the crosses made by knife scars, and says disdainfully he would have lasted more than six hours on the cross. He rises to go, saying he must *meet* a transport of oil.

The man's future is made to seem harder than Peter's, and lonelier. When he reveals his name and we realize what it is that weighs upon his soul, he becomes in his opposite way as morally significant a figure, and we see that the ironic parallels of the story are the parallel paths to salvation of saint and hero—paths that never meet until infinity. " ' "What is your name?" ' " Peter asks.

"He turned around and looked at Peter with hauteur and a slight scorn. He looked a magnificent figure. 'Did you not know my name?' he asked him. 'My name was cried all over the town. There was not one of the tame burghers of Jerusalem who did not shout it with all his might. "Barabbas," they cried, "Barabbas! Barabbas! Give us Barabbas." My name is Barabbas. I have been a great chief, and, as you said yourself, a brave man. My name shall be remembered.' And with these words he walked away."

The repetition of the name is masterly and shows how in the mythical kind of story the revelation of a name is the revelation of a state of soul. Barabbas reminds us in his last sentence that he was indispensable to the famous drama he helped enact. Barabbas, Judas, Pilate, Caiaphas fascinate Isak Dinesen as the tragic figures in the divine comedy of the Passion. They were tragically sacrificed, their suffering is endless, in order to make possible Jesus's comic sacrifice, the happy outcome of which was never in doubt.

The story is punctuated by the longest pause in Isak Dinesen, a pause of a page and a quarter during which Jonathan rises, rejoins his wife, the two fall asleep, and Miss Malin continues to be transfigured before our eyes. Earlier we were told that "she looked like a corpse of twenty-four hours", now she "looked as if she were not going to sleep for all eternity", in the end she has "on her shoulders that death's-head by which druggists label their poison bottles". Finally, as if to answer the question of the point of the story, which has been standing between them, the Cardinal removes the blood-stained bandages from his head. " 'My name,' " he says, echoing Barabbas, " 'is Kasparson. I am the Cardinal's valet.' " He killed the Cardinal before the boat arrived to rescue them that morning. "The Wine of the Tetrarch" has been the vehicle of his self-revelation and self-defense.

Miss Malin's eye for nobility has been impugned, and she demands to know with whom she has passed the night. Kasparson reveals that he is what must be, for a Legitimist like Miss Malin, the most shocking thing possible—the bastard son of a moral bastard, of Philippe-Egalité, that Duke of Orléans who " 'voted for the death of the King of France' ". He is an actor by profession. As a child he danced in ballet, later he became a courtesan to the elderly noblemen of Berlin; he has been a barber in Spain, a printer of revolutionary papers in Paris, a dogseller in London, a slavetrader in Algiers, and the lover of a dowager principessa of Pisa. He has had a life the very opposite of the Cardinal's. Yet it is no less appealing to our imagination. We cannot, as a matter of fact, be sure that this new figure is not as much a fabrication as that of the Cardinal. The account of Kasparson's career sounds like a comic aria in an opera by Mozart or Rossini.

Beginning to regain confidence in her eye, Miss Malin joins in this new game. When Kasparson says that he has " 'stood in the great triangular shadow of the great pyramid' " in Egypt, she, not to be outshone in imagination, comes out with her wildest witticism. Obscene, grotesque, like nothing she has said before, it is a sign that she is joining hands with this new partner, that their dance of wit is becoming, as his unmasking and her transfiguration into a death's-head shows, a *danse macabre*. The mounting intensity of the comedy corresponds to the mounting intensity of the tragedy as morning approaches. " 'Ah,' " she says, " 'in Egypt, in the great triangular shadow of the great pyramid, while the ass was grazing, St Joseph said to the Virgin: "Oh, my sweet young dear, could you not just for a moment shut your eyes and make believe that I am the Holy Ghost?" ' "

The little story seems wildly irrelevant, until Kasparson responds with an equally fantastic allusion. Kasparson is itself a pseudonym, he reveals, which, when fleeing the law in Copenhagen, he took " 'in remembrance of that proud and unfortunate boy of Nürnberg who stabbed himself to death in order to make

Lord Stanhope believe that he was the illegitimate son of Grand Duchess Stephanie of Baden' ". The allusion is to Kaspar Hauser, whose life relates to that of Kasparson[1]; for Kasparson is committing suicide, both literally and in Miss Malin's esteem, in order to prove that he is the illegitimate son of the Duke of Orléans. The situation is archetypal, and relates to Miss Malin's little joke, in which the legitimate husband can only hope to be mistaken for the illegitimate. Did not Jesus sacrifice his life to prove that he was the illegitimate son of the Holy Ghost?

Without knowing it, Miss Malin has foreseen the substance of Kasparson's self-defense—that he wanted to show what he was capable of being, to manifest the Holy Ghost in himself. When Miss Malin asks why he wanted this role so much, Kasparson answers, " 'Not by the face shall the man be known, but by the mask' "—because the mask allows you to play out your unrealized potentialities.

Now we see why Kasparson was in a position to understand Louis-Philippe; he is his older brother and, as usurper of the Cardinal's role, he can understand the usurper of the throne of France. Like Barabbas, Kasparson is the criminal who usurped the right to live that should have been the saint's. Through the story of Barabbas, however, Kasparson is saying that the usurper

[1] Notorious in his time, Kaspar Hauser was a German youth who appeared mysteriously in Nuremberg in 1828 with hardly any capacity for speech or knowledge of the world. It came to be believed that he was the Crown Prince of Baden, that he had been kidnapped from his cradle, and that a dying baby had been substituted in his place in order to secure the succession to a collateral line. The English Earl Stanhope took up Kaspar's cause and then turned against him, denouncing him as an impostor. Kaspar died of a knife wound in 1833, but it was never determined whether he stabbed himself or whether, as he alleged, he was stabbed by a stranger. According to the interpretation Isak Dinesen is following, Kaspar Hauser would have committed suicide in order to give Lord Stanhope the impression that he had been murdered by the usurper's party and was therefore the son of Grand Duchess Stephanie. According to this interpretation, Kaspar would have been an impostor in his manner of trying to prove that he was not an impostor.

This has interesting implications for our Kasparson, who may be lying about being the illegitimate son of Philippe-Egalité, in order to prove that he was not an impostor in all that he said under the guise of the Cardinal. Even more interesting is the fact that Kaspar Hauser wanted to prove that he was the *legitimate* son of Grand Duchess Stephanie. Isak Dinesen's change to *illegitimate* makes the allusion comically preposterous, and relates it to her theme of illegitimacy—of, in other words, the Holy Ghost. Isak Dinesen would have seen in Kaspar Hauser a man who managed to excite the imagination of Europe, because he was a great charlatan. (See E. E. Evans, *The Story of Kaspar Hauser* [London: Swan Sonnenschein, 1892] and Andrew Lang, *Historical Mysteries* [London: Smith, Elder, 1904]).

is redeemed by the spirit of the good man whose place he has taken. We see by Barabbas's distaste for the old pleasures that the spirit of Jesus has possessed him, yet its effect is to make him more himself than ever. In the same way, Kasparson is possessed by the Cardinal's spirit at the climax of his career as actor and charlatan. Like Jesus with Barabbas, the Cardinal would in any case " 'have sacrificed his life for mine' ". And Kasparson has now the chance to die for these peasants and fishermen whom, as his mother's people, he loved like nothing else in the world. He would have served them had they called him master, and died for them had they worshipped him.[1] Tonight, he concludes, " 'they have seen the face of God in my face' ". Like all Isak Dinesen's greatest characters, Kasparson wants nothing less than to play at being God.

The unmasking of the Cardinal negates the validity of everything he has been saying. Even the heroism is negated; for, as Miss Malin discreetly observes, if Kasparson is a murderer, then he is doomed whether the boat comes back to rescue them or not. With his whole performance negated morally, Kasparson proceeds to re-establish its validity in esthetic and existential terms. He is pleased to have created this night, and he has thoroughly enjoyed playing the role of the Cardinal.

"For I have lived long enough, by now, to have learned, when the devil grins at me, to grin back. And what now if this—to grin back when the devil grins at you—be in reality the highest, the only true fun in all the world? And what if everything else, which people have named fun, be only a presentiment, a foreshadowing, of it?"

What if "we shall enjoy ourselves hereafter," speculates Keats in his *Letters*, "by having what we called happiness on Earth repeated in a finer tone". The romanticist wants not renunciation or conversion but the intensification of life as it is. To grin back at the devil is the very opposite of changing your ways; it is to intensify your own character to the point where, as Keats says of the intensity of art, "all disagreeables evaporate, from their being in close relationship with Beauty and Truth". The Minds that follow their own bent, says Keats, "would leave each other in contrary directions . . . and at last greet each other at the

---

[1] This is the dream Isak Dinesen herself realized in her relation with her Negro servants in Kenya. Her love for them, she told me, was the greatest passion of her life.

Journeys end".[1] Art carries character to its journey's end, revealing in such opposite personalities as Kasparson and the Cardinal the same Holy Ghost.

Miss Malin, who has also created this night, and who has lived her virginity with such passion as to become one in erotic imagination with her opposite, the whore—Miss Malin breaks out with an utterance like song.

"And I too, I too," said Miss Malin in a voice which, although it was subdued, was rich and shrill, and which seemed to rise in the flight of a lark. As if she wanted to accompany in person the soaring course of it, she rose straight up, with the lightness and dignity of a lady who has had, by now, enough of a pleasant entertainment, and is taking her leave. "I have grinned back at him too. It is an art worth learning."

Her body follows the trajectory of her soaring emotion, just as Prince Potenziani's bullet follows the line of the song he is about to send forth when he dies of love. Kasparson having risen with her, she looks at him with radiant eyes and they consummate their "marriage" with a duet as well as a *pas de deux*.

"Kasparson, you great actor," she said, "Bastard of Égalité, kiss me."

"Ah, no, Madame," said Kasparson, "I am ill; there is poison in my mouth."

Miss Malin laughed. "A fig for that tonight," she said. She looked, indeed, past any sort of poison. She had on her shoulders that death's-head by which druggists label their poison bottles, an unengaging object for any man to kiss. But looking straight at the man before her, she said slowly and with much grace: *"Fils de St Louis, montez au ciel!"*

This is the climax of absurdity and beauty—that the skinny old maid offers her lips as a stairway to heaven, and that she addresses to Kasparson the words reputed to have been addressed to Louis XVI by the priest who officiated at his execution. The beauty is in the imaginative penetration to the potentiality which the absurdity symbolizes by its very extravagance, its equivalent amount of energy. It is because they have made an artwork of the night, made of it an occasion for intense and stylized gestures, that we can see through the old maid to the *donna angelicata* of the high old Western tradition of ideal love, and through the bastard to the true son of St Louis, the exemplary ancestor of the

---

[1] To Benjamin Bailey, November 22, 1817; To George and Thomas Keats, December 21, 27 (?), 1817; To John Hamilton Reynolds, February 19, 1818.

royal line of France. He kisses her, and she concludes the dance with one of the most finely executed flourishes in all Isak Dinesen. "With a majestic and graceful movement she lifted up the hem of her skirt and placed it in his hand. The silk, which had been trailing over the floor, was dripping wet. He understood that this was the reason why she had got up from her seat." Brought back with such wit and style, the tragic note blends with the comedy and poetry to make the story's concluding chord.

The water, which had risen to the level of the hayloft, threatens the young couple asleep on the floor, and it is to stop Kasparson from waking them that Miss Malin suggests, through a swift recapitulation of her life, the sense in which they are all to be saved.

She took one of the actor's hands in hers. "Wait a moment," she said softly, so as not to waken the sleepers. "I want to tell you. I, too, was once a young girl. I walked in the woods and looked at the birds, and I thought: How dreadful that people shut up birds in cages. I thought: If I could so live and so serve the world that after me there should never again be any birds in cages, they should all be free—"

She stops, because she sees between the boards the symbol of their liberation—the dawn which brings them not the rescue boat but death. The image of bird flight, which in her climax of under-standing she had only demonstrated by her voice and motion, she now uses to epitomize her life as leading to that climax. For she has freed them all from the conditions which would have made the hayloft a prison. By turning the hayloft into a stage of the free play of the imagination, she has given them the freest hours of their lives—hours which have prepared them to make death their ultimate triumph over conditions. After such words and gestures, rescue would come as an anti-climax; it would turn the night into a burlesque, as the old lord of "Sorrow-acre" would have turned Anne-Marie's ordeal into burlesque had he stopped it. The end of life is not safety but self-realization.

It is because they are, in meeting death blithely, going to be everything they want to be, that they are saved. Additional years of life could take them no farther toward self-realization. There are, however, two kinds of blitheness. The sleeping young couple will meet death perfectly, because they are innocent of the water, the "dark figure, like that of a long thick snake" on the floor of the loft. The sleepless old couple will meet death perfectly, because they have outstared it, they have grinned back at the snake in the Garden, they know everything. That is what Miss Malin means when she says in effect: Do not wake them, I too was young and knew freedom as potentiality, do not confront their freedom with conditions for they will not have time to regain it as we have. Innocence and Innocence Regained! The two couples together symbolize the whole progress of the imagination in the romantic version of the myth of the fall.

Chapter 3

THE MYSTERIES OF IDENTITY:
SEVEN GOTHIC TALES

SEVEN GOTHIC TALES (1934) is Isak Dinesen's wittiest book. This makes it important. For Isak Dinesen excels among contemporary writers in her wit and her treatment of nature. Her wit is amazing in that it exalts and magnifies and never diminishes its object. Partly it goes back to the great Renaissance tradition according to which wit is the verbal expression of high manners and therefore expresses itself in compliments and in a playfully competitive exhibition of dialectical and verbal skill, the witty tone of which declares that the speaker is bringing all his resources of mind and spirit to the service of the social occasion. She adds to this the nineteenth-century sense that the occasion is not merely social but a work of art, that the speakers are creating for each other a world different from and better than the ordinary world around them. Whereas the world is generally hostile to imagination, they encourage each other to be as imaginative as possible; they spur each other on to higher and higher flights of imaginative thought.

I have suggested that her style of wit is distinctively romantic, because it combines eighteenth-century irony with imaginative activity. I want to distinguish the romantic wit I mean, however, from the sentimental humor that actually dominates most nineteenth-century English and German writing. There are very few nineteenth-century writers whose irony is hard enough and fine enough to make, when it is absorbed in a life-enhancing imaginative vision, the effect I have in mind. Stendhal epitomizes the style I mean. In his combination of satire and romance—in which a heroic or other affirmative posture is subjected to eighteenth-century satire and maintained against it—things are affirmed and denied with the same breath, yet maintain an integrity that transcends the dialectical impasse. The same kind of wit is to be found in much of Dostoevsky—in the Grand Inquisitor episode, for example, in *Brothers Karamazov*. It is to be found in Kierkegaard and Nietzsche.

73

It is, I think, because the Danes did not at first understand Isak Dinesen's style of wit that they objected to *Seven Gothic Tales*. The Danes were offended by what they took to be the book's blatantly reactionary politics and its decadence. Frederick Schyberg, in his review of the book, said it made its appeal through snobbery and perversity. Annoyed that Isak Dinesen's success should have come to Denmark as a *fait accompli*, accomplished in America, he said that *Seven Gothic Tales* would have appealed to just the cheap American sense of old-world aristocratic decadence as glamorous. He condemned the book as a brilliant fake, sensational but without meaning.[1]

Schyberg's review raises all the questions that have to be answered in connection with Isak Dinesen's work. It is true that Americans, for whom aristocracy is not a political issue, can afford to take a kind of tourist's interest in Isak Dinesen's aristocratic point of view. But this, once the first superficial bewitchment is over, qualifies us for understanding her point of view. For Isak Dinesen treats her aristocrats ironically. She "revives" them in the same anachronistic spirit with which she revives the tale and calls her tales Gothic. "When I used the word 'Gothic'," she told *The Atlantic Monthly* editor Curtis Cate, "I didn't mean the real Gothic, but the imitation of the Gothic, the Romantic age of Byron, the age of that man—what was his name?—who built Strawberry Hill, the age of the Gothic revival."[2] Romantic wit has precisely to do with the revival of an age that was acknowledged to be barbarous and cruel, but which was also felt to be beautiful and stirring to the imagination. Romantic wit is a way of affirming with the imagination what has been denied with the reason. It is a way of salvaging the enduring or existential values that lie beneath the values that have been superseded historically.

"Deluge" offers us, in the aristocrats who go down under the waters with a fine gesture, a perfect example of Isak Dinesen's irony. Nor is aristocracy treated as only a social category. It is also, as the illegitimacy of the two men suggests, a condition of the imagination. The two men inherit from their spiritual, as

---

[1] *Berlingske Tidende*, September 25, 1935. Harald Nielsen continues this line of attack in his book *Karen Blixen* ([Copenhagen:] Borgens, 1956).

[2] "Isak Dinesen", *Atlantic Monthly*, December 1959, p. 153; *Cornhill*, Winter 1959-60, p. 129.

opposed to their official, fathers the aristocracy that the two women have as a biological and official inheritance.[1] But all four are "off-beat" aristocrats. The normal aristocrats have fled from the chance to display the aristocratic virtues. The two men are artists and Miss Malin, who is a bit mad, lives in the imagination. Her heroism is as much an artistic performance as Kasparson's, and his defense of aristocracy could serve as a defense of art. For once aristocracy has been cut off from social function, its code becomes an esthetic code prescribing that the "thing" be done for its own sake.

The aristocratic virtues are in fact salvaged through art. The sinking hayloft cuts our four aristocrats off from society; it makes them derelicts who create their splendid night after every moral and practical reason for doing so has been negated. Isak Dinesen's treatment of aristocracy is ironical and modern, because she displays the aristocratic virtues at that verge where in the modern world the artistic virtues have been driven—among outsiders who dare to deny the whole structure of bourgeois and scientific reality. The ruined chateaux become centers of dissidence in literary history at about the same time as the garrets of Bohemia. Isak Dinesen's aristocrats are in many cases elegant Bohemians.

As far as their politics go, they are as likely to be Jacobins or

[1] Isak Dinesen says in "Sorrow-acre" that it is the women who uphold like caryatids the purity of the noble houses. The idea and image are expanded in "The Caryatids: An Unfinished Gothic Tale," which appears in *Last Tales* but was originally written for her first volume. Her notebooks of the African period show that nine tales were originally planned for her first volume and that her first idea for a title and pseudonym was *Tales by Nozdref's Cook*. (Nozdref's or Nozdyov's cook, in Gogol's *Dead Souls*, put anything around into the pot, sure that some taste or other would result.) "The Old Chevalier" is called "Nocturne" in the notebooks, and "Deluge" does not appear. The three stories that appear in the notebooks but not in *Seven Gothic Tales* are "Caryatids", "Glass" and "Carnival".

No trace of "Glass" has been found. "Carnival", which was originally conceived in Danish as a marionette comedy and was then turned into a story in English (a fairly complete version exists in typescript), shows how Isak Dinesen evolved through marionette comedy to her mature style. It also shows her evolving a technique for speaking with one voice of the twentieth century and the *ancien régime*. The story takes place in 1926, and the characters, four men and four women, who are very 1920's in their attitudes, are having supper after an Opera Carnival at Copenhagen dressed in costumes of the past. The point of the story is to defend the past against the present, by suggesting that the past with its inequality and violence had more notes to its scale so that you could play more beautiful melodies with it. Although "Carnival" contains characters, ideas and passages that are recognizable in many of the published stories, the main situation suggests that "Carnival" may well be a preliminary version of "Deluge".

Bonapartists as Legitimists; for some of them feel, as does Athena in "The Monkey", that the true aristocratic energy is to be found in the revolutionaries rather than in the effete eighteenth-century nobles. Their "decadence", too, is a way of calling attention to the decline of the old order. The high premium on virginity that has poisoned Miss Malin's life is shown as beautiful in the description of the Somali women in *Out of Africa*. By calling attention through the decadence of old virtues to the period when they flourished, Isak Dinesen is at the same time criticizing the new order. Without suggesting that the old virtues can be perpetuated, she is suggesting that the new order will have to find equivalents for them. She does not, in defending the aristocracy, attack other classes. Even the middle class is praised for its special virtues. If she rallies to the defense of the aristocracy, it is because they are the underdogs of our time and because their virtues are obsolete. It is because their cause is so hopeless in a political sense, that she can use their obsolete virtues as a stance from which to understand and criticize modern values.

Isak Dinesen's work, backward-looking as it is, is modern, because she appointed herself the voice of memory. She liked to speak of herself as 3,000 years old. She meant by this, as she explained in two talks on the Danish radio, that her own personal memory went back, through the reminiscences she had heard as a very young child from very old people, to that first third of the nineteenth century about which she liked to write, and that she was able as a woman steeped in the tradition to use cultural memory as an extension of personal memory.[1] Now to appoint yourself the voice of memory in an age when cultural memory has been almost lost, and when we are about to take off from the earth itself, is to take upon yourself a modern job. It is to make modern people see what their world is like by making them see how very new and how very curious it is. It is, even more importantly, to help them salvage their humanity, which might be defined as precisely those values that can be salvaged after the whole of the past has been negated. We see how this is done in "Deluge" through the ironical revival of the old order on the sinking hayloft. It is because the lives of our four aristocrats,

[1] January 1 and 7, 1951; published as *Daguerreotypier* (*Daguerreotypes*) (Copenhagen: Gyldendal, 1951). She quotes Goethe as saying, " 'He who cannot account for at least 3,000 years is living from hand to mouth' " (p. 9).

particularly their sexual deficiencies, are a sign that the old
values of Europe have turned poisonous, that they can, as a *jeu
d'esprit*, blow all the old values up again, like a gorgeous bubble,
restoring for an instant their beauty and validity just because
they are offered as illusory.

Desexualization, only one of the themes in "Deluge at
Norderney", is the subject of the two smaller stories that follow—
"The Old Chevalier" and "The Monkey". "The Old Chevalier"
starts in the twentieth century and carries us back through the
recollections of an obsolete type, the Danish Baron von Brackel
(the old chevalier of the title)[1] to amorous adventures in the
Paris of the 1870's—"in the early days", we are told, "of what we
called then 'the emancipation of woman' ". We have progressed
to a new point in the history of desexualization, but the style of
the Baron's story is elegantly nostalgic. The story itself, however,
is critical; for we are made aware (by the title and the frame, to
start with) that it is being filtered through the nostalgia of a
man who finds himself a stranger among an efficient and machinelike twentieth-century generation. The upholstered atmosphere
of the '70's, which subtly recalls Maupassant and French novels
of the period, is made to seem as old-fashioned as possible, in
order to suggest that if the seeds of trouble were present even
then how much worse things have grown since.

Baron von Brackel's story turns on the juxtaposition of two
amorous adventures that befell him on the same rainy winter
night of 1874—the first one looking forward to our time, the
second looking back to the past. In the first, his mistress tries to
poison him. Although she receives him in the silk-lined boudoir
characteristic of the period, one sees emergent in her the flapper
of the 1920's. She is "blonde", "pale", "colorless", "cool",
"frail" with "an unrivaled energy". She is jealous not, as women
used to be, of other women, but of men. She competes with men,
and is thus among "the young women of the highest intelligence"
who were for the first time in those days "coming out of the
chiaroscuro of a thousand years". Isak Dinesen characterizes

---

[1] The Danish title, "Den Gamle Vandrende Ridder" ("The Old Wandering
Chevalier"), suggests that von Brackel tried forever after to recapture the perfect
experience described in the story. This is not really borne out by the story, but Isak
Dinesen told me that she often changed titles in translating because they sounded
better that way in the other language.

these women as witches—her way of talking about sexual deficiency in women.

It is after von Brackel detects poison in the coffee his mistress hands him, and rushes out of the house, that the second adventure occurs. A foreign girl comes up to him in the rain, her "black hat with ostrich feathers drooping sadly", her eyes were like stars, "her round young neck shone in the light of the gas lamp". This is a period piece down to the sentimentalized prostitute, but the literary associations quite remarkably reinforce the genuineness in this case of the contrast between the girl's innocence and the role she is trying to play.

He takes her to his smart bachelor apartment—also a period piece, the equivalent of the silk-lined boudoir. He asks no questions, but accepts her as "a little wild spirit", a gift (it makes a nice contrast with their ostensibly commercial transaction) out of the Paris night; and he thinks now that he "must also have symbolized something to her, and that I hardly existed for her as an individual". It is because they have both stepped from a brutal reality (hers would be the thing that drove her into the streets, or her experience on the streets) into a romantic story of the '70's, that they exist for each other as symbols and can achieve a perfect night together.

The first adventure turns to poison because the psychological situation is incongruent with the setting. Although the lady is in her silk-lined boudoir, the symbol in that period of femininity, she resists the role of Woman. The second adventure turns into innocence the poison in von Brackel's heart and in the girl's ostensible role, because the psychological situation is congruent with the setting, the individuals lose themselves in their roles of Man and Woman. The scene in which he undresses her, for example, is charming, managing to be both innocent and sensuous. It is interrupted by the witty digression on clothes, which is perhaps the most memorable thing in the story and which explains the contrast von Brackel has already suggested between the individual and the symbol.

Von Brackel derides the "few perpendicular lines" of the clothes women wear nowadays. " 'In those days a woman's body was a secret which her clothes did their utmost to keep. . . . Clothes then had a being, an idea of their own. . . . A woman was then a work of art, the product of centuries of civilization.' "

Like the priests who preside over famous miracles, the women of those days dedicated their lives to the service of a mystery which they knew all about. It would be too simple to say that they disbelieved in it, for they believed in the efficacy of the idea—they saw its transforming effect not only on the men but on themselves: on the little girl who in growing up was gradually "inaugurated into the rites of the cult, and finally ordained. Slowly the center of gravity of her being would be shifted from individuality to symbol, and you would be met with that particular pride and modesty characteristic of the representative of the great powers—such as you may find again in a really great artist."

The girl's clothes, as they fall, combine with the décor to evoke the heavily draped interior of the period within which the lovers can achieve perfect happiness just because the external world is shut out. The perfection ends when von Brackel awakes out of the sleep that follows love—suddenly cold, suddenly distrustful of the future as if he had heard himself asking: " 'I am to pay for this; what am I to pay?' " It is a sign that he has returned to the ordinary sphere of existence, and there follows as a consequence the ironic deflation of the symbols the story has been at such pains to develop. She rises to go, and gets "back into her black shabby disguise"—that disguise which had been given so much significance. " 'And you will give me twenty francs, will you not?' " she asks. " 'Marie said that—she said that I should get twenty francs.' " She has not changed, her clothes have; she emerges from them as freshly innocent as ever. It is he who now sees their happiness together as an illusion. Their happiness, which had seemed a symbol of the ideal, turns into a ghostly transparency which brings him back to that same reality which had stared at him out of his mistress's cup of poison. "A great clearness came upon me then, as if all the illusions and arts with which we try to transform our world, coloring and music and dreams, had been drawn aside, and reality was shown to me, waste as a burnt house."

Yet, as in "Deluge", the symbols are reinvalidated, too, in a new sense. He advances in perception in realizing that he has achieved his perfect night by regarding her only as a symbol and ignoring her humanity. But it is too late to reconcile his perceptions of her as real and ideal. It is because he cannot reconcile them that he gives her the twenty francs and lets her go. The price is so absurdly disproportionate to the gift that he can only explain her demand and his response as a ritual the meaning of which has been forgotten, like a response in church. She has no sooner gone than he wants to rush out and get her back, but— it is the final comic reduction of the clothes symbolism—he has no clothes on. He has been stripped of the symbolic means of recovering the ideal; and by the time he gets his clothes on and can go out, they have lost their efficacy—she has disappeared forever.

Isak Dinesen reminds us, through an allusion to the old highwaymen of Denmark, that the automatic response calls forth the robbers of the ideal. This is her answer to the question, with which the story starts, as to whether one ought to forsake "an inclination for the sake of principle". One ought to follow genuine as opposed to conventional inclination. For the ideal disappears when we try to apprehend it through outworn symbols.

In trying to account for the girl as a real human being, von Brackel recalls that the episode took place "only a short time after the fall of the Second Empire, that strange sham millennium. . . . This was also the time of Nihilism in Russia, when the revolutionaries had lost all and were fleeing into exile." The girl was probably one of these exiles. She must have fallen swiftly from some high place to this "last step of the ladder". It is a sign of the revolutionary times that the ideal Woman, who ought to have been dressed as a lady, wears instead those clothes of the prostitute which have always parodied the lady's clothes. The Second Empire was a "strange sham millennium", because it tried to revive the symbols of an order that was already dead. Aided by its artificial drapery, von Brackel managed to revive for a moment the old idea of Woman, then saw it disappear. The fall of the Second Empire is the period, after the turn of the nineteenth century, that Isak Dinesen likes most to write about. The earlier period saw the death of the old order; the later period saw the death of its ghost.

Von Brackel does not finally understand the case in its real and ideal aspects until he encounters the myth of Orpheus and Eurydice at a performance of Gluck's opera. Then he realizes that he tried like Orpheus to revive a ghost. Von Brackel lost his Eurydice, because he looked back. He had forced the experience back into the old conventional mold by asking, in a moral sense of course, what he was to pay. The goddess Nemesis had answered, " 'Twenty francs' "—thus forcing him to treat the girl as what she was, according to the conventional mold, a prostitute. What was required were the new concepts and symbols that would have given him "the strength . . . and the right, to move her destiny and mine". It is significant that the girl was a revolutionary; he was, after all, only a dandy of the Second Empire.

The young man's despair is superbly rendered through the retrospective distance of the urbane and ironical old gentleman. The author's technical achievement here is to have put forward such a complex story in the guise of a handsomely turned little anecdote. The anecdotal style justifies, I think, the old gentleman's final recollection—which some readers may find too sensational and literary—that he "saw" the girl once more in a *fantaisie macabre*, when fifteen years later in Paris a painter showed him the skull of what had been a remarkably beautiful young woman. The *fantaisie macabre* reminds us that von Brackel saw the girl for the first time in a kind of fantasy, and it is a fitting conclusion to the theme of physical change which, with that of historical change, makes the reality the story is talking about.

"The Monkey", which is a longer story, develops the theme of desexualization through even larger contrasts—the contrast between the nineteenth century and the whole European tradition back through the Middle Ages to Greece; the contrast between Christianity and paganism; the contrast between Europe and Africa. This is the story of *Seven Gothic Tales* in which Africa figures most overtly.

We are introduced to a peculiar institution of the Lutheran countries of Northern Europe—the secular convent, where spinsters and widows of noble birth can in their autumn and winter years enjoy the trappings of conventual life without its religious substance. It is beautiful still that early nineteenth-century world in which the story takes place, but the spirit has departed from it. We get a sense of its old age; and the story, which occurs in October, projects in its landscapes and interiors a sumptuous autumnal atmosphere.

The Virgin Prioress, who matches Miss Nat-og-Dag in strength of mind and character, has also a night-and-day nature. Her night nature is made palpable (we only hear about Miss Nat-og-Dag's) by means of her monkey, which darts with a strange, disrupting power through the polished precincts of Closter Seven. The monkey has been brought to the Prioress as a gift from Zanzibar, the island off the coast of Kenya; and Isak Dinesen suggests with remarkable swiftness a certain unholy intimacy between them. During the periods when the monkey is absent from the convent, the Prioress "would become silent and the victim of a particular restlessness, and would seem loth to act in the affairs of the house".

It is during one of these periods that the Prioress's young nephew, Boris, a lieutenant in the fashionable Royal Guards, arrives in a state of agitation. He has been involved, with his regiment and circle of highly placed friends, in a scandal the nature of which has reached the ladies' ears as having to do with the "romantic and sacred shores of ancient Greece".[1] This way of putting it is not only appropriate to the style of humor with which the events at Closter Seven are being narrated, but it suggests that Boris's homosexuality has in it the freshness of the early world, that it is, like the ladies' celibacy, a tribute to a high ideal of innocence and love. Boris's homosexuality receives quite different treatment from Count Platen-Hallermund's.

Boris has come to tell his aunt that he would like to marry. The Prioress understands that he needs a badge of respectability to avert scandal, and counsels duty. Since duty, for this fiercely aristocratic old woman, consists of making an advantageous marriage, she decides that Boris must marry Athena Hopballehus, whose father has, we gather, just won a lawsuit over estates in Poland.

The mixture of motives by which the pious old lady can move ruthlessly to serve not only her family but also, in a deeper sense, the most primitive biological forces, all this is admirably represented—it is the best thing in the story—by the identification of the monkey with the Prioress. The thing Isak Dinesen is getting at in her characterization of the Prioress is the shocking union of

---

[1] Isak Dinesen had in mind the Eulenburg Affair, the homosexual scandal involving high figures of the Prussian court in the years preceding World War I. Although "The Monkey" is not specifically located, it seems to take place in Prussia, somewhere between 1818 and 1845.

refinement with barbaric force. When the Prioress announces her plan to marry Boris to Athena Hopballehus, he

got such a terrible impression of strength and cunning that it was as if he had touched an electric eel. Women, he thought, when they are old enough to have done with the business of being women, and can let loose their strength, must be the most powerful creatures in the whole world. He gazed at his aunt's refined face.

Boris journeys to Hopballehus through a luminous autumn landscape that speaks to him, on his way to propose marriage, of the end of youth. He thinks of the life force, which he associates with the strength of women, that pushes us on inexorably to the next stage of existence. And he thinks sadly "of all the young men who had been, through the ages, perfect in beauty and vigor", and who "had been changed, against their wishes, into supporters of society, fathers-in-law, authorities on food and morals". Boris's homosexuality is an attempt to maintain that unchanging state of youth and innocence which we conceive through the cluster of symbols we call the pastoral tradition.

Hopballehus is in the realm of pastoral. It is fantastic like its name, enormous, grand; it is described as Olympus and as a giant's castle. The old Count is a giant, and Athena, who is six feet high, is the giant's daughter. A great huntress, she is also compared to the virgin goddesses Athena and Diana. Hopballehus is removed from time, and thus contrasts with that other retreat, Closter Seven, which by its very pretension to be a convent, shows its worldliness and involvement in time. Unlike the Virgin Prioress, Athena knows nothing about money or society. Boris wonders "if she had ever heard of love". Athena demonstrates her innocence by the question she asks regarding the old Wendish idol of the goddess of love, which "had the face and façade of a beautiful woman" but "presented at the back the image of a monkey". How did they know, she asks, "which was the front and which the back?" The story poses in the end the same question regarding the Prioress's double nature— which side is good and which bad.

It is a sign of the epic primitiveness with which Isak Dinesen is trying to endow Athena that she makes her stand on one leg, as the Masai warriors do in *Out of Africa*. In Athena, the characteristic is disturbing; she never does come together as a figure you can picture. The Hopballehus episode is more interesting as intention than accomplishment; the whole story sags, as a matter of fact, whenever the Prioress is not on the scene.

Leaving the Count to communicate his proposal to Athena, Boris returns to Closter Seven. Its lamps look in the distance like the Pleiades, but on approaching it suddenly came upon Boris that "strange powers were out tonight". He has a terrified sense of "the wild life of dead things all around him". His carriage lamps "suddenly shone into a pair of glinting eyes. A very small shadow ran across the road and was gone into the deeper black shadows of the Prioress's shrubbery." The shift from stars to monkey shows the convent as a paradise lost, where an ideal has died and turned poisonous. The reference to the Pleiades explains the convent's curious name; for there are seven stars in the Pleiades, and *closter* combines *cluster* and *cloister*. In the Greek myth, Zeus changed the seven daughters of Atlas into the Pleiades to save them from the amorous pursuit of the hunter Orion. The Pleiades is used here as an apotheosis of virginity.

Athena, too, is identified with a constellation, the Great Bear, because she is a huntress like the nymph Callisto who was changed into the Great Bear, and because of the Great Bear's connection with the North Star. Athena figures in Boris's mind as an unchanging ideal, a Pilot Star.

It is because Boris knows he is violating his own ideal in his designs on Athena, that he feels, as he sits down to the supper the Prioress has left for him, like Don Giovanni in the last act of the opera. And that is why he quotes, later in the story as he passes through the halls of Closter Seven to seduce Athena, the lines in Aeschylus's *Eumenides* where Orestes, having been "strangely changed" by the consequences of his crime of matricide, prays to Pallas Athena for help in his forthcoming trial. In violating his own ideal of chastity, Boris is perhaps in a psychological sense killing his mother, in tribute to whom he practises the ideal.

When a letter from the Count the next morning announces that Athena will not marry, the Prioress's repressed fury makes Boris see himself "as a marionette, pulled alternately by the deadly determined old lady and the deadly determined young lady". The two women would seem to represent the opposite ideals that a young man growing up in our culture encounters. On the one hand, there is the Dionysian injunction to be a Don Giovanni and serve the life force. On the other hand, there is the

84

Apollonian injunction to be chaste and serve an ideal in the sky. Homosexuality and heterosexuality are being treated as stages in the process of coming to terms with these ideals.

All this is intelligent; yet it is labored and obscure. The narrative picks up when, at the supper to which she invites Athena that night, the Prioress tells two very small stories—one about Europe and one about Asia-Africa. The first is amazing, among the best of Isak Dinesen's inset stories. It is about a visit of the Holy Family to Paris, during the Christmas of 1721, under the Regency[1]—a licentious period. The hopeless inadequacy of the Court to cope with the situation, the inadequacy of their highest gifts and of the base analogies by which they try to understand the situation, are brilliantly funny, and make us realize that we have been missing in "The Monkey" the wit that in Isak Dinesen is a sign of tension, a sign that thought has been perfectly transformed into an imaginative activity.

Wearing all his jewels, the Regent, accompanied by his daughter, the Duchess of Berri, and other members of his Court, proceeds in state to the stable of Bethlehem which has been mysteriously moved to Paris. At the sight of the Virgin, the Regent has a mincing little transport:

"he went into a strange ecstasy. He swayed and uttered little screams. You will know that the beauty of the Mother of the Lord, while without equal, was of such a kind that it could awaken no sort of earthly desire. This the Duke of Orléans had never experienced before, and he did not know what to do. At last he asked her, in turn blushing scarlet and deadly pale, to come to a supper at the Berri's, where he would have such food and wine served as had never been seen before, and to which he would make the Comte de Noircy come, and Madame de Parabere.

"The Duchess of Berri was at the time in *grossesse*, and evil tongues had it that this was by her father, the Regent. She threw herself at the feet of the Virgin. 'Oh, dear sweet Virgin,' she cried, 'forgive me. You would never have done it, I know. But if I could only tell you what a deadly, what a damnably dull Court this is!' "

The Regent cries out desperately in the end, " 'She will never, never come' "—thus equating the denial of Grace with the refusal of an invitation to supper.

This is a thoroughly wicked story, which is designed to corrupt

[1] The Danish edition corrects the year given in the American and British editions, 1727; the Regent died in 1723.

Athena, and suggests that the Prioress is now possessed by the monkey. Yet the story is in its irony moral, too. It is Apollonian in that it measures the distance Europe has fallen from the Christian ideal. The Regent and his pregnant daughter are a fallen image of the Trinity, for in a sense the Virgin did do as the Duchess of Berri.

The other story, of Asia-Africa, is Dionysian. It proceeds from the Prioress's monkey nature, which manifests itself in the course of the supper. She scratches herself delicately, nibbles at cloves and dreams of Zanzibar. This story is mellifluous and dark in contrast to the clear, brittle brilliance of the first. It is about an African elephant, which is a wild elephant, bigger and more magnificent than the domesticated Indian beast, that is sent to the Indian King of Ava in Yandabu.

"The elephants of Yandabu and their herdsmen were terrified of the . . . elephant—such as Africa always frightens Asia—and in the end they made the King have him put in chains and a barred house built for him in the menagerie. But from that time, on moonlit nights, the whole city of Yandabu began to swarm with the shades of the elephants of Africa, wandering about the place and waving their large shadow-ears in the streets. . . . No people dared any more be out in the town after dark had fallen. Still they could not [i.e. dared not] break the cage of the captive elephant."

In the first story, we see how good, abstracted from the flesh and spiritualized, renders our animal nature evil just to the extent that we try to reconcile ourselves with spirit. It is, in the second story, when our animal nature is caged that it throws an evil shadow. Both stories contrast humanity with an inhuman ideal, whether the Virgin Mother or the wild elephant. Athena, as virgin and star on the one hand, and as she-bear on the other, represents both ideals; and the Prioress works against both. In working to bring about the violation of Athena's virginity, the Prioress is a Dionysian force; but she is Apollonian in her attempt to cage the splendidly wild and free young girl. The monkey is thus an agent of both forces. Athena clearly identifies herself with the elephant; for when she is told, in response to her questions, that he died in the cage, she grows pale and retires to her room for the night. Insisting that Boris follow Athena to her room, the Prioress gives him an Asian-African aphrodisiac.

There ensues in Athena's bedroom a wrestling match, which is designed to be comic and epic, but is merely boring. Boris finally forces a kiss, which fills them both with "deadly disgust", Athena faints and he departs. Quite comically, the kiss has the next morning all the consequences of a rape; and Boris feels like the seducer Valmont in Laclos' *Liaisons dangereuses*. Treating Athena like a fallen woman, the Prioress insists that Athena marry Boris since she is likely to have a baby.

Athena rises to new heights in her reply. " 'If I have a child,' said Athena, from her quaking earth thrusting at the heavens, 'my father will teach him astronomy.' " She turns something sordid into something magnificent—thus pulling victory out of defeat, Boris thinks. Having quoted, on his way to seduce Athena, Orestes's prayer to Pallas Athena before his trial for matricide, Boris now quotes Orestes's prayer of thanksgiving to her for having worked his exoneration.[1] After the nymph Callisto had been changed into a bear, her son on a hunt was about to kill her. It was then that Zeus, to prevent the crime of matricide, changed her into the Great Bear. In transporting herself to the stars, Athena would seem, for some psychological reason that is obscure, to have helped Boris overcome the sense of guilt about sex that is associated in his mind with matricide.

Mutual innocence, however, is not the thing that prepares the two young people for love. For that, they must eat of the apple together. When the Prioress reminds Athena that her child will be a bastard, Athena agrees to marry with the understanding that she will kill Boris at the earliest opportunity. Things have thus reached an impasse, when we come to the great scene of the story. A knocking is heard at the window. The Prioress is struck with terror. It is the monkey. Breaking the glass, it jumps into the room and chases the Prioress up the wall, which she mounts "with the most surprising, most wonderful, lightness and swiftness", then down to the floor. It jumps upon her, gets hold of her lace cap and tears it from her head. The face she turns toward the young people is that of a monkey, and where the monkey had been, there "rose, a little out of breath from the effort, her face still a deep rose, the true Prioress of Closter Seven."

The monkey comes finally to rest on the marble head of a bust of Immanuel Kant; and the young people turn and look into

---

[1] The lines, from Aeschylus's *Eumenides*, are in the American and British editions unaccountably attributed to Euripides.

each other's faces. They have finally seen evil because they have seen it in the face of good; and because they have had the moral experience together, are bound together in guilt, they are ready for human love—the kind Milton gives to Adam and Eve when he describes them in the end as taking, "hand in hand, with wandering steps and slow", their "solitary way" out of Eden.

In the final line of the story, the Prioress says in Latin to the young couple, " 'Obey the law, and do not hold the gods in contempt.' " The question is which law and which gods, for the monkey is a god too. Which of the two Prioresses, for that matter, is good and which evil? One sign that we have the original Prioress back is the repetition in Latin of her admonition to Boris to follow the path of duty. Once we saw what was meant by duty, however, the monkey seemed to enter.

Isak Dinesen said in regard to this story: "When men by way of their conventions have got themselves into difficulties, then let the monkey in, he will find the unattainable solution." Let in the irrational, unconscious, biological forces. The monkey that is finally let in, however, contains not the Dionysian but the Apollonian Prioress, who has herself let in the other. The meaning of her reappearance is, I think, explained by the delightful image of the original monkey sitting on the head of Kant. For Kant was the philosopher who conquered for the reason the vast domain of the irrational. What was once below is after Kantian or imaginative apprehension on top. The Apollonian Prioress must reappear for the Dionysian Prioress to turn into a monkey— for the young people to know, in other words, that they have seen good and evil.

Obey, the Prioress is saying in the end, both Apollo and Dionysus. Boris learns what Miss Malin, who had taken "the words of Scripture *au pied de la lettre*" had to learn—that living is like playing the concertina, the field of action lies between opposite ideas. But homosexuality in men and frigidity in women, which is associated in "Deluge" with the decline of the old order, is treated here as a necessarily recurring phenomenon, a phase in the process of growing up in Western culture. In scope, "The Monkey" is as ambitious as any of Isak Dinesen's stories.

In spite of Isak Dinesen's reputation as a writer of fantastic tales, the sort of blatantly supernatural situation which we find

in "The Monkey" is to be found only twice again in her fiction
—in "The Supper at Elsinore" in *Seven Gothic Tales,* and "The
Sailor-boy's Tale" in *Winter's Tales.* In the first two at least, the
supernatural situation is so embedded in a symbolic framework
as to leave little of the unrationalized aura that gives the effect
of weirdness. Isak Dinesen is not a writer of hair-raising tales.[1]
Her stories are fantastic in the way wit is—in the jubilant
freedom with which possibilities are stretched and ideas combined.

I have already suggested that wit creates an intensity in some
of Isak Dinesen's stories, sets the story in the atmosphere of the
imagination where life can be explored in depth. In other stories,
a thoroughly evoked natural setting has an equivalent effect.
"The Supper at Elsinore" is one of these. It adds to the evocation
of nature, a thorough localization, an evocation of place and
historical period, that gives texture to states of mind and feeling.
The story was suggested to Isak Dinesen by a dignified, old, gray
eighteenth-century house in Elsinore, the seaport town just up
the coast from Rungsted at the narrowest point of the Sound
between Denmark and Sweden.

The house in Elsinore recalled the town's old shipowning
families and its most romantic period—the time of the Napo-
leonic wars. From Elsinore, one would have witnessed Denmark's
humiliation, when in 1807 her fleet was led captive by the British
up through the Sound. And one would have seen shortly afterward the gallant privateers set sail from Elsinore to take revenge
by preying, with the unofficial blessing of the Danish Crown, on
British shipping in the Baltic. To the English-speaking reader, of
course, Elsinore means Hamlet. Since this is a story about
beautiful, brilliant young people who are melancholy and self-
destructive because they will settle for nothing less than everything, the Hamlet of the romantic tradition figures in the background, as does his castle of Kronborg.

Because of the importance of its natural setting and its Danish
reverberations, "Supper at Elsinore" is closer in style to *Winter's
Tales* than to *Seven Gothic Tales.* Isak Dinesen considered that her
stories fall into the two classes of Gothic and Winter's tale, which
seem to divide along the lines of art versus nature—with the

---

[1] She expressed to me, for example, her poor opinion of Poe's tales. "He scares
you but that's all."

Gothic tale on the side of art: witty, extravagant, cosmopolitan; and the Winter's tale, Danish, provincial, natural.

"Supper", which in the American edition follows "Roads Round Pisa", starts with the reminiscences of the old house in Elsinore, that turn into the reminiscences of the old housekeeper who has lived alone in the house ever since the family abandoned it in 1813. In the supernaturally cold winter of 1841, Madam Bæk's reminiscences materialize into the ghost of the last De Coninck son, Morten, who, after a period of heroic exploits as captain of a privateer, disappeared on his wedding day. For his grief-stricken parents, he ceased to exist. But he became for his two sisters the ghost of their unfulfilled longings, the symbol of that romantic ideal of infinite experience to which they remained faithful all their lives. Rumors reached them that he had died on the gallows. As Madam Bæk's reminiscences merge into the sisters', Morten's ghost materializes for them too.

The young De Conincks are like the young Angels in "Copenhagen Season" (*LT*)—and therefore like the Dinesens as the author conceives them—abundantly endowed with every grace and talent except the ability to live successfully. The De Coninck sisters and their brother are ruined in opposite ways by their romantic ideal of experience. He does everything, and ends up cold and a ghost. They do nothing—for they feared to give away any possibilities "in order to make a definite choice and come down to a limited reality"—and they, too, end up cold and ghostly.

"Supper" is clearly no ghost story in the ordinary sense, since the ghosts are the mental atmosphere in which the sisters live. Morten's ghost is the materialization of that atmosphere; it emerges from the cold of that winter and the sisters' internal cold. Since Isak Dinesen makes the sisters' ghost life more real than the bodies they send forth into the world, she turns their ghostly reality into a reality of death; so that—brilliant in society and melancholiac in private, capable of making others love them but incapable of loving in return—they become in the end dead women who send forth apparitions that pretend to be alive. Their frigidity, which is analyzed with even greater precision than Miss Malin's, stems from their lack of connection with the apparitions they send forth.

The sisters are giving a party the evening Madam Bæk arrives in Copenhagen to bring them the news of Morten's appearance.

They are now old maids in their fifties—"a pair of prominent spiritual courtesans", who like Miss Malin seduce their admirers with the charms of wit and imagination. The conversation at their party skips lightly over all the themes of the story.

The theme of ghosts is introduced at the start, when the guests sing old songs and one of them, a bishop, proposes the ancient toast to the old generation. The talk passes on to angels' wings, and Fanny De Coninck expresses her desire to fly. The bishop protests that

"In woman, the particularly heavenly and angelic attributes, and those which we must look up to and worship, all go to weigh her down and keep her on the ground. The long tresses, the veils of pudicity, the trailing garments, even the adorable womanly forms in themselves, the swelling bosom and hip, are as little as possible in conformity with the idea of flying. We, all of us, willingly grant her the title of angel, and the white wings, and lift her up on our highest pedestal, on the one inevitable condition that she must not dream of, must even have been brought up in absolute ignorance of, the possibility of flight."

The energetic, imaginative women who rebel against such restrictions, who like men imitate the angels by daring to fly, are called instead witches. There is the suggestion that the De Coninck sisters might be considered witches, along with Miss Malin, von Brackel's mistress, Athena and the Prioress. There is also the contrary suggestion—borne out by the angelic imagery used in connection with Athena—that it is perhaps these women who are really the angels. In any case, angels and witches are two sides of the same coin, both sides contrasting with von Brackel's Russian girl.

The De Coninck sisters would seem to represent the two sides of the coin. The sisters are not clearly differentiated, but Fanny, the stronger, more intellectual sister who is dark and has lost her looks, seems to be the witch; whereas the younger, gentler, fair Eliza, who was always the more beautiful and is fading with time "into an even more marble-like loveliness", seems to be the angel. The distinction does not always hold, however, for the two sisters often act as one—combining both sides of the coin at once. They are intended, as characters, to merge and separate, merge and separate. The sentimental commodore at the party identifies the angels' wings of old-fashioned women with poems and sailing-ships, thus merging the sisters and Morten in a single vision of the ideal.

On the day before the sisters return to Elsinore, Fanny walks alone in the Rosenborg Gardens where she has a vision of evil—she falls. She understands for the first time the cruelty involved in Morten's career of experience. She has a vision of him in the house, gazing at the clock stopped dead, and she understands that he is gazing at his mother's death of grief for him and at the broken heart of the bride he abandoned. Even more remarkably, she sees him as an image of herself. What he has done and what she has ruthlessly aspired to do have the same moral quality.

We sense a contrary idea in the question that keeps coming to Fanny's mind during this scene: "What is Eliza thinking now?" Not, however, until the question develops into a recurring theme of the story (the story ends with the question and an answer to it), can we understand that what Eliza thinks is the story's enigma, the answer to which is the timeless answer, the unchanging ideal, they are all seeking. Time has told on Fanny and Morten; it has turned them into one kind of ghost. But Eliza, in her angelic aspect, is another kind of ghost—the ghost of their ideal in its original simplicity. Retrospectively, we can understand that Fanny is measuring the distance she has fallen by the question: "What is Eliza thinking now?"

The house in Elsinore is for the sisters a ghost that brings the past alive, and accuses them of having changed. It is when the sisters sit down to just such an adventurous supper as they used to have secretly with Morten, that his ghost materializes. The signs of all he has been through, of all the life he has had that the sisters have not had, are superbly rendered.

Before the brother and sisters can entirely regain their old communion, a common stand must be taken on the disturbing question of Adrienne Rosenstand, the girl Morten abandoned at the altar. Morten disposes of her by reminding them of an old satire on the French Revolution that they used to sing. The point seems to be that just as Marat had only the shirts he had stolen from the aristocrats, so Adrienne never had an existence to destroy. Whatever existence she had came from Morten.[1] The song re-establishes their old cruelly exclusive communion.

---

[1] In the original (found by Mrs Merete Klenow With of Odense in a collection of M. Marchant's, called *La Constitution en Vaudevilles*, Paris: chez les Libraires Royalistes, 1792, pp. 150-56), the revolutionist is the Girondin journalist, Gorsas, who announced that the shirts of the King's aunts belong to him. The joke is that the

The actual account Morten gives of his life, of his five wives and his career as a pirate, is mainly dull. The one fine episode is Morten's original crime, which was an affair of the heart. He stole a schooner because he fell in love with it, and he named it *La Belle Eliza*. Eliza admits she had heard of a pirate ship of that name, and suspected it was Morten's. This secret, "which the old maid had guarded from all the world", explains her difference from Fanny—why she grew lovelier with time and remained in their original paradise.

The name brings together all the themes of the story. It makes manifest the sexual element in the attraction between the sisters and their brother. None of Morten's wives ever boarded *La Belle Eliza*. He remained faithful to his sisters, and they remained faithful to him in not marrying. It is suggested that they remained faithful in return for his abandonment of Adrienne, which overtly they deplored. Such psychological analysis is never in Isak Dinesen an end in itself, but always an aspect of a spiritual drama. The sexual attraction of the sisters and brother is an aspect of their narcissism and their fixation at a stage of adolescent idealism. Their sexual failure is an aspect of their spiritual failure. *La Belle Eliza* is the ideal to which they have all remained faithful and which has ruined them—led them all, as Fanny realized in the garden, to commit crimes.

It was after Morten lost *La Belle Eliza* that he died spiritually, and entered that state of sleeplessness and cold in which we find the sisters. Morten became in a spiritual sense a floater, like the demonic women of the party conversation who fly. Only his element was water rather than air—which fits Isak Dinesen's symbolic system in which air is a masculine element, attractive to women, and water a female element, attractive to men. The ghost of Morten can return when the Sound is frozen because there is then a spiritual meeting-ground between the elements of air and water, between the sisters and the brother. The frozen Sound is the objective image of the cold hell in which all three exist.

The cold, that pervades the story, takes over at the end.

---

populace understand this to mean that the King's aunts have stolen Gorsas' shirts; whereas Gorsas was announcing his right to all the property of the Royalists. Isak Dinesen may have deliberately changed to the better known Marat. But she told Mrs With that she did not remember having read the song anywhere, only to have heard it quoted—a sign of how far back the oral tradition went with her.

Morten says he has learned from all his experiences " 'that you
cannot eat your cake and have it' ". It is the ironic lesson that
every romantic must learn; for the romantic is the kind of person
who wants both to stay in Eden and go out into the world, to have
his career of experience without moral consequences. The sisters
kept their cake, Morten ate his, and they have all ended in the
same condition—they are cold, used up. Morten reminds them
that they are gathered again in that pleasant room, just as they
used to be. They are back where they started, but with the
difference that is to emerge so powerfully when Morten reminds
them of their romantic aspirations to get away from Elsinore.

His elder sister suddenly turned her old body all around in the
chair, and faced him straight. Her face was changed and drawn with
pain. The long wake and the strain began to tell on her, and she
spoke to him in a hoarse and cracked voice, as if she were heaving it
up from the innermost part of her chest. "Yes," she cried, "yes, you
may talk. But you mean to go away again and leave me. You! You
have been to these great warm seas of which you talk, to a hundred
countries. You have been married to five people—Oh, I do not know
of it all! It is easy for you to speak quietly, to sit still. You have never
needed to beat your arms to keep warm. You do not need to now!"
Her voice failed her. She stuttered in her speech and clasped the edge
of the table. "And here," she groaned out, "I am—cold. The world is
bitterly cold around me. I am so cold at night, in my bed, that my
warming-pans are no good to me!"

This, to a ghost—one kind of ghost speaking to another. Fanny
finally expresses the envy she had sensed in herself in the garden,
that envy of the male which differentiates her aspiration from
Eliza's and accounts for her witchlike character. The recollection
that Morten is a ghost breaks upon her when the clock strikes
midnight. This is the stopped clock of her vision in the garden,
which she herself—once again the destroyer of her own happiness
—wound up that afternoon. It is a cry of supreme frustration;
for she "meant to go on speaking, and to lift at last all the deadly
weight of her whole life off her", but "she could not out-talk the
clock, and her mouth opened and shut twice without a sound".
All this is involved in the nice ambiguity of the cry, " 'Oh, hell,
to hell!' " which is ambiguous in its effect too. She both has and
has not—by uttering the cry and winding up the clock—caused
the apparition to dissolve. Throwing herself toward Morten
across the table, she wails out a lifetime of unfulfilled love and

94

longing. " 'Morten!' she cried in a long wail. 'Brother! Stay! Listen! Take me with you!' " At the last stroke of the clock, she finds herself, indeed—after the brief return to their original paradise—back in hell when, at the sight of Morten's empty chair, she lets her head fall down on the table. She hears the ice breaking up outside. "What is Eliza thinking?" she wonders dully.

The De Conincks' lives are not all failure, however; nor is the story an attack on the romantic life. On the contrary, it glorifies the romantic life as tragic—triumphant in its failure. The triumphant element is in Morten's account of his request, before they hung him, for one minute more of life so he could " 'think, with the halter around my neck, for one minute of *La Belle Eliza*' ". If Morten's failure is reflected in Fanny's final despair, his triumph is reflected in Eliza's answer to Fanny's unspoken question. Fanny looks up and sees Eliza pulling at the streamers of her cap as "long, long ago, when angry or in great pain or joy", she used to pull "at her long golden tresses. Eliza lifted her pale eyes and stared straight at her sister's face. 'To think,' said she, ' "to think, with the halter around my neck, for one minute of *La Belle Eliza*." ' "

The old ideal remains, mysteriously comprehending anger and great pain in joy. Fanny's thoughts turn toward it in her despair, just as Morten's did. Given the sisters' heroic imagination, the fact that nothing has happened to them becomes a gloriously intense tragic fate like Morten's. Each sister has her own tie to Morten. Eliza is his pilot star, Fanny shares his ambivalent moral condition. Together they give Morten the complete relation that Boris has with his pilot star, Athena, after they have witnessed together the Prioress's metamorphosis into a monkey.

It is by now apparent that all the stories of *Seven Gothic Tales* are on the same complex of themes, but that in each story the emphasis is different. What was subsidiary in one becomes central in another; an implication in one is explored in depth in another and then in a third pushed through to an unheard-of dimension. The effect, if you read the book from beginning to end, is of an accumulating revelation—showing new aspects and new depths of a single vision. As the penultimate and last major story, "The Dreamers" does the spectacular job of pulling together the themes of the volume, of showing what the whole volume was driving at.

We have read in *Seven Gothic Tales* about people who have passed through a catastrophe to a tragicomic realm of indifference, where all things are alike. We have read about women who are in a psychological sense witches, and about people who have extraordinary powers because they know how to appropriate the powers of nature and tradition, to merge their minds with the collective mind and their identities with archetypal identities. These themes are brought together in such a way in "The Dreamers" that they are seen as aspects of what turns out to be the main psychological theme of the volume—the mysteries of identity.

We understand that the volume has all along been asking the following questions. How do we navigate between experience and tradition, between fact and myth, and among conflicting facts and myths, to achieve an identity; and where, among the different aspects we show to people, and among the metamorphoses we pass through in the different stages of our life, is our identity? Until now, the question has been how we get over from the flesh-and-blood individual to the mythical person who puts forth those magical powers from which all value and culture derive. In "The Dreamers", the question is reversed. The story reads backward from a mythical identity to the flesh-and-blood woman behind it. It asks what happens to a woman who has outlived her mythical identity.

"The Dreamers" is about Pellegrina Leoni, the greatest opera singer of her time. She is a mighty and potent myth, a goddess to whom all the world, rich and poor, pay tribute and from whom they draw spiritual nourishment. She loves her admirers in the manner of a deity; she would die for them as long as they worship her and feed upon her. She herself lives in the service of her own myth. " 'She worked in the service of Pellegrina Leoni like a slave under the whip, weeping, dying at times, when it was demanded of her,' " says the fabulously rich Jew, Marcus Cocoza, whom she has drawn into the service of her idol as a kind of high priest.

Pellegrina does not quite lose her life in a theater fire. As a result of shock, she loses instead her voice. This is the ultimate catastrophe. Although she rises bodily from the dead, she is spiritually dead like Morten De Coninck after he loses *La Belle Eliza*; only the situation here is so much more fully articulated that it helps us understand the meaning of the earlier catastrophes. For spiritual death means in this story the death of an identity, and identity means an identifying myth. A Pellegrina who does not sing is no longer in that sense Pellegrina. She therefore makes Marcus tell the world she died; while she herself begins a career of wandering, assuming a different name and character in each place. She commits a kind of suicide to keep her myth intact.

What, then, happens to her qualities—her vitality, intelligence, imagination—after she has ceased to be Pellegrina? She is a great artist still, but an artist in life, playing roles as she used to on the stage and giving happiness through these roles. But the person who in life plays roles without being committed to them is an anarchic force, ambiguously vitalizing and demonic. Pellegrina has become a witch, a high-flying lady, in the sense we have been talking about. We understand here that the thing the witch refuses to be tied down to is a single identity. Like the De Coninck sisters, the witch sends forth images into the world but keeps her identity intact or potential, and this is why she remains psychologically and spiritually a virgin even if she gives herself bodily to men. Pellegrina makes men fall madly in love with her. But she does not love in return; and when the time comes for consequences, she disappears and assumes another role elsewhere. She is *par excellence* the "spiritual courtesan" that the De Coninck sisters are to a degree and that Miss Nat-og-Dag dreams of being.

Pellegrina's power is magical because she is invulnerable. Having no hope, she does not look before or after, but rides the currents of life with the passivity and indifference of a natural force. There is also of course such witchcraft in art; for art is the means by which thought-distracted human beings recover a power like nature's. All magic is dangerous, and white magic becomes black when the power of art is let loose into life and a human being takes on the quality of a natural force. Each of the men who love Pellegrina under her other names catches sight at one point, when her hair is thrown back, of a long scar that runs "like a little white snake" from her left ear to her collar bone. This is the witch's brand, and though her lovers do not all recognize it as such, it gives them all a sense that Pellegrina's vitality comes from her inhumanity rather than her humanity, from a life beyond death. One of her lovers compares her quality to that *pourriture noble*, or noble putrefaction of the grapes, which gives to certain rare wines their extraordinary flavor.

Her scar of course comes from her burns, as does her witchlike spiritual quality. "The Dreamers" is more supernatural in its effect than any other of Isak Dinesen's stories; yet it has always, as in this case, a naturalistic explanation of the supernatural effect. The most remarkable scene in the story is the one in which Pellegrina becomes a bird and begins to fly. The metamorphosis turns out to be an optical illusion and the cause of her death. Yet it loses nothing in supernatural effect; it is, if anything, more stunning than the Prioress's metamorphosis. For the supernatural, when sacrificed as physical truth, transfers its aura of suggestiveness to the psychological and poetic truth.

"The Dreamers" is among other things a great nature poem, demonstrating that "natural supernaturalism", that trick of psychologizing the supernatural, of which Goethe speaks and which is at the heart of romantic literature. The natural-supernatural is most effective when our credulity is stretched to the breaking point but not finally broken. Our scientific habit of mind must be enlarged but not destroyed, for a psychological attitude—the deepest, but still psychological—is wanted. A good case in point is the treatment of Marcus Cocoza. When Pellegrina becomes a witch, he becomes the Mephistopheles who makes her witch's career possible through his extraordinary wealth and intelligence. Since he does not speak until the end of the story, but appears as a silent, mysteriously ubiquitous old Jew of apparently infinite potency, he goes farther even than Pellegrina in threatening to break our credulity by turning out to be the devil. Instead, it is he who in his account of Pellegrina's life restores her humanity and his own. Again, there is no loss of supernatural effect. For Pellegrina and Marcus turn out no less great as human beings than they seemed as supernatural beings. By sacrificing the supernatural as fact, Isak Dinesen makes it a symbol of human greatness, taking us over the line between the flesh-and-blood individual and the mythical person.

The natural-supernatural effect is mainly achieved by the brilliance of Pellegrina and Marcus in utterance and gesture. It is enhanced, however, by the wealth and variety of mythological allusions through which their characters are presented. We have already seen how Isak Dinesen adds depth to her characters through such allusions—through the faint outlines of the witch, for example, behind so many of her women. But only in Athena have the allusions been so explicit as here. The natural and the supernatural do not quite come together in Athena for two reasons. Because the allusions are not various enough, we tend to allegorize her as the virgin goddess and she loses humanity; as a human being, on the other hand, she is rather a stick who does not live up to the high claims made for her.

In Pellegrina, the allusions are so various and shifting that we cannot identify her with any one of them, and she gains depth and roundness by our sense that they are all aspects of a mysterious, living entity. In her aspect of penitential pilgrim, she recalls the Wandering Jew; Marcus's presence helps us make that connection. Marcus calls her a Donna Quixotta de la Mancha: " 'The phenomena of life were not great enough for her; they were not in proportion with her own heart.' " This connects her with Faust, still another wanderer; and since the force that makes her so effective in her metamorphoses as whore, revolutionary and saint is an erotic force, she is also a female Don Juan. It is surely to make this connection that Isak Dinesen has the fire break out when Pellegrina is singing Mozart's *Don Giovanni*.

Isak Dinesen especially notes the place in the opera where Pellegrina is interrupted. It is when Pellegrina as Donna Anna begins the second-act recitative: "Cruel? Ah, no, my love. It grieves me all too much to defer the happiness for which we both have yearned so long." Donna Anna has deferred her marriage to Don Ottavio until he avenges her father's death at the hands of Don Giovanni. Don Ottavio has just accused her of cruelty for refusing to anticipate the happiness of the next day when the revenge will be accomplished. She suggests in her recitative that they have still a great deal of suffering to pass through before they can be happy. The implication would seem to be that Pellegrina must pass through the fire, that now breaks out in the theater, before she can be happy.[1]

[1] This particular point in the opera seems to have been suggested by E. T. A. Hoffmann's story, "Don Juan", in which the narrator writes: "Even Donna Anna's scene in the second act: Crudele (which, considered superficially, refers only to Don Ottavio), expresses in secret harmonies, in the most wonderful inferences, that inner state of the soul that consumes all earthly happiness. What other meaning can we

Marcus Cocoza is the alter ego—the Mephistopheles to her Faust, for example—that often accompanies the archetypal Wanderer. In characterizing him, Isak Dinesen has exploited superbly the associations which the figure of the Jew calls up in the European imagination. Not only does he recall the Wandering Jew, but his wealth is fabulous, and his Dutch nationality and Portuguese name recall the Jewish philosopher, Spinoza. The Jew is associated with wealth and wisdom in the European imagination; the question is whether these gifts are of God or the devil. The exaggerated fear and respect felt for the Jew take one construction when Marcus seems satanic, and quite another when he turns out the noblest character in the story.

After Pellegrina has lost her identity, one of her lovers asks about the mysterious Jew who spends so much time in the street outside her house. Have you not noticed, she says, " 'that I have no shadow? Once upon a time I sold my shadow to the devil, for a little heart-ease, a little fun.' " The man is " 'this shadow of mine, with which I have no longer anything to do' ".

The incident alludes to *Peter Schlemihl*, the novella of the German romanticist Chamisso, about a man who sells his shadow to the devil for unlimited gold. The lack of a shadow is apparently an unimportant thing; yet the deficiency fills all beholders with the existential horror we feel for a freak. The deficiency becomes therefore a powerful symbol of the nameless, inexplicable crime, the only crime that really matters for it is not an action or intention but a state of being—a state of being that separates you from humanity. Chamisso's supernatural situation is entirely psychologized in Isak Dinesen's story. It is only in a psychological sense that Pellegrina has no shadow. She considers her loss of voice that order of crime, but the things she sells to the devil are her penance for the crime together with regret for the past, hope for the future and present moral responsibility— all the things that add up to the memory of her identity. Marcus, who carries the memory, leaves Pellegrina free to be an amoral natural force—to be Don Juan as Kierkegaard, from whom Isak

---

find in the passage added and altered by the poet: forse un giorno il cielo ancora sentirà pietà di me! [perhaps one day heaven will again smile on me]." (Trans. in *Tales of Hoffmann*, ed. Christopher Lazare, New York: Grove Press, 1946, p. 114.) The fact that Hoffmann's narrator writes all this in a letter may account for Isak Dinesen's curious misstatement that "Donna Anna comes upon the stage, with Ottavio's letter in her hand".

Dinesen seems to derive her ideas of Don Juan, conceives him.[1]

Kierkegaard considers the Don Juan legend specifically Christian, for only Christianity abstracts sensuousness as a principle opposed to spirit. He connects Don Juan and Faust as related medieval ideas, since Faust is the part of intellect and spirit that Christianity excludes. Don Juan and Faust are the sensuous and spiritual demonic.

Pellegrina combines Don Juan and Faust; for she overcomes not only like Don Juan through the power of physical desire, but through the power of the erotic idea as a force that takes hold of the imagination. It is significant that she is a singer; for music, especially music with words, is, according to Kierkegaard, the art of the demonic. Kierkegaard wrote his essay to show that Mozart had in *Don Giovanni* the perfect subject for music, and that music is the only medium which could adequately express the legend of Don Juan as the life force that exists in immediacy, that is always on the point of becoming an individual but which never finally does, for if it did it would disappear in reflection and rationalization.

Pellegrina, after she loses her voice, is the spirit of music let loose into life. She is demonic not only in her metamorphoses as whore and artist-revolutionary, but even in her metamorphosis as a saint. For she is a saint in the manner of Mary Magdalen, which is why every one is so attracted to her. If we consider that the three metamorphoses correspond to Dante's three realms of being, we might say that the saint is the demonic force in the realm of orthodoxy-theology-Paradise; the whore, in the realm of biology-Hell; and the artist-revolutionary, in the realm of intellect-Purgatory.

"The Dreamers" is a fable of the European spirit, and we gain a view of Europe as a totality from the elaborate frame which takes place off the coast of Kenya, within the sphere of Arabian civilization. This is the closest Isak Dinesen gets in her fiction to an African setting. The story of modern Europe is told to Asian-Africans, who are removed from it not only by place and culture but by time; they seem to belong to the legendary past, they might be out of *The Arabian Nights*. As if to symbolize its foreignness to these Asian-Africans, the scene changes from the tropical

[1] In "The Immediate Stages of the Erotic, or The Musical Erotic", *Either/Or*, Vol. I. Isak Dinesen expressed to me her admiration for this essay.

night of the frame to a nocturnal snowstorm in the Swiss Alps. Yet the same moon shines on both scenes. These people can, we learn in the end, understand the story as an archetypal myth that recurs eternally in the universal moon of the imagination.

Three people are grouped around a lantern on a dhow which, "on a full-moon night of 1863 . . . was on its way from Lamu to Zanzibar". They are Said, a princely warrior on his way to a deed of revenge; Lincoln Forsner, an Englishman; and the famous old storyteller, Mira Jama, once the favorite of princes, now poorly dressed, with his nose and ears cut off. Lincoln asks him why he does not tell them one of his famous tales, such as make the blood run cold. Mira answers that he no longer tells stories, because he has "become too familiar with life; it can no longer delude me into believing that one thing is much worse than the other' ". Mira Jama is in that realm of indifference where we find Pellegrina after the fire.

Only in his dreams can Mira feel again, because there the emotion is cut off from cause and object. He can enjoy his feelings, even the horrible ones, because he knows they belong to an autonomous realm cut off from the world of Necessity. " 'But what particularly pleases me about dreams,' " Mira says, " 'is this: that there the world creates itself around me without any effort on my part.' " Through the metamorphosis of the reality around him, he finds himself always at the intense heart of experience, without the low-intensity business of having to get to the experience or of having to come away from it through a chain of consequences. " 'The air in my dreams,' " says Mira, " 'and particularly since I have been in prison with Said, is always very high, and I generally see myself as a very small figure in a great landscape, or in a big house.' " There is a sense of freedom in that comic or diminutive view of himself, which defines the quality of tragicomic romance. For he takes that view of himself in the midst of emotion, and it does not make his emotion ridiculous.

The high air of his dreams is the air of so many scenes in *Out of Africa*. It is the air of Isak Dinesen's own dreams as she describes them when writing in *Out of Africa* about her happy faculty of dreaming.[1] The faculty is characteristic of the Dinesens (the De Conincks have it, and so do the Angels in "Copenhagen

[1] New York, pp. 87-88; London, pp. 95-96.

Season"). Mira, who has given up storytelling for dreaming, is like Pellegrina who, after she stops singing, makes for herself a dreamlike mode of life. Both have found the realm of reconciliation out of which Isak Dinesen seems to have written *Seven Gothic Tales*—the realm she herself seems to have found by reversing their careers, by moving from life to art, from Africa to the composition of her first book. We see in a passage at the end of *Out of Africa* that the book has in fact described the catastrophe in her life that stands behind the catastrophes of Mira and Pellegrina. When in the end, she says, the day she could not believe in came, the day on which she was going away from Africa, she

learned the strange learning that things can happen which we ourselves cannot possibly imagine, either beforehand, or at the time when they are taking place, or afterwards when we look back on them. . . . *Those who have been through such events can, in a way, say that they have been through death,—a passage outside the range of imagination, but within the range of experience.*[1]

When Lincoln Forsner says that he hardly ever dreams, Mira replies: " 'You dream indeed more than I do myself. Do I not know the dreamers when I meet them? You dream awake and walking about. You will do nothing yourself to choose your own ways: you let the world form itself around you, and then you open your eyes to see where you will find yourself.' " This is a good description of the wellborn Englishman who drifts around exotic places. The dreamer is here a psychological type. By a lovely analogy, Mira connects the type with art and neurosis.

"If, in planting a coffee tree, you bend the taproot, that tree will start, after a little time, to put out a multitude of small delicate roots near the surface. That tree will never thrive, nor bear fruit, but it will flower more richly than the others. Those fine roots are the dreams of the tree. As it puts them out, it need no longer think of its bent taproot. It keeps alive by them—a little, not very long. Or you can say that it dies by them, if you like. For really, dreaming is the well-mannered people's way of committing suicide."

If you want to go to sleep, says Mira, think of a deep well.

"In the bottom of that well, just in the middle of it, there comes up a spring of water, which runs out in little streamlets to all possible sides, like the rays of a star. If you can make your thoughts run out with

[1] New York, pp. 385-86; London, p. 413. Italics are mine.

that water, not in one direction, but equally to all sides, you will fall asleep. If you can make your heart do it thoroughly enough, as the coffee tree does it with the little surface roots, you will die."

The artist dies in this sense, by letting his thoughts and his heart run out in all directions in his various characters. Here, it is Pellegrina who dies in this sense in a career of experience analogous to art. Said is by way of contrast the man of action. Said is praying to God, he still wants things. " 'By the time when you have finished praying to God . . . that is when you begin to dream,' " says Mira. The dreamer represents in this passage not a psychological type but a stage of spiritual development. The word is used in both senses throughout.

Lincoln begins the story of Pellegrina, the woman who taught him to dream, taking us back twenty years to a moonlit, snowy night when he was twenty-three and sat in a hotel at a pass of the Swiss Alps. In telling how he came to be there, he describes the conflict between himself and his father. His father is the Western and modern counterpart of the man of action. He is a puritan and a utilitarian, a type difficult to explain to Mira. It is a sign of what Isak Dinesen has in mind that she uses again the situation of her early satire, "The Family de Cats", in which the exemplary bourgeois family requires, in order to maintain its virtue, that the family produce one black sheep in each generation. Lincoln was considered by his father to be the current black sheep, which in this story means the dreamer. The dreamer stands opposed to the man of action in modern Western culture; he is his necessary complement in the traditional culture represented by Said and Mira. In a brothel in Rome, Lincoln falls madly in love with a supernaturally remarkable prostitute named Olalla.[1] After Lincoln makes Olalla promise to marry him, she disappears and he searches everywhere for her. It is the search that brings him to the pass in the Swiss Alps.

[1] The name derives from Robert Louis Stevenson's story, "Olalla". Stevenson's Olalla belongs to a degenerate noble family of Spain, in which the human spirit has died. The beauty of Olalla's mother is enhanced by its animal quality. The mother turns out to be a vampire; while Olalla herself is apparently a beautiful saint. Isak Dinesen must have been struck in Stevenson's story by the idea that extraordinary beauty is both more than and less than human. It is characteristic of her that she combines Olalla and the mother in the ambivalent figure of Pellegrina. The vampire theme emerges when she returns to the story of Pellegrina in "Echoes", *Last Tales*. Stevenson's story is simply a thriller. One has only to read it to see how Isak Dinesen turns such subjects into serious art.

An acquaintance of Lincoln's, a German of noble family named Hohenemser, turns up at the hotel, accompanied by a Swedish Baron Guildenstern. They are both nonentities; the Baron's name recalls the two undistinguishable nonentities in *Hamlet*, who on the surface share common experiences with Hamlet. Hohenemser very proudly tells the story—a story within a story within a story—of his love for Madame Lola, the greatest practitioner of the milliner's art in Europe, whose atelier was the revolutionary headquarters of Lucerne. In her appeal to both the great and the humble, Madame Lola repeats Pellegrina's career as diva. When street fighting breaks out, Madame Lola rushes Hohenemser to the barricades with her. He kills a man, is himself wounded, and spends the three happiest weeks of his life being nursed by Madame Lola who, after she has cured him, departs with a kiss. Hohenemser has been looking for her ever since.

Not to be outdone, the Baron recounts his adventure with a beautiful saint in France. Madame Rosalba is the pet of " 'a curious community of old ruined Legitimists of the highest aristocracy, who had lost all that they had in the French Revolution' ". Since they had not the money to marry, they had produced no younger generation " 'and with them to be young was synonymous with being of the second-best circles' ". Recalling the correspondence with Dante, we see that Legitimist virgins make the proper milieu for the orthodox realm of Paradise. In contrast to Madame Lola, Madame Rosalba had been mistress to the Spanish General Zumalacárregui (as it is rightly spelled), who in 1835 died leading the Carlist rebellion in the interest of Legitimacy. To honor his memory, Rosalba dressed in white and lived the life of a saint. "For all this she was highly thought of. . . . The collection of old maids of both sexes were . . . much intrigued by the idea of experience in this holy person."

The two tales are comic, and the two nonentities make beautiful foils to Pellegrina since they lack an identity in quite a different sense than she does. When a lady passes quickly through the room followed by Marcus, the three men decide she is their mistress. But when Lincoln inquires after her, he learns she has already gone. Lincoln decides that the sight of the Jew must have driven her away.

The three men take a coach up the pass in the wild snowstorm. The coach gets stuck in the snow and they continue the pursuit on foot, Lincoln ahead of the others. It has stopped snowing, the moon is bright, the winds are terrible. Lincoln comes upon Olalla's coach, also stuck in the snow; she has continued on foot. The Baron catches up, and by the light of the two coach lanterns his face appears, "in the moon-cold night" "flaming scarlet". One recalls the opening scene on the dhow, where the slave's red cap glows in the moonlight.

The two men proceed together. Then, "through the mist of the loose whirling snow", Lincoln

caught sight of a dark shadow . . . which might be a human figure. At first it seemed to disappear and to appear again, and it was difficult in the night and in the storm to keep your eyes fixed upon it. . . . She walked, on this steep and heavy road, as quickly as I myself did, and my old fancy about her, that she could fly if she would, came back. The wind whirled her clothes about. Sometimes it filled them and stretched them out, so that she looked like an angry owl on a branch, her wings spread out. At other times it screwed them up all around her, so that on her long legs she was like a crane when it runs along the ground to catch the wind and get on the wing.

Knocking the Baron down, Lincoln leaps past Olalla and catches her in his arms. "In a moment we were under the wild winter moon, in a tight embrace. Pressed to each other by the elements themselves, we both panted for breath." But when she turns up her terrified face—"white as bone, with its big eyes like two pools"—he knows she was running, not from the Jew, but from him.

Many years later, on crossing the Mediterranean in a storm, I looked, for one moment, into the face of a falcon which had tried many times in vain to hook itself to the rigging of my ship, before it was blown off and down into the sea for good. That was again the face of Olalla in the mountain pass. That bird, too, was wild and mad with fear, broken by overstrain, without hope.

The falcon desperate among sea winds is an image of natural force that expresses something deep in Isak Dinesen. It may have been suggested by an incident in her father's *Hunting Letters*.[1] She has made it into a story in "The Sailor-boy's Tale" (*WT*), where the falcon turns out to be a witch and is called a peregrine falcon. Since *peregrinus* is Latin for *pilgrim*, Pellegrina is being called falcon as well as pilgrim and, as her last name suggests, lion. The

---

[1] Boganis, *Jagtbreve*, No. 19.

animal metaphors work like the mythological allusions to give Pellegrina a superhuman stature.

The artistry of this scene is tremendous; for, after the apparently supernatural tales about Pellegrina, she is more supernatural than ever when she actually appears. "She stood still and let me kiss her. It might as well have been the snowflakes and the wild air pressing themselves upon her lips as my face and mouth. 'Olalla,' I said, 'I have sought you all over this world my whole life. Can we not be together here now?' "

Lincoln takes shelter with her under a great rock, where there .is no wind and where she sat "as a little girl would sit in a flower meadow". In Dante, the Earthly Paradise is at the top of the mountain of Purgatory. Lincoln is experiencing the Earthly Paradise at the top of this mountain; just as Hohenemser experienced it in the garret of Madame Lola's house, and the Baron in Rosalba's boudoir in the tower of her chateau. There is a moment of hope. Then the other two approach, carrying a lantern from Olalla's coach and looking "like two big birds of ill omen". They accuse her by calling out her different names, and demand to know who she is.

Her appearance renders such a question irrelevant. "By the light of the lantern I saw that Olalla's clothes were stiff and shining with frozen snow." The light of lantern and moon recalls the double light in which the Baron appeared at Olalla's coach and the double light on the dhow. The lantern seems to represent the human imagination as a specialized aspect of the universal light of the moon. Olalla appears to Lincoln as she would by moonlight—in the guise he described to Mira when he spoke of her as "self-luminous" like a star. There begins here a fulfillment of Mira's description of death as a running-out of thought and feeling in all directions, "like the rays of a star". For if she must be all three women at once, she can be no one.

When Olalla turns to Lincoln for help against the other two, he cries, " 'Tell them who you are!' " Like St Peter, he sides with the crowd against her three times. Then she acts out the rest of Lincoln's story about the falcon that tried to hook itself to the rigging of his ship, "before it was blown off and down into the sea for good".

She did not turn, or look at me. But the next moment she did what I had always feared that she might do: she spread out her wings and

flew away. Below the round white moon she made one great movement, throwing herself away from us all, and the wind caught her and
spread out her clothes. I have said already that on her flight from me
up the hill she had looked like some big bird which runs to catch the
wind and get on the wing. Now again she behaved exactly like a black
martin when you see it throw itself out from a slope or a roof to get
off the ground and take flight. For one second she seemed to lift
herself up with the wind, then, running straight across the road,
with all her might she threw herself from the earth clear into the
abyss, and disappeared from our sight.

Natural-supernaturalism can go no farther; for in leaping over
the precipice, she really does fly for a moment. They rescue her
body as the Jew appears. She is discovered to be still alive,
though apparently unconscious, and they drive her to a nearby
monastery where, as she lies dying, the Jew tells the story, the
most brilliant of the inset stories, that reveals her true identity.

In the scene on the mountain, Pellegrina and Marcus do not
exchange a word until she revives and takes up her life at the
point just before the fire. He answers in the language of her
delirium, so that they speak together symbolically. This keeps
their relation at the highest pitch of intensity. It would have been
well had Pellegrina not spoken in the mountain scene until this
moment. Marcus announces the second act of *Don Giovanni*, and
as she repeats after him the words of her recitative,

a wave of deep dark color, like that of a bride, like that in the face of
the old Jew, washed over her white and bruised face. It spread from
her bosom to the roots of her hair. The three of us who were lookers-on
were, I believe, pale faced; but those two, looking at each other,
glowed in a mute, increasing ecstasy. Suddenly her face broke, as the
night-old ice on a pool was broken up when, as a boy, I threw a stone
into it. It became like a constellation of stars, quivering in the universe. A rain of tears sprang from her eyes and bathed it all. Her
whole body vibrated under her passion like the string of an instrument."

Prince Potenziani blushed that way before he died of love. The
image that describes the breaking-up of her face into water and
starlight recalls the breaking-up of the ice in "Supper" and
Mira's description of death as " 'water, which runs out in little
streamlets to all possible sides, like the rays of a star' ".
Knocking three times with his walking-stick, " 'Donna
Pellegrina Leoni,' " Marcus cries out, " *'En scène pour le deux.'* "

She gave him a glance from her enormous dark eyes. In one mighty movement, like that of a billow rising and sinking, she lifted the middle of her body. A strange sound, like the distant roar of a great animal, came from her breast. Slowly the flames in her face sank, and an ashen gray covered it instead. Her body fell back, stretched itself out and lay quite still, and she was dead.

The roar represents the closing note of all tragedies. There is a pitiful irony in it; yet there is triumph, too, for it is the quint-essence of that singing which was itself a quintessence of energy and desire.

Mira says he knows the tale, he has made it himself. Lincoln's story is framed on either side by brief tales of Mira that define its archetype. At the beginning, Mira tells of a sultan who wanted a true virgin but found her, after she had finally been procured, looking with love upon a young water-carrier. The sultan had the two buried alive together, and he sat wondering by their grave " 'at how he was never to have his heart's desire, and he had a young boy to play the flute to him' ". The story of Pellegrina is also about infinite desire and hence about music. At the end, Mira tells of a Sultan Sabour who carried out the will of God with fire and sword, but was betrayed by a woman and reduced to beggary. In order not to be known in his beggar's state, " 'he has become, like your woman, many persons' ". Only his slave knows who he is and " 'this slave, I now remember, has had his nose cut off for Sabour's sake' ". The corollary of infinite desire is the ideal, and the ideal, when it falls among the conditions of this world, expresses itself through metamorphosis, through a restless using up and casting away of forms. In his last sentence, Mira humorously connects himself with Marcus as servants of the ideal. The story of Pellegrina suggests that the ideal dies if you try to nail it down to any one of its forms.

Pellegrina's tragic death is also followed by a little parody of her career in that Friederich Hohenemser takes on a pseudonymous existence as Fridolin Emser and is finally happy. "Since he himself, from the beginning, knew Fridolin to be nonexistent, he was never worried by efforts to make him exist"; whereas earlier he had been unable to make Friederich Hohenemser exist, because "he could not imagine what Friederich Hohenemser was to be like". Because we see the possibility of not existing under many names, we understand the intensity of Pellegrina's existence and the reason for it—that an identity is a work of imagination.

This little parody works, along with Mira's translation of Pellegrina's story into an archetype and Lincoln's final picture of her as, had she lived, a playful jackal, to put her story into a comic perspective. Mira says in the end that he has made friends with God. " 'To love him truly you must love change, and you must love a joke, these being the true inclinations of his own heart. Soon I shall take to loving a joke so well that I, who once turned the blood of all the world to ice, shall become a teller of funny tales, to make people laugh.' " It is from the tragicomic realm defined by Mira that Lincoln, who has called his tale a " 'lesson for Said' ", now asks, " 'What says Said?' " The lesson would be the elusiveness of the ideal in this world. But Said is not at the stage of life to heed this lesson, he has still to walk through tragedy. He only says " 'We shall be in Mombasa at dawn.' "

Of the three major stories in *Seven Gothic Tales*, "Deluge" excels in wit and "Roads" in color and extravagance. But "Dreamers" is the most poetic and explores with the most thoroughness the working of imagination itself. One's order of preference among them depends on personal taste and is likely to change with rereadings.

"The Poet", the last story of *Seven Gothic Tales*, is to be understood in connection with the story which was intended to stand first in the volume, "The Roads Round Pisa". The connecting link is Count Augustus von Schimmelmann, who turns up thirteen years later in "The Poet", which takes place in 1836. He is now in his early forties, but spiritually he is just where we left him at the end of "Roads". He understands that there is in life a wonderful happiness, and he has studied its manifestations in flowers, art and friendship. "But the road leading from it all into the heart of things he had not found."

A dreadful thing had, however, happened with time to this older Schimmelmann; "one thing had become to him as good as another". He is in that state of indifference where we found Pellegrina; but Pellegrina entered it after walking through the fire, and he has not walked through anything. He, too, has made his peace with his lot, but it is the peace of despair, quite different from the radiance of the tragicomic vision. He is aware, however, of the thing he is missing, and that makes him the type of the critic who knows about something he cannot be or do.

The man to whom he is a foil starts out in the story in apparently the same position as Count Augustus. He is Councilor (what we should call Councilman) Mathiesen of Hirschholm, a charming country town three miles from Rungsted. An intelligent, cultured, worldly man in his late fifties, the Councilor is an old friend and former tutor of Count Augustus. He loves poetry and knows all about it, but quickly decided after some early efforts that "he was no poet". Poetry now figures for him in its public and institutional aspect, as giving power and prestige. Weimar, the little German state of which Goethe was Privy Councilor, is his elysium, and it is Geheimerat Goethe, the poet turned public figure, whom he worships and to whom, in the most memorable experience of his life, he addressed the words: " 'I am Your Excellency's respectful servant.' " Councilor Mathiesen has for some time been playing Maecenas to a young peasant poet, Anders Kube, and he considers himself so far superior to the poet that he thinks he knows better than Anders what is good for him and his poetry. Having perceived an attraction between Anders and Fransine, a pretty young Italian widow who recently moved into the neighborhood, he decides that the two must marry as part of his plan to keep Anders anchored and under his control.

But then one early May morning before sunrise, the Councilor passes Fransine's house and, through the French windows of the sky-blue garden room, sees Fransine dancing on tiptoes in a diaphanous ballet dress. She looks "as if she were really rising from the ground and about to fly". It is a beautiful scene, designed to recall the early morning of the world, that colorless gray hour between the creation, which brought light, and the fall, which broke the light up into many colors. Remembering the conversation in "Supper" about high-flying ladies, we see why the Councilor thinks Fransine may be the witch, Lilith, rather than Eve, and that she is in any case not the lady to anchor Anders. He decides to marry her himself as a way of keeping both Fransine and Anders in his possession.

The Councilor's decision to marry Fransine himself comes from some compulsion in him to bring about the fall. In this compulsion, he plays the role of the devil, but the devil as an aspect after all of God. He also plays the role of the artist. When the idea first struck him of a love affair between Anders and Fransine, he thought of it as the first chapter of a simple idyllic romance like Goethe's *Hermann und Dorothea*. But when he injects himself into the romance, he envisions a more complicated and interesting story, rather more like *Werther*. "These are the thoughts", we are told, "which only such a man can allow himself who has within the structure of his mind a perfectly swept room to which he is absolutely sure that no one but himself has the key." The swept and locked-up room describes the detachment and self-awareness of the critical mind.

It is in front of Count Augustus that the Councilor, in order to stage "a bit of drama", first announces to Anders his plan to marry Fransine. Seeing Anders's disturbance, the Count realizes that he has once more come upon a vein of events from which he has been left out. Count Augustus appears just long enough to mark for us the difference between himself and the Councilor, to make us see that the Councilor is about to involve himself in the heart of things by involving himself in the lives of the two young people, by doing something dreadful to them. The Councilor has already, we learn, involved himself in life through a crime. He has been responsible, through subtle psychological aggression, for the death of his wife. He began his destruction of her in a garden, in a highly colored evening scene which is the obverse of the scene at Fransine's house.

Count Augustus helps us understand that the Councilor is not a critic but a poet, and that the contrast between the Councilor and Anders is a contrast between two kinds of poets. The Councilor is like Goethe a modern poet, who contains and transcends the critical intellect. The peasant Anders, instead, is a pre-modern or mythical poet. Anders does not so much think as he *sees*. He does not deal in the moral way with what ought and ought not to be, but rather in the mythical way with what must be. He foresees in a vision of Caiaphas and the other priests the role the Councilor is to play in his own life. Ye the does not judge the Councilor or seek to forestall him.

All through the summer of their engagement, Fransine accomplishes her fiancé's purpose by keeping Anders always with them and by playing out with him, before the Councilor's delighted eyes, an idyllic romance. In not allowing herself to think that the

summer will ever end, she, too, like the Councilor, tries to turn
life into an artwork.

This is something Anders does not do; he moves from life to
art but never the other way. That is why he is the only completely
engaged, completely tragic character in the story. He plans to
drown himself on Fransine's wedding day, so that he gives the
summer idyl a meaning not consciously intended by its author—
though he might be said to fulfill, as characters do who run away
with a story, the author's unconscious intention. From time to
time, he recites to Fransine and the Councilor parts of a great
poem he is writing on the sea, which unknown to them is to be
his swan song.

The old man was very much impressed, filled with an admiration
which at times came near to idolatry. It seemed to him, too, that he
had come out into a new sort of space and time, into the ether itself,
until he was swimming and flying in the blue, and in a new kind of
harmony and happiness. He thought it the beginning of great things.
He discussed it much with the poet, and even advised him upon it,
so that not a few of the Councilor's own ideas and reflections were,
in one way or another, echoed within the epos, and he was, during
these summer months, in a way making love, and writing poetry, to
his bride by proxy.

We see again the theme of vicariousness that recalls Prince
Potenziani in "Roads". The theme has more than one meaning.
It suggests, first of all, an unsavory sexual motive that is appropriate to the Councilor's hypocritical respectability. There is just
such a mixture of idealism and voyeurism in Karl Gutzkow's
scandal-making novel, *Wally, die Zweiflerin* (*Wally, the Skeptic*,
1835), after which the Councilor models his dénouement. The
novel, which arrives from Germany two days before the wedding,
is about Wally who, having promised to marry a rich man she
does not love, shows herself naked on her wedding morning to
the man she does love to symbolize their spiritual marriage.
Wally, however, does this at her lover's request; whereas it is the
Councilor who calls Fransine's attention to the novel, pointing
out that the lovers in the novel meet in a place like her own little
summer house. He clearly wants to create an erotic situation
which will have within it an outcome he instinctively senses to be
right—though he does not yet know what it is to be.

Wandering restlessly the night before his wedding, the Coun-

cilor is led to Fransine's summer house by the moon—symbol of
the imagination that tells us what we really want. The Councilor's
mind shoots back forty years to a scene in which he was the object
of vicarious eroticism—a scene he looks back on with pleasure, as
a little wild flower "in the garland of his life". "Would this
night put a rose into the garland?" We come here to the other
meaning of vicariousness. It is the morally ambivalent way the
artist involves himself in his characters' lives, in order to bring
about their fulfillment by bringing about their fall.

Without a sound, the Councilor approaches Fransine's summer
house, which is built with Greek columns. The lovers are there
as on a moonlit Greek stage. "For the second time a lurker" on
Fransine's grounds, the Councilor has like Satan in Eden come
back to finish his work. Fransine is wrapped in a cloak; she is
naked beneath it. Anders is drunk and carrying a gun. The fall
has already taken place, for Anders now sees Fransine's angelic
qualities as destructive. He calls her a witch for the spiritual
eroticism she has planned. She flees like Arethusa, the Greek
nymph who fled her Alpheus to whom she was not united until
the two came together as rivers in Sicily, the land of pastoral
poetry, the poetry of innocence.

Anders turns around and is brought face to face with the
Councilor. He is not surprised, for behind the witch there always
lurks the devil. When he shoots the Councilor, "the roar and the
sudden, overwhelming pain struck the old man as one thing, as
the end or the beginning of the world"—as fall and rebirth.
Upon regaining consciousness, the Councilor thinks he can still
save himself if he can manage to crawl to Fransine's house; so he
draws himself along, "like an old snake which has been run over
on the road, but still wriggles on".

But it was the serpent, according to the party conversation in
"Supper", who "opened the eyes of man to the arts". The
Councilor, when he raises himself again, finds that he is in
Weimar. "The sweetness of this discovery nearly overwhelmed
him. Weimar, then, was so easy to get to." As he falls again and
rolls over on his back, gasping for breath, he understands that
King Lear felt so exceptionally safe, in spite of his dreadful
situation, because he knew he was in the hands of Shakespeare.
By the time the Councilor reached the fence of Fransine's garden,
he "understood everything in the world". He had got not only

to Weimar, but "inside the magic circle of poetry. He was in the world of the mind of the great Geheimerat."

He had opened the locked-up room in his own mind and let in another mind; that is why he felt inside that other mind. He had got past the critical reservation that had kept him on the outside of things, had kept him from merging his own will with the author's and from seeing that all things are right because necessary to the author's plan. When the Councilor repeats the words he had addressed to Goethe: "I am Your Excellency's respectful servant", they no longer seem a mere overstated homage to power, but appropriate and true. For now that the Councilor speaks from inside Goethe's mind, the great Geheimerat has become another name for God.

Hearing Fransine's wild sobbing, the Councilor thinks of Margaret in *Faust* and understands that it was necessary for the Geheimerat to treat Margaret so cruelly. He drags himself up to the terrace of the house to bring this message to Fransine. " 'My poor girl, my dove,' " he says to her, " 'listen. Everything is good. All, all! Sacred, Fransine,' " he says, " 'sacred puppets.' "

The change in Fransine is portrayed with power and economy, showing the advantage of symbolic notation. Her doll's face, "dissolved and ruined by tears", is the counterpart of Anders's death by water. Her body is now witchlike, shrunken to a stick, but she is spiritually no longer a doll, no longer an angel-witch, but a woman. The sign of this, if we remember "Supper", is that her despair keeps her upright by weighting her to the ground, "like the lead in the little wooden figures which children play with".

Fransine has been weeping because of Anders's cruelty to her, but when she sees the old man with the blood running out of his body, she realizes that Anders has shot him and will be hanged if the old man dies. The conviction that in shooting the old man Anders has proved his love for her releases all her woman's nature. One motive for what follows is her desire to save Anders from hanging by killing the old man herself. But there are also older, more instinctive motives that cause her to lift up with both arms an enormous flat stone, press it to her bosom "as if it had been her only child, which the old sorcerer had managed to turn into stone", and finally, raising it above her head, fling it down upon the Councilor, crushing out his life. "And I will put enmity between thee and the woman," the Lord said to the serpent, "and between thy seed and her seed; it shall bruise thy head, and thou shalt bruise his heel" (Genesis 3: 15).

Before the stone falls, the Councilor, "afraid that his lips had given no sound when he had tried to speak to her, . . . dragged his right hand along the ground until it touched her bare foot". She understands through his touch his intention to tell her that the world is good and beautiful. That is the bruise to her heel; for it is just such idealistic sorcery that has turned her children to stone. " 'You!' " she cries as she flings the stone. " 'You poet!' " The irony is tremendous—because Fransine means "You liar!" and because we now see that the title of the story applies not to Anders but the Councilor.

The Councilor's assertion about the world was a lie until he had himself come to understand through catastrophe the sense in which it is true. Fransine is right in accusing him of bringing about the tragedy. But she does not know—it would spoil her involvement in the moment if she did—that he has given her thereby her humanity and that her accusing words, echoing in his ears as he is flung headlong "in three or four great leaps from one cataract to the other" into "the engulfing darkness", give him his triumphant, his properly tragic death. The water imagery connects his death with the transformation by water of Anders and Fransine.

Not only do we have all the proper elements of a tragic dénouement in which the major characters achieve apotheosis and death, but there is conducted throughout the story a comparison between two kinds of tragedy—traditional tragedy made by circumstances beyond the hero's control, and romantic or Faustian tragedy where the hero creates the drama in which he himself stars. Anders is the hero of the first kind of tragedy, the Councilor of the second.

In comparing the two kinds of tragedy, Isak Dinesen explores again that change in the mind and culture of Europe which is the large subject of *Seven Gothic Tales*. The subject is given its most explicit treatment in this the closing story of the volume, and it is Goethe's presiding presence in the story that makes the treatment explicit. For Goethe is the representative figure of German romanticism, *Faust* is its bible, and German romanticism formulated for Europe the implications of the transition from the eighteenth century to the nineteenth.

Anders, Count Augustus and the Councilor represent what German romanticism held to be the three main phases of the European mind. The peasant, Anders, represents the archaic myth-making mentality; the aristocratic Augustus represents the critical intellect of the eighteenth century; the bourgeois Councilor represents the nineteenth-century attempt to employ the critical intellect to reach back across the eighteenth century and recover, by a supreme act of criticism, the primitive mode of thought. Anders and Count Augustus are in their different ways defeated figures; only the bourgeois Councilor triumphs. The Councilor brings Anders to light as a poet and a tragic hero in the way the romanticists glorified peasants and brought to light the folk mind and folk art of Europe. Although the Councilor shares Count Augustus's critical intellect, he becomes a poet as Augustus cannot, because he exploits Anders as Goethe exploited the old Germanic ballads, folk tales and oral epics. "The Poet" offers us a miniature history of Europe that is actually sketched out for us in the opening account of Hirschholm's past.

In comparing the two stories that in the British and Danish editions frame *Seven Gothic Tales*, Aage Henriksen speaks of Prince Potenziani's "terrifying innocence".[1] It is true that Prince Potenziani overcomes the consequences of the fall through style, through immersion in a complete civilization that has prepared a ritualized response to and a final value for every aspect of reality. Dante and the absolutism of the medieval aristocratic and Catholic order stand behind "Roads", just as Goethe and the relativism of the modern bourgeois and romantic order stand behind "The Poet". That is why the tragic events of the first story turn into a divine comedy, why "Roads" is tragicomic; while "The Poet" is mainly tragic, even though the Councilor does achieve a tragicomic vision at the end. When we are told that the Councilor lay dead on the ground "like a bundle of old clothes", we are meant to recall Fransine sinking down upon the floor, at the end of her early-morning dance, "in a graceful heap", and to realize that he has regained the utter passivity of innocence which she has now lost. The difference between the two images is the difference between innocence and innocence regained, between pastoral and tragicomedy.

As the only tragedy, "The Poet" is the least witty story in

[1] *Karen Blixen og Marionetterne*, p. 22.

Seven Gothic Tales and the most nearly naturalistic in its depiction of character. This accounts for the story's shortcoming—that the characters have not the extravagant, fantastic qualities of Isak Dinesen's most successful characters, and that the prudent, calculating, comfortable Councilor has the wrong kind of flaws for an entirely successful tragic hero. Although one admires "The Poet" rather more than one likes it, it is as intelligent and as beautifully wrought as any story in *Seven Gothic Tales*. The position it occupies in the book makes it, moreover, indispensable. For it establishes in its connection with "Roads" the large historical and cultural range that makes *Seven Gothic Tales* a great book about Europe.

Chapter 4

AUTOBIOGRAPHY AND MYTH
IN THE AFRICAN MEMOIRS

SEVEN GOTHIC TALES is a great book about Europe, because Isak Dinesen's experience of Africa stands behind it; and Europe stands, in the same way, behind every word of *Out of Africa*. That is why *Out of Africa* (1937) is literature and not just another memoir of an interesting life.

While a great deal of *Seven Gothic Tales* was "thought of", as Isak Dinesen says in the foreword to the Danish edition, "and some of it written in Africa", *Out of Africa* was, as she made clear to me, entirely conceived and written after she got back to Europe. In assuring the Danish readers of *Seven Gothic Tales* that the parts about Denmark "have to be considered more as the fantasies of a Danish emigrant than as an attempt to describe reality", she is saying that a Denmark conceived from the standpoint of Africa is not everybody's Denmark. But the apologetic tone is an attempt to forestall hostile criticism; for the imagination works by just such reconciliation of opposites, and there is no doubt that she considers her imagined Denmark more real than the Denmark of ordinary observation.

Her Africa is not everybody's Africa either. I have already suggested that it is an Africa of certain romantic expectations come true—expectations as to the possibility of recovering in primitive places that unity of man with nature which yields psychological and social unity as well: expectations as to the possibility of recovering a kind of life that prevailed in Europe before the Industrial Revolution, that unique event, cut Europeans off from nature and the past, and consequently from all other civilizations. Her Africa is also seen retrospectively, as something already lost even to her. It is seen in a way she herself could not have seen it while she was in the midst of the experience and did not know it was to end. It is because Africa figures as a paradise lost—both in Isak Dinesen's life and in the life of Europe—that *Out of Africa* is an authentic pastoral, perhaps the best prose pastoral of our time.

Because it is divided into five parts, *Out of Africa* has been compared to the five-act French tragedies Isak Dinesen loved.[1] Although there are similarities, its structure is not quite that of tragedy; for tragedy takes place in a fallen world where we see from the start those seeds of trouble that give a moral rationale to the final catastrophe. In *Out of Africa*, however, we have four acts of pure idyl, followed by a fall which is unaccountable except on grounds of physical necessity—the necessity by which things change and we grow up and die. The seeds of trouble, in other words, lie outside the story; there is a breaking in of the fallen world upon the unfallen. Adam and Eve lost Eden because Satan had already fallen from heaven. And adverse forces of nature and historical change cause Isak Dinesen to lose her African Eden. It is because she assimilated her African memories to the myth of the fall that Isak Dinesen made a unified book of what started out to be a series of disconnected anecdotes.

A letter of hers provides an interesting clue to the genesis of *Out of Africa*. Writing to her American publisher, Robert Haas, on March 24, 1934, just before the American publication date of *Seven Gothic Tales*, she authorizes him to reveal her true identity if and when he sees fit. She then concludes as follows:

> Now that this secret is out in any case, I have got a few short, quite truthful recounts of my life on the African farm, particularly about my relations with the Natives. I have to have these published under my real name, as they deal with real facts and people. I should like to get them out in a *good* magazine, if possible, and I suppose that this can not in any way interfere with our contract, since the stories can not in any way be classed as a book. Will you give me your kind assistance to find such a magazine, if you think it could be found?[2]

The emphasis on the truthfulness of the account raises the interesting critical question. For *Out of Africa* makes such an immediate appeal that the critic does not need to explain it as he does the stories. He has, on the contrary, to complicate the obvious in order to demonstrate the book's artistry—to dispel the idea that, because the book is autobiographical, all Isak Dinesen had to do was write down what happened. The book renders the "feel" of Africa, takes us inside an experience of it, by making us

[1] By the Danish critic, Hakon Stangerup, *Nationaltidende*, October 6, 1937.
[2] The correspondence with Robert Haas quoted herein is in the Random House files.

take Africa inside us. It does this by making Africa part of an intensely personal experience, in which we participate, of growing up morally—of arriving at a new settlement with reality after the old one has been smashed. The personal story emerges, at the same time, as a re-enactment of every profound European story of moral development, just because it takes place in an Africa which is at once so "real", so different from us, and yet, miraculously, the materialization of European myths about otherness—about nature, the past and the unfallen world. To render all this, the facts about Africa and about Isak Dinesen's life there have had to pass through a very special imagination and to be set forth with a great deal of conscious art.[1]

Oddly enough, the publication of *Out of Africa* in 1937 did little to dispel the mystery about Isak Dinesen. In America and England, where she went on publishing under the name of Isak Dinesen, people went on asking who she was. And even in Scandinavia where she began, starting with *The African Farm* (as it is called in the Scandinavian editions), to publish under the name of Karen Blixen, she remained a legend whom people did not know as they knew other people. *Out of Africa* is largely responsible for creating her legend. For while it personifies the voice behind *Seven Gothic Tales*, giving it a history that accounts for its knowledge and its point of view, it tells us little not relevant to that voice. It is remarkable how the author manages to keep her name out of the book (her name appears only three times—twice as Karen Blixen, once as Tania), and you would have to look hard to gather from the book that she was married and divorced while in Africa. She is vague about chronology in order to separate out the idyl from the fall. There were troubles with the farm all along since it was too high up for profitable coffee growing.[2] But these did not fit the shape given to her experience of Africa by the succession of catastrophes which finally separated her from what in retrospect figures as an unalloyedly golden time.

---

[1] In *The Anatomy of Criticism*, Northrop Frye makes the very sensible suggestion that we not confine the word *fiction* to only the novel, but apply it to any "work of art in prose" (p. 303). Such an enlargement of the word *fiction* helps us account for the fact that fine autobiographies often turn out upon examination to be as elaborately "worked" as any novel and less "true to fact" than is claimed, while autobiographical novels often turn out to be more "true to fact" than is claimed.

[2] Thomas Dinesen describes her continuous difficulties with the farm and with ill health, in his memoir of her in the Karen Blixen memorial anthology.

The biographer who tried to gather material from *Out of Africa* would find that it does not answer many questions he would have to raise. It does not tell us whether Denys Finch-Hatton was more than a friend, or what the people around her, black and white, really thought of her. We have only her own feeling that she was surrounded by a circle of adoration, just as we have only episodes that tell to her advantage. That this does not offend us is a sign that the book operates in the manner of art—that its validity and general significance derive from the personal nature of its vision. Because we recognize Isak Dinesen's Africa as a personal dream come true, we recognize it as a cultural dream come true. In our psychic life, the golden time was the time we remember, or dream we remember, when people saw us as we see ourselves, in our full potentiality, and consequently stood in the relation to us that we most deeply desire. And in the cultural tradition, the Golden Age was the time when all our potentiality was manifest, when we were like gods.

This does not impugn the truthfulness of her account. She has achieved the main aim of romantic autobiography which, whether in verse or prose, is to pull the ideal out of the real by calling in as witness not the authority of traditional myths but one's own experience. The aim is to achieve a perfect union of fact and myth, to show how the myth came to pass in one's own life; and it is because she does this that her true accounts fall so naturally and inevitably into the shape of stories. But to do this, the writer must arrogate to himself a humanity grander and more intense than ordinary. We accept this because we know he is acting out for us our own potentialities, that he is walking through the paces of his life to make the myth come to pass, to make us see the mythical outlines around the naturalistic person.

There is no danger of a paranoiac atmosphere as long as the writer knows precisely what he is doing. To show that Isak Dinesen knew what she was doing in *Out of Africa*, one has only to point to her portrayal of Pellegrina Leoni as a woman who had deliberately turned herself into a myth. Two people are described as doing this in *Out of Africa*. The first is an old, blind, down-and-out Dane to whom Isak Dinesen gave a bungalow on her farm. Old Knudsen was a man after her own heart, who must have gone into the making of many of her fictitious characters. For he was a born rebel in the cause of the old lost heroic tradition. "He liked to talk of kings and royal families, jugglers, dwarfs and lunatics, for them he took to be outside the law. . . . But for the good citizen he had a deep contempt, and law-abidingness in any man was to him the sign of a slavish mind." He always spoke of himself in the third person, as Old Knudsen, and with much boasting. His boasting, however, was not like the boasting of people who represent only themselves. For the impotent old man before her was the servant of the mighty mythical figure of Old Knudsen.[1] Old Knudsen's case helps explain the relation between the author of *Out of Africa* and the lady in the book.

The second case is that of an artist, the Swedish actor, Emmanuelson, a shady character who gets periodically run out of places for what we gather to be homosexual practices. Known to Isak Dinesen only as headwaiter in a Nairobi hotel, he appears one evening at the farm and announces his intention to start the next morning on a three-day walk through the Masai Reserve, where there is no water and the lions are bad, in order to reach Tanganyika. It is almost certain death, but he has clearly to get out of Nairobi. Isak Dinesen becomes interested in him when he reveals that he is by profession a tragic actor.

When she tries to console him by suggesting that he may get a lift from a lorry, he shows himself unwilling to be deprived of any fraction of his tragic destiny.

"Yes, but there are the lions," said Emmanuelson, "and the Masai."
"Do you believe in God, Emmanuelson?" I asked him.
"Yes, yes, yes," said Emmanuelson. He sat in silence for a time. "Perhaps you will think me a terrible sceptic," he said, "if I now say what I am going to say. But with the exception of God I believe in absolutely nothing whatever."[2]

That last sentence makes Emmanuelson a man after Isak Dinesen's own heart. After he says it, she offers him money and determines to drive him the next morning the first ten miles of his way. Her question is the one Carlotta asks Count Schimmel-mann in "Roads". Emmanuelson's answer expresses Carlotta's position and Isak Dinesen's. For Isak Dinesen's question really is: Do you believe in the significance of life, do you believe that your death will have significance? And Emmanuelson points to the

---

[1] New York, pp. 190, 59; London, pp. 204, 63.
[2] New York, p. 201; London, p. 215.

grandeur of the imagination, or to the grandeur of the world as perceived by the imagination, to show that life has significance, though he does not know what that significance is.

We are to understand the meaning of his answer from the scene where she lets him out of her car the next morning. We are to understand that he has, through the power of his imagination, turned himself from a shabby fugitive into a mythical figure, an archetype of all heroic wanderers.[1] I do not think the transformation quite comes off. To understand what Isak Dinesen saw in and through Emmanuelson, we have to consider the fictitious character who is clearly modelled after him. I mean Kasparson of "Deluge", who helps give significance to the death of himself and his companions in the way Emmanuelson gave significance to his own death—by turning it into an artwork, assimilating it to deaths already seen and understood under the aspect of imagination. To do this, both men need an audience; for the transformation into significance takes place in the eyes of the beholder. It was probably to secure a worthy audience that Emmanuelson made his way to the farm.

The combination in Emmanuelson of shady character and actor-charlatan is exaggerated in Kasparson, who is both more criminal and more brilliant, and who acts the part of hero and saint. The shady character who can bring to life our highest ideals typifies for Isak Dinesen the mystery of all value, all transcendence—in which there is always an element of charlatanism because transcendence is by definition not justified by the facts. The other kind of person, the Louis-Philippe, who claims no grandeur not justified by the facts, is the predictable, law-abiding citizen whom Old Knudsen despised. The same distinction is made in this episode when we learn that Emmanuelson did after all get through to Tanganyika, having been taken in by travelling Masai whom he entertained, by some trick of pantomime, with stories of his adventures. Isak Dinesen reflects that Emmanuelson had found with the Masai his proper audience, for the same reason presumably that he had found it with her.

The true aristocracy and the true proletariat of the world are both in understanding with tragedy. . . . They differ in this way from the bourgeoisie of all classes, who deny tragedy, who will not tolerate it,

<hr>

[1] New York, p. 202; London, p. 216.

and to whom the word of tragedy means in itself unpleasantness. Many misunderstandings between the white middle-class immigrant settlers and the Natives arise from this fact. The sulky Masai are both aristocracy and proletariat, they would have recognized at once in the lonely wanderer in black, a figure of tragedy; and the tragic actor had come, with them, into his own.[1]

Aristocracy, proletariat and Africans see the world as symbolic. For the bourgeois, however, a fact is just a fact (Emmanuelson would have been a man in want of a ride and a new coat), and tragedy is therefore an unpleasantness which might have been avoided by better social arrangements and an improved technology.

In writing about the feudal society of her farm in relation to the rhythms of Africa—to the slow-moving apprehensions of its people, the special stillnesses of its wild animals, and its shimmering landscapes—Isak Dinesen is reconstructing that organic life of the European past projected by the romantic mythology. When the modern world breaks in and she loses her farm through bankruptcy, we see re-enacted in miniature the crisis of modern Europe, the breakup of a social organization based on love and mutual obligation. In the end she goes back to Denmark to become the author of stories about the difference between the old order and the new—thus fulfilling the myth of fall and redemption by recovering in the imagination what has been lost in the external world.

We see the relation of nature, the old order and the sense of tragedy in the story of her people's insistence on remaining together after she sold the farm. They were to be resettled in the Kikuyu Reserve, where there was not a stretch of unoccupied land big enough for all of them. She spent her last months in Africa haunting Government offices on their behalf. Her efforts were finally successful. But when the authorities suggested that there was really no need for all her people to remain together, she thought of King Lear and his reply to the ungrateful daughters who wanted to strip him of the last few symbols of his royal identity. " 'Oh reason not the need,' I thought, 'our basest beggars are in the poorest things superfluous.' " This is the essence of the tragic view, that it is symbols not things that matter to human beings.

[1] New York, p. 204; London, p. 218.

"All my life," Isak Dinesen continues, "I have held that you can class people according to how they may be imagined behaving to King Lear"—according to how well, in other words, they understand the importance of symbols. "You could not reason with King Lear, any more than with an old Kikuyu, and from the first he demanded too much of everybody; but he was a king."[1] The African had not, as had Lear, given his land away; he had had it taken from him. But like Lear he knew who he was through familiar sights and circumstances, and now the world around him had changed. The connection between place and the sense of identity is even more important among primitive than modern people, because the former have not learned to abstract subject from object. When the outside changes, they do not know where to look for the inside, and it was consequently their very existence that Isak Dinesen's people were demanding when they insisted on retaining familiar faces around them.

It has been observed that Lear is the stupidest of Shakespeare's tragic heroes. Isak Dinesen's treatment suggests that he is the most primitive, and therefore the most kingly and the most tragic. Lear's emotion is as unreasonable and irresistible as the storm in which he rages because there is at stake in it his existence as a king and therefore—his kingliness being what it is—his existence as a man and an animal. Such an emotion is possible only in a world where one's personal and social identity is as sure and firmly rooted as one's biological existence.

It is knowledge of such a world that Isak Dinesen brings us in *Out of Africa*. It is a sign of her artistry that she makes it at once familiar and remote. We are allowed to know it, but never to confuse it with our world. The humanity of her Africans is very real, just because we are so aware that their sense of themselves is quite different from ours, that they move to a different drummer than we do. The most striking example is their extraordinary capacity to communicate through silence and stillness.

The enigmatic stillness of the Africans is a sign of their otherness. They communicate throughout the book as nature does, without ever yielding their final secret. Her characterization of the Africans bears out her statement that they "were Africa in flesh and blood".[2]

---

[1] New York, p. 377; London, p. 404.
[2] New York, p. 21; London, p. 22.

It was not easy to get to know the Natives. They were quick of hearing, and evanescent; if you frightened them they could withdraw into a world of their own, in a second, like the wild animals which at an abrupt movement from you are gone,—simply are not there. . . . If we pressed or pursued them, to get an explanation of their behaviour out of them, they receded as long as they possibly could, and then they used a grotesque humorous fantasy to lead us on the wrong track. . . . When we really did break into the Natives' existence, they behaved like ants, when you poke a stick into their ant-hill; they wiped out the damage with unwearied energy, swiftly and silently,— as if obliterating an unseemly action.[1]

Wordsworth has a poem, called "Anecdote for Fathers", in which a child obliterates the unseemly action of his father as the Africans do here. The little boy expresses an instinctive preference for one beautiful place over another. When the father asks for a reason, the boy blushes with shame, and finally, after being pressed for a reason three times, puts his father off with just such a grotesque humorous fantasy of a "reason" as the Africans give the Europeans.

The thing the Africans feared from the Europeans is indicated in *Shadows on the Grass*, where we are told of the Africans' deadly fear of hospitals. "They had deep roots to their nature . . . which, like all roots, demanded darkness." "Their hearts in an instinctive deadly nausea" turned from the spirit of the hospitals, which is the spirit of the floodlight, of a civilization which has not feared "to floodlight" its "own inmost mechanisms".[2] Again we see how the Africans were trying to maintain their identity by maintaining that "umbilical cord of Nature" which, as Isak Dinesen says in *Out of Africa*, "has, with them, not been quite cut through".[3]

Their morality, as a consequence—which is based on the knowledge "lost to us by our first parents . . . that God and the Devil are one"[4]—approaches the morality a rock would have were it conscious that it was taking the same attitude toward the sun that shines on it or the storms that batter it. This attitude gives the Africans their tremendous strength in passivity and their ability to endure the hardest lot of any race in the world. Their

---

[1] New York, pp. 18-19; London, pp. 19-20.
[2] New York: Random House, 1961, pp. 90-92; London: Michael Joseph, 1961, pp. 67-68.
[3] New York, p. 162; London, p. 175.
[4] New York, p. 20; London, p. 21.

moral simplicity is the point to which the highest moral sophisti-
cation comes back full circle; so that Isak Dinesen can speak of
"the unprejudiced Kikuyu" who "know of no code. They have
it that most people are capable of most things, and you cannot
shock them if you want to. . . . The very poor people of Europe,
in this way, are like the Kikuyus. They judge you not, but sum
you up."[1]

By combining what she heard from old people with her own
observation of Danish peasants and aristocrats, Isak Dinesen
acquired an almost personal memory of the European past, the
range of which she extended in Africa. She saw in Africa the
myth-making mind still in operation—in the way the Africans
turned the Europeans into myths by giving them characterizing
names, usually of animals (they named her Lioness), and by
turning them into brass serpents or talismanic cure-alls. Her
friend, Lord Delamere, was such a brass serpent. When the
grasshoppers came and left not a blade of grass behind them, the
Africans were in despair until she told them she had seen the
hoppers on Delamere's farm. They then "became quiet and
almost at ease. They asked me what Delamere had said of his
misfortune, and again asked me to repeat it, and then they said
no more."[2]

She learned in Africa what it had been like a hundred years
earlier in Denmark, when the plain people first had "the world of
the written word" opened to them. She tells the charming and
touching story of the illiterate Jogona, who in connection with a
legal dispute had to dictate to her an account of his life. When
in reading it back to him she read out his name,

he swiftly turned his face to me, and gave me a great fierce flaming
glance, so exuberant with laughter that it changed the old man into
a boy, into the very symbol of youth. . . . Such a glance did Adam
give the Lord when He formed him out of the dust, and breathed
into his nostrils the breath of life, and man became a living soul. I had
created him and shown him himself: Jogona Kanyagga of life ever-
lasting. When I handed him the paper, he took it reverently and
greedily, folded it up in a corner of his cloak and kept his hand upon
it. He could not afford to lose it, for his soul was in it, and it was the
proof of his existence. Here was something which Jogona Kanyagga

---

[1] New York, pp. 127-28; London, p. 138.
[2] New York, p. 107; London, p. 116.

had performed, and which would preserve his name for ever: the flesh was made word and dwelt among us full of grace and truth.[1]

Her accounts of the Africans have always this light, tender touch that sets strings vibrating. She makes comedy of their passion for cows:

The people of the farm did not have it in them to remain silent where a cow and calf were being discussed. Everyone present gave out his opinion. The old men seized one another by the arm and shook out their last asthmatic breath in praise and condemnation of the cow. The shrill voices of their old women fell in and followed them up, as in a canon. The young men spat out short deadly remarks at one another in deep voices. In two or three minutes the open place by my house was boiling over like a witch's caldron.

But she also makes poetry of it when she says that their passion for livestock "smells of the stone-age, like a fire you strike with a flint".[2]

We get a sense of the stone age, too, in her description of the Ngomas or big dancing parties where the dances were of immemorial antiquity. The young men were stark naked but very formal, with elaborate coiffures and bodies covered by a pale red chalk that gave them "a strangely *blond* look". She speaks of the dancers' "sweetness and fire", and says of a dance where the girls stand demurely on the men's feet, clasping them round the waist, while the men make protective motions, she says that "as the dance went on for hours the faces of the dancers took on an expression of angelic ecstasy, as if they were really all ready to die for one another". What she manages to suggest is not how barbaric but how civilized—that somehow this is the essence of civilization, man's earliest expression of the social principle. The Ngomas, where all ages and conditions had their appointed places, become the model of society as it has always existed—not only in its unchanging rhythm, that keeps time to the rhythm of the natural cycles, but in its texture, in its many sweetly intimate human details.[3]

It was all like that glorious sight—in the middle of a very hot day, at the center of the Ngong Forest—of the rarely seen Giant Forest Hog. "He came suddenly past me, with his wife and three young pigs, at a great speed, the whole family looking like

[1] New York, pp. 120-21; London, p. 130.
[2] New York, pp. 152-53; London, p. 164.
[3] New York, pp. 158-64; London, pp. 169-76.

uniform, bigger and smaller figures cut out in dark papers, against the sunlit green behind them. It was a glorious sight, like a reflection in a forest pool, like a thing that had happened a thousand years ago."[1] The whole of *Out of Africa* presents just such a glorious sight. For Africa is used to give us both an acute sense of history and a sense of the timeless life of nature at the unseen heart of things, where men and animals merge with each other and the landscape and the seen event merges with all its unseen occurrences. The glorious sight is a transformation of the author's very particular vision of otherness, of life as it is in itself apart from human perception. The forest pool is the absolute eye referred to by the showman of "In the Menagerie" (*Out of Africa*, Part IV), when Count Schimmelmann doubts the reality of wild animals in a wild landscape where nobody sees them. " 'God sees them,' " says the showman. All the elaborate technique of the stories is designed to project the glorious sight— to project absolute through relative vision.

Because *Out of Africa* gives evidence that Isak Dinesen has been at the heart of things, both as a historical and an ever-present perceptual condition, it justifies the ageless and authoritative voice behind the stories, the voice of the archetypal storyteller who knows all the stories and has therefore all the memories and wisdom of the culture. The voice is one answer to the main technical question of fiction—the question of how the narrator knows the story and is in a position to judge it. In the early novels, the author, speaking in his own person, offered himself as the criterion of knowledge and validity. But he seemed an intruder who broke the illusion, and since he was just another person like you and me he offered a criterion of only relative validity. The solution was to make a virtue of necessity, to invent the point-of-view character through whose knowledge and judgment the novel could be filtered, and thus make the novel acknowledge through its form its characteristically subjective and relativistic view of life.

For an absolute view, the author must still speak out in his own voice. But to do this, he must speak not as an ordinary, but a mythical person. The voice must have character, so we can discern in it a whole spectrum of memories and values that will give meaning to the story. But it must be larger than life. Hence

[1] New York, pp. 65-66; London, p. 71.

that voice which was perhaps the most exciting thing about *Seven Gothic Tales* when it first came out—a voice individual to the point of strangeness and yet so impersonal that it hardly seemed as though it could belong to any one person. Continental and aristocratic, it seemed to be the voice of European civilization. *Out of Africa*, when it appeared, explained the other thing about the voice—that it seemed at once so primitive and so civilized and that the one quality seemed to derive from the other. *Out of Africa* accounted for the character of Isak Dinesen's voice; and it is interesting to see how in her Danish radio talks, in her American recitals in 1959, and in *Shadows on the Grass*, she has been able to do what few writers nowadays can do—speak directly and intimately to an audience whom she can rely on to know her legend as set forth in *Out of Africa*.

The case is instructive, and should make us revise our ideas about the relation of an author's life to his work. The old, simple idea was that the work is an expression of the life, and the current reaction is to say that there is little connection between them. The fact is that the connection is more important in some writers than in others. But where it is important, the work has as much effect upon the life as the life upon the work.

One thinks of Byron who made his life into the legend required by characters like Childe Harold and Don Juan. Yeats moved into a ruined medieval tower in order to give himself the setting required by the speaker of his poems, in order, as he says in "Meditations in Time of Civil War", to grow his symbolic roses in his own garden. It was as he brought his life and art into conjunction and made of his personal voice a mythical voice, that he was able to write the increasingly personal poetry of his later years. Isak Dinesen in the same way made her life a part of her *œuvre*. Using Africa and her Danish estate, Rungstedlund, as appropriate settings, she made herself into the combined figure of the aristocrat and artist that she so consistently admired in her writing—a figure of extraordinary, indeed sometimes frightening force for so frail a lady, because representative of the great powers outside herself, the powers of a tradition so profoundly under-stood that it reaches back through cultural memory to the point where culture has its origin in nature.

When in one of our conversations I asked Isak Dinesen what qualities she thought the aristocracy served as models for, whether she thought they were more virtuous than other people, she said they certainly were not more virtuous. What they had above all was courage, that was the main thing, and after that taste and responsibility. It is because Isak Dinesen had courage—both courage in the ordinary sense and the existential courage to be one's self and to follow the logic of one's own nature—that her life and work are all of a piece: that she was able to write stories distinguished by the courage that in art we call style, and to create for herself a life and personality as audacious, extravagant, surprising and, yes, as shocking, too, as her stories.

Out of Africa is in its structure like a dream that materializes out of the African landscape, growing ever more tangible and complex only to burst in the end, lingering on as dreamlike memory. We start with the landscape, the chief feature of which is the air, a pervasive blue luminousness that breaks down the distinction between earth and sky, so that you recognize your life there as the fulfillment of a dream. The animals are seen as moving bits of landscape, and the Africans are seen as variants of the wild animals. "When you have caught the rhythm of Africa, you find that it is the same in all her music. What I learned from the game of the country, was useful to me in my dealings with the Native People." Her discovery of the dark races was, like all cases of love at first sight, a recognition. "If some one with an ear for music had happened to hear music for the first time when he was already grown up; their cases might have been similar to mine. After I had met with the Natives, I set out the routine of my daily life to the Orchestra."[1]

Part I, "Kamante and Lulu", is about Isak Dinesen's relation with a single Kikuyu and a single wild animal—the little savage, Kamante, and the little gazelle, Lulu, both of whom she brought up in her own house. They represent her link with the wilderness, and she moves in her description of them back and forth across the line between nature and civilization. Each has qualities that are the highest ideals of civilization. Kamante has genius, and Lulu has the grace and elegance of a princess. But the isolation of these qualities in creatures who are otherwise wild and unknowable enhances our sense of both nature and civilization.

[1] New York, pp. 15-18; London, pp. 17-19.

The son of one of her squatters, Kamante was an undersized, deformed little boy whose legs were covered with terrible running sores which she undertook to cure. Suffering had made him, even in that setting, the wildest of creatures, a human being who was "by a sort of firm deadly resignation, completely closed to all surrounding life. I could make him answer when I questioned him, but he never volunteered a word and never looked at me. He had no pity whatever in him."[1]

Finding his case beyond her medical powers, she sent him to the Church of Scotland Mission from whence he returned cured and converted to Christianity. She took him into her service and taught him cooking. He turned out a genius at the highest, most refined European cuisine. Yet he did not understand the real meaning of the art he practised (he never could get the order of courses straight), he felt contempt for it, and did not himself like to eat the delicacies he prepared. He preferred the maizecobs and the roasted sweet potatoes of the Kikuyu. She derives much fine comedy from the incongruity, but without patronizing him; for Kamante was formidable in all his dealings. He was shrewd in money matters, though he thought money worthless. He had observed the medical techniques of the Mission and became an excellent medical assistant to her. He could do better than other people all the things they thought worth doing; he had mastered existence, "but he had no high opinion of it".

Kamante showed his genius in the questions he asked, and even his misunderstandings showed that he had understood everything there was to be understood once you left out the requisite context of cultural experience. The genius makes all the more apparent the alien sensibility, the "strong strain of malice", the "shrill delight in things going wrong", which is common to all Africans, but which Kamante brought to "a rare perfection, even to a special self-irony, that made him take pleasure in his own disappointments and disasters, nearly exactly as in those of other people". The quality is made to seem, like the Kikuyu "lack of prejudice", both very primitive and the last fruit of long historical experience. On the other hand, Kamante felt toward her some special form of that gratitude which the Kikuyu are supposed to know nothing about. He looked upon the trouble she had taken to get him cured "as upon a piece of hopeless eccentricity", but

[1] New York, p. 26; London, p. 28.

in gratitude took it upon himself to look after her in her foolish-ness.[1]

As a man, he retained the appearance of a dwarf and the uncanny ability to produce crocodile tears at will when she scolded him.

His flat wooden face, on these occasions, sank back into the world of darkness and infinite loneliness, in which he had dwelt for many years. Such heavy, dumb tears he might have wept as a little boy on the plain, with the sheep round him. They made me uneasy, and gave to the sins for which I scolded him a different aspect, a smaller look so that I did not want to go on talking about them. In a way it was a demoralizing thing. Still I believe that by strength of the true human understanding which existed between us, Kamante knew in his heart that I looked through his tears of contrition and did not take them for more than they were,—indeed that he himself looked upon them more as a ceremony due to the higher powers, than as any attempt to deceive.[2]

It is amazing how deep her understanding goes and yet how ironical it remains. The affectionate satire enables her to main-tain the admirable precision of her portrait, to show Kamante to full advantage without sentimentalizing him.

The story of Lulu works in an opposite way suggested by its opening sentence. "Lulu came to my house from the woods as Kamante had come to it from the plains." In Kamante, we see a rich humanity in the sort of grotesque excrescence that would stand out on a plain. In Lulu, we see an alien life in a beauty perfectly harmonious with the beauty of the forest. The episode opens with a description of the African Forest as "a mysterious region. You ride into the depths of an old tapestry... marvelously rich in green shades."[3] The allusion to art, and to a notably stylized two-dimensional art, gives us a view of the forest as design, a design in which the animals are marvelous embodiments of the strange plays of light. Lulu is a shining copper-red bush-buck antelope.

Tapestry also recalls the Middle Ages and prepares us for the fairy-tale quality of Lulu's story. The baby bushbuck was offered twice to Isak Dinesen by some Kikuyu children. Twice she refused the fawn because her head was full of business matters, but she woke up that night in terror thinking the fawn might

---

[1] New York, pp. 33-35; London, p. 38.
[2] New York, pp. 50-51; London, p. 55.
[3] New York, p. 64; London, p. 70.

meet a cruel end. She woke up all her houseboys and, like the queen in fairy tales who threatens beheading, threatened them with dismissal if they did not bring her the fawn by morning.

The fawn is delicately anthropomorphized as the found princess of the fairy tale. "She had such delicate legs that you feared they would not bear being folded up and unfolded again, as she lay down and rose up. . . . Her diminutive hoofs gave her all the air of a young Chinese lady of the old school, with laced feet." She was named Lulu, which is Swaheli for a pearl, and she is compared to expensive things. She swiftly established dominion over the house. Even the dogs acknowledged her precedence, and Kamante, who brought her up on a sucking bottle, became her servant. He received a hard butt when he did not do what she wanted. We see the relation between the two episodes in the observation that Kamante and Lulu together made "a new paradoxical illustration to the tale of the Beauty and the Beast".[1]

We do not arrive at the final metamorphosis of the fairy tale, however, for this is a true story and Lulu was not "really gentle, she had the so called devil in her". She was like a woman at the point where femaleness is a biological force that, frustrated, brings out witchlike characteristics. The "war-dance" she performed on the lawn at high points of her female discontent "looked like a brief zig-zagged prayer to Satan". Isak Dinesen's response was itself a kind of prayer to nature, a paean of praise that strikes a remarkable balance between anthropomorphization and realism.

"Oh Lulu," I thought, "I know that you are marvellously strong and that you can leap higher than your own height. You are furious with us now, you wish that we were all dead, and indeed we should be so if you could be bothered to kill us. But the trouble is not as you think now, that we have put up obstacles too high for you to jump, and how could we possibly do that, you great leaper? It is that we have put up no obstacles at all. The great strength is in you, Lulu, and the obstacles are within you as well, and the thing is, that the fullness of time has not yet come."[2]

Lulu did in the fullness of time run away, and it was Kamante, the link with the wilderness, who reported that she had married and came with her *bwana* most mornings before sunrise to eat the maize he left out for her. She came up to the house, but her

---

[1] New York, p. 68; London, p. 74.
[2] New York, pp. 71-72; London, p. 78.

husband did not dare to. Isak Dinesen's sight of her is rendered as an epiphany, a revelation of the life of things. The growing illumination of the sky, while the silver dew still lay on the grass and the gray mist on the hills, corresponds to the movement from one state of apprehension to another. As in so many epiphanies, the atmosphere of insight is externalized by rendering one sensation in terms of another—by rendering, as she does here and elsewhere in *Out of Africa*, air as water. "Standing like this in the limpid shadow, looking up toward the golden heights and the clear sky, you would get the feeling that you were in reality walking along the bottom of the Sea, with the currents running by you, and were gazing up towards the surface of the Ocean."

In this transformed atmosphere, she saw as in an apparition— "a turning round one of the boys' huts brought her upon us"—a transformed Lulu. "Lulu of the woods was a superior, independent being, a change of heart had come upon her, she was in possession." The metamorphosis had finally come off. "If I had happened to have known a young princess in exile, and while she was still a pretender to the throne, and had met her again in her full queenly estate after she had come into her rights, our meeting would have had the same character." Only this was not a metamorphosis. It was Lulu fulfilling her own nature; and since her nature was distinctly not human, she is seen in the epiphany not as a human princess but as one of those pagan deities who were originally intensifications of animal existences, of a nonhuman otherness. "For a minute she gazed at me; her purple smoky eyes were absolutely without expression and did not wink, and I remembered that the Gods or Goddesses never wink, and felt that I was face to face with the ox-eyed Hera."

Lulu came regularly, with her *bwana*, and eventually with her *toto*, a small male fawn at her heels. "The free union between my house and the antelope was a rare, honourable thing. Lulu came in from the wild world to show that we were on good terms with it, and she made my house one with the African landscape, so that nobody could tell where the one stopped and the other began." That view of her house is the essence of the pastoral vision, in which the line between nature and civilization is distinct but passable. The virtues of the one state correspond to the virtues of the other, and civilization draws constantly new influxes of grace from nature.

Lulu brought grace because she had the knowledge Isak Dinesen had a glimpse of when she saw the Giant Forest Hog.

Lulu knew the place of the Giant Forest-Hog's lair and had seen the Rhino copulate. In Africa there is a cuckoo which sings in the middle of the hot days in the midst of the forest, like the sonorous heartbeat of the world, I had never had the luck to see her, neither had anyone that I knew, for nobody could tell me how she looked. But Lulu had perhaps walked on a narrow green deerpath just under the branch on which the cuckoo was sitting.

Then, in a magnificent leap of imagination, Isak Dinesen shows that civilization has its counterpart to the heart of the forest in the inner sanctum from which god-kings emerged to convey grace to the world. Those symbols of animal, king and god by which nature and civilization have been contemplated side by side, are drawn together when she compares Lulu with her fawn to the Empress of China. "I was then reading," she continues,

a book about the old great Empress of China, and of how after the birth of her son, young Yahanola came on a visit to her old home; she set forth from the Forbidden City in her golden, green-hung palanquin. My house, I thought, was now like the house of the young Empress's father and mother.[1]

In the Kamante episode, we have even shepherds. The little Kikuyu boys, who took their fathers' herds of sheep and goats to graze on her lawn, made "a link between the life of my civilized house and the life of the wild. . . . The heads of the children and of the goats swam through the bush and long grass of the forest like heads of frogs in a pond."[2] One side of pastoral is perfectly expressed in that last sentence, which by its imagery connects children, animals and innocence with the origins of life in the water.

Perhaps the best expression of the other side is Isak Dinesen's reflection on Kamante's culinary genius. "This natural instinct in a Savage for our culinary art . . .," she says, "made me take another view of our civilization; after all it might be in some way divine and predestinated."[3] If the capacity for our most civilized accomplishments can be found in nature—as they are in Kamante's genius and Lulu's elegance—then those accomplishments acquire an absolute value and a civilization can be judged by the extent to which it is congruent with nature.

[1] New York, pp. 74-77; London, pp. 83-84.
[2] New York, pp. 46-47; London, p. 50.
[3] New York, p. 37; London, p. 40.

This is the controlling vision of *Out of Africa*, a vision according to which the old European order is praised and the new condemned. Its opposite political judgment distinguishes the vision from eighteenth-century Rousseauism. It is also distinguished by another implication, which is worked out in the stories. This is that civilization, the right kind of civilization, is our way of recovering the natural virtues lost in the fall; so that the way to fulfill the pastoral vision is through more and higher civilization —another bite of the apple, according to Kleist's idea. Art, the most stylized art, is our equivalent for nature.

The pastoral vision is further elaborated in Part II, where we see the society of the farm in successful operation. Called "A Shooting Accident on the Farm", this part is organized like a novel around a central act of violence which, because it leads to a legal process and transfers of property and has ramifications involving people of different social classes, gives the writer a chance to exhibit both the principles and actualities of the society as well as the forms that character and manners take in it.

Several children of her squatters were playing with a shotgun one night, when one boy fired the gun at the others. Three were slightly wounded, one had his lower jaw shot off, one died soon afterward, and the culprit disappeared. The accident led to a Kyama, an assembly of the old people of a farm, which is authorized by the Government to settle local differences among the squatters according to native laws. Her own position in these Kyamas was curious, for she was supposed to be the judge. "It is likely," she says, "that the Kikuyu of the farm saw my greatness as a judge in the fact that I knew nothing whatever of the laws according to which I judged."[1] This was a sign of "their mythological and theological mentality"[2]—a sign that sovereignty was for them a magical principle different from expertise, and justice a ritual not for solving the mysteries of life but for coping with them.

The Native will not give time or thought to the weighing up of guilt or desert; either he fears that this may lead him too far, or he reasons that such things are no concern of his. But he will devote himself, in endless speculations, to the method by which crime or disaster shall be weighed up in sheep and goats.[3]

Since Kaninu, the father of the boy who shot the gun, was a

[1] New York, p. 106; London, p. 115.   [2] New York, p. 104; London, p. 114.
[3] New York, p. 100; London, p. 109.

rich man—with thirty-five head of cattle, five wives and sixty goats—while Jogona, the father of the boy who was killed, was a poor man, with only one old wife and three goats, we get a good view of Kikuyu economic and social distinctions. The chief purpose of this Kyama, we are told, was to fleece the rich Kaninu. The shooting accident involves the Masai across the river, for Kaninu had daughters married to Masai and his son Kabero, who had shot the gun, took refuge, as it turns out, among the Masai. The case of the wounded boy takes us into the hospital for natives in Nairobi, and even brings forth an African witch, the boy's grandmother, who cast a spell on Kaninu's cattle so that they were going blind.

The night Isak Dinesen heard about this, she sat up late thinking of witchcraft as an ugly presence that "had come up from an old grave to flatten its nose upon my window-panes". Hearing a hyena wail, she remembered stories of old Kikuyu women who were supposed to run in the night as hyenas. "It seemed a reasonable thing, so many things are about, at night, in Africa." She even thought in Swaheli that "this old woman is mean", and "this accident and the things which have come from it, are getting into the blood of the farm, and it is my fault. I must call in fresh forces, or the farm will run into a bad dream, a nightmare."[1] There is something about her transformed vision of the African night and the transformation of her thoughts into an African tongue that recalls the Prioress's metamorphosis in "The Monkey". One recalls also the monkey's face at the window pane at the end of that story.

"A Shooting Accident" begins with a description of the African night—where after the heat of the day things come to life again—as like a dream, a good dream. "The thing which in the waking world comes nearest to a dream is night in a big town, where nobody knows one, or the African night. There too is infinite freedom: it is there that things are going on, destinies are made round you, there is activity to all sides, and it is none of your concern."[2] The return, at the end of the section, to the same sense of things going on in the African night shows that Isak Dinesen is as careful here as in the stories about symbolic texture. The shot that rang out in the night would seem to have turned

---

[1] New York, pp. 137-40; London, pp. 150-51.
[2] New York, p. 88; London, p. 96.

the good dream into a nightmare, but the society of the farm was at this point functioning successfully. It had its own white magic to counteract the black. It had the magic of kingship, which is why she sent for the Chief of the Kikuyu, Kinanjui.

The portrait of Kinanjui is a *tour de force* because Isak Dinesen manages to pull the very essence of kingliness out of incongruous modern circumstances which to the unsympathetic European eye would make Kinanjui absurd. In response to her appeal, Kinanjui arrives in a great big flashy automobile which he bought from the American Consul.

I found Kinanjui sitting up straight in the car, immovable as an idol. He had on a large cloak of blue monkey-skins, and on his head a skull-cap, of the kind which the Kikuyu make out of sheep's stomachs. . . . Kinanjui now did not open his mouth or wince while I paid him my compliments on the car, he stared straight in front of him in order that I should see his face in profile like a head struck upon a medal. As I walked round to the front of the car, he turned his head so as to keep his regal profile towards me, perhaps he really had in his mind the King's head on the Rupee. One of his young sons was driver to him, and the car was boiling hard. When the ceremony was over, I invited Kinanjui to come out of the car. He collected his big cloak round him in a majestic gesture and descended, and in that one movement he stepped back two thousand years, into Kikuyu justice.[1]

Kinanjui brings the case of the shooting accident to a conclusion by making the father of the wounded boy sign a document in which he accepts Kaninu's cow and calf as final settlement of all claims.

The social scene is widened in Part III, which deals with African and European visitors to the farm. The point about the European visitors is that they fitted into the African society already described, because they either were aristocrats, like her English friends (the then Prince of Wales came on one occasion), or else they had, like Knudsen and Emmanuelson, the aristocratic point of view. In *Shadows on the Grass*, Isak Dinesen says that the "white people to whom the past was still a reality—in whose minds the past of their country, their name and blood or their home was naturally alive—would get on easier with the Africans and would come closer to them than others, to whom the world was created yesterday, or upon the day when they got their new car".[2] Such Europeans could meet Africans at the African stage

[1] New York, pp. 144-45; London, pp. 155-56.
[2] New York, p. 91; London, p. 68.

of civilization; and it is clear in *Out of Africa* that they liked doing this, that they were themselves ill at ease in modern Europe and had taken refuge in Africa in order to find an equivalent for the European past.

The sense of being castaways, like the aristocrats in "Deluge", seems to have bound together Isak Dinesen and her two closest friends—the Englishmen Berkeley Cole and Denys Finch-Hatton. "It was a curious thing," she writes, "about Berkeley and Denys", who were wellborn and much loved in England and the Colony, "that they should be all the same, outcasts. It was not a society that had thrown them out, and not any place in the whole world either, but time had done it, they did not belong to their century." Berkeley was a Restoration wit. Denys, who was poetical and heroic, might have been an Elizabethan, but would have been at home in any period of our civilization before the industrial nineteenth century.[1]

It was a sign of the thing the three had in common that Africans felt an instinctive attachment toward them. They built around this fundamentally right thing a civilized environment that seemed somehow congruent with it—an environment compounded of wit, much talk, books, music, fine wine and fine food. All this went on at her house which was also theirs when they were at Ngong. They contributed the wine, books and records. Berkeley's own farm was on Mount Kenya, and Denys, who was a white hunter, had no home other than hers when he was not on safari. Their friendship was a joint imaginative venture. The excitement of their conversations is, one may suppose, behind the dances of wit in the stories.

Berkeley was small and nimble, and Isak Dinesen may have combined his wit and grace with the bulk and cynicism of another English friend, Hugh Martin, to create Prince Potenziani. Lincoln Forsner of "Dreamers" is modelled after Berkeley whose dream it was that they should "buy a dhow and go trading to Lamu, Mombasa and Zanzibar".[2] In the three idyllic parts of *Out of Africa*, Berkeley's death of a heart attack is the only event that points toward the reversal of Part V.

The idyllic section ends with the chapter called "Wings", on the greatest friendship of her life, the friendship with Denys

---

[1] New York, pp. 213-15; London, pp. 228-30.
[2] New York, p. 217; London, p. 232.

Finch-Hatton. Denys, who was a younger brother of the Earl of Winchilsea, had for Isak Dinesen everything. He was, she told me—and photographs confirm her—as handsome as a Greek statue; he wrote poetry and was a man of action; he had a moral perfection that corresponded to his aristocratic spirit. His life, she says in *Out of Africa*, led in an unbroken line from Eton to his grave in the Ngong Hills.[1]

It was to Denys that she told stories in the evenings. He would settle on cushions before the fire, while she sat cross-legged on the floor like Scheherezade herself. Denys taught her Latin and Greek and to read the Bible and bought her her gramophone. They hunted together, as on the memorable New Year's morning when he shot the lioness and she shot the lion that fed on the dead giraffe. Their feeling for each other is beautifully evoked by descriptions of the things they loved in common—in this case the lions they were shooting, whose close relation is a counterpart of theirs. Her happiness as she watched Denys and his boy skin the lions has the quality of an epiphany, its atmosphere inseparable from the cold, fresh early-morning air of the highlands. She writes again of that happiness in *Shadows on the Grass*: "I knew then, without reflecting, that I was up a great height, upon the roof of the world, a small figure in the tremendous retort of earth and air, yet one with it; I did not know that I was at the height and upon the roof of my own life."[2]

Denys had a small airplane from which they had wonderful views of the landscape and animals. The point of these descriptions is that nature seen from above, in its unapproachable fastnesses, is nature as it is in itself, as God sees it. Once when she was giving a tea party, Denys landed on the lawn and refused to get out of the plane. " 'The Buffalo are out feeding in the hills,' he said, 'come out and have a look at them.' " She said she had a tea party. " 'But we will go and see them and be back in a quarter of an hour.' " "This sounded to me," she says, "like the propositions which people make to you in a dream." They had a view which was like being "taken into the heart of the Ngong Hills by a secret unknown road", and returned to find the teapot still hot. "The Prophet had the same experience when he upset a jug of water, and the Archangel Gabriel took him, and flew

[1] New York, p. 360; London, p. 386.
[2] New York, p. 60; London, p. 47.

with him through the seven heavens, and when he returned, the water had not yet run out of the jug."[1] The heaven to which she mounted with Denys makes the appropriate climax to the idyllic section of *Out of Africa*. For it was from that height, and largely from that airplane, that her happiness came crashing down in ruins around her.

Part IV, "From an Immigrant's Notebook", presents a problem in that it is an apparently miscellaneous collection of fables, observations and meditations, that breaks the narrative line. Isak Dinesen told me that she did not keep this kind of notebook in Africa; nor has it, since her death, turned up among her papers. Since she told me that the section was composed in Denmark with the rest of the book, we can assume that it was composed and placed where it is for a purpose.

The section accomplishes several things. It reiterates all the themes of the book, thus giving us a sense of the rich experience behind the author's ideas—an experience from which she might have adduced many other instances. It also enables her to use episodes, like the story of her wartime safari to transport supplies to the British army, that did not fit into the four main centers of organization of the narrative proper. Standing between the idyl and the reversal, it prolongs the duration of the idyl; so that the proportions of the book make clear that the reversal came all at once at the end of her stay in Africa. At the same time, the difference between Part IV and the preceding Parts creates an intermission that makes the reversal all the more impressive; and in this, Part IV is like the "hopeful" fourth act of many five-act tragedies. The hopefulness of the fourth act, however, is usually an ironic deception. But the serenity of Part IV differs from that of the preceding Parts, because it anticipates the wisdom Isak Dinesen arrives at after the catastrophes of Part V.

The incident of the cock and the chameleon, through which she achieves reconciliation in Part V, might be a fable in the "Notebook". Indeed, the "Notebook" might come at the end to sum up the wisdom she acquired in Africa. The fact that it comes before the reversal is the most artful touch of all, for it prepares us to view the reversal serenely, and thus it maintains the serenely retrospective, the pastoral, quality of the whole

[1] New York, pp. 242-43; London, pp. 259-61.

book—in which, if paradise is remembered by one who has lost it, the fall, too, is remembered by one who has recovered from it.

There are several very slight things in Part IV, but all the pieces are interesting and a few are remarkable. The animal fables are unequalled in any modern writer I know of. They recommend themselves to modern taste because the animals do not dissolve away in the moral. The reality of the animals, their resistance to moralization in the ordinary sense, is the moral.

The first piece is about a young ox, bred by the Masai from cattle and wild buffalo, which could not be trained for the wagon or plough. " 'To break the heart of this ox' ", Isak Dinesen's manager had him thrown in the paddock with his legs tied up and a rein round his muzzle, "and even then, as he was lying dumb on the ground, long scalding jets of steam stood out from his nose and terrible snorts and sighs came from his throat." The manager went to bed and dreamt of seeing this black ox under the yoke. But he was awakened that night to find that a leopard had eaten a hind leg off the tied-up ox. The manager shot the ox. "We would never come to see him in the yoke now."[1] The moral is in the title: "The Wild Came to the Aid of the Wild". The wild animals are, through the fineness of their energy, emblems of the aristocratic spirit.

There is another, even more beautiful fable about the ordinary oxen from whom we have taken all the satisfactions of life. "In reward we have claimed their existence for ourselves. The oxen walk along within our own daily life, pulling hard all the time, creatures without a life, things made for our use. They have moist, limpid, violet eyes, soft muzzles, silky ears, they are patient and dull in all their ways; sometimes they look as if they were thinking about things."

The animal types have their counterparts in human types. In the story of Esa, her old cook before Kamante, she evokes a patient, enduring life of service like the oxen's. In the story of Esa's death, we see what happened when Esa for once showed some spirit and took a second wife—a young girl who finally poisoned him and ran away to live with the Native soldiers in Nairobi. It shows the artful arrangement of Part IV that the two stories about Esa are widely separated to suggest the passage of time between them.

[1] New York, p. 250; London, pp. 267-68.

In the magnificently told story of Kitosch, the African suffers as much injustice as the oxen. Kitosch's passive resistance, however, is like the ferocity of the wild ox. The difference is that the nature of the domesticated oxen is not being violated; while the nature of Kitosch and the wild ox is. Kitosch was ordered by his white employer to bring home a mare. He was told to lead the mare not ride her, but he was seen riding her. The employer had him flogged and tied up in his store, where late that night Kitosch died. These are the bare facts of the case, and the story is told from the point of view of the European jury who have to decide whether it was a case of murder. What emerges from the ironically slanted narrative is the inadequacy of the European point of view for understanding the African. The employer testified that he asked Kitosch forty or fifty times who had given him permission to ride the mare. It was because Kitosch finally answered the inane question with dignity, saying he was not a thief, that the employer had him flogged for insolence and then, feeling that he had still not mastered him, tied him up in the store. The little Native boy who spent the night with Kitosch testified that Kitosch said "he wanted to die. A little while after, he rocked himself from side to side, cried: 'I am dead!' and died."

Although the jury did not commit themselves on the so-called " 'wish-to-die theory' ", their verdict was "Guilty of grievous hurt" and the sentence was only two years. The Africans would only have asked that compensation be paid to Kitosch's people; they would not have asked about intention. Now, it was "the African, in his grave" who had by his intention to die "saved the European" from a conviction for murder. The African had a victory in the same sense as the wild ox.

It seems to you, as you read the case through, a strange, a humiliating fact that the Europeans should not, in Africa, have power to throw the African out of existence. The country is his Native land, and whatever you do to him, when he goes he goes by his own free will, and because he does not want to stay.

In the figure of Kitosch "is embodied the fugitiveness of the wild things who are, in the hour of need, conscious of a refuge somewhere in existence; who go when they like; of whom we can never get hold".[1]

[1] New York, pp. 280-83; London, pp. 298-304. Isak Dinesen's English publisher wanted to omit the story of Kitosch from their edition, as too critical of the British in Kenya; but she insisted on retaining it.

In the lovely meditation, " 'I Will Not Let Thee Go Except Thou Bless Me' ", Isak Dinesen draws from a variety of incidents the lesson of the title. The title is Jacob's answer to the man with whom he wrestled, when the man asked to be let go (Genesis 32: 26). After receiving the blessing and letting the man go, Jacob realized he had seen in the man the face of God. The lesson is that each thing that happens to us, good and bad, is a blessing. We must learn to see it that way, take from it everything it has to give in the way of experience, and then let it go; for it is only by letting it go that we turn it into a blessing, a contribution to the grand design of our life. The need to let go is the main lesson of Part V, and it was because Isak Dinesen was already the successful writer in Denmark, looking back on the terrible events of Part V, that she could see how letting go contributed to the design of her life.

Part V, "Farewell to the Farm", is short, swift, intense. Catastrophe piles up on catastrophe, and the phrase connecting them is "the same year". The year was 1930-31. The price of coffee fell, and in the same year the grasshoppers came. The description of their depredation adds to the picture of man in nature a cruelty that only deepens and complicates its beauty. By the end of 1930 she had sold the farm, but she stayed on through May 1931 to see the coffee crop picked and shipped. Since the truth underlying everything, that the farm was no longer hers, "made no difference to things from day to day", she lived during these months with a curiously rearranged sense of reality whereby she both knew and did not know that she was to leave.

In that same year Chief Kinanjui died, and she failed him on his deathbed; whereas before, their friendship had always gone right. He sent for her to ask a favor. A lorry was coming to take him into the Mission hospital and, dreading hospitals, he wanted her to take him into her house before the lorry came. At any other time she would have done this, but now everything was going badly for her, the house was no longer hers, Kinanjui would die and she would be blamed. "I had not got it in me any longer to stand up against the authorities of the world."[1] It is a sign of how far she was violating the noble old code of the natural community, of which she felt herself a member, that when at last

---

[1] New York, p. 338; London, p. 363.

she told Kinanjui she could not take him, she heard the cocks outside crow twice—a symbol to her of betrayal.

She saw in Kinanjui's funeral another betrayal. For the funeral was taken over by the Christians and the Europeans, who buried the big pagan—which itself went against the Kikuyu custom of exposing the dead to the birds and hyenas—in a coffin too small for him. The generally dismal circumstances of Kinanjui's death are artfully connected with her own loss of the farm to suggest the passing of an old order rooted in the African landscape.

Finally there was Denys's death in May of that year. Like a death in a tragedy, it was preceded by premonitions and adumbrations. Denys had been looking for a place to live after her house closed, and was persuaded to look at some bungalows in Nairobi. "He came back so repelled with what he had seen that he did not even like to talk about it. . . . He had been in contact with a kind of existence the idea of which was unbearable to him." He said he would be happy with a tent in the Masai Reserve and that she might be "well out of the sort of civilization that we were going to get in Africa".[1]

Denys was planning a flight to Mombasa and back by Voi, and the last days before the journey he was absent-minded and melancholy. She asked to go with him, and for the first time he refused to take her. Later she learned that Denys broke a propeller in Mombasa and that the Airway's boy who brought him the necessary spare parts from Nairobi refused to fly back to Nairobi with him, although he had flown with Denys before. Denys took his own boy Kamau with him, and they were both killed when the airplane crashed and burned up after taking off at Voi. Denys would not have taken Kamau with him if he had intended to kill himself. Yet you cannot help wondering whether there was not an unconscious suicidal intention behind his death.

A week after Denys's death, she woke one morning and asked for a sign, something which would explain, after all these catastrophes, the coherence of things. If in the right state of mind "you ask for a sign," she says, "the answer cannot fail you; it follows as the natural consequence of the demand". She came out of the house and the sign came up to meet her.

[1] New York, pp. 344-45; London, pp. 369-70.

Fathima's big white cock came strutting up before me. Suddenly he stopped, laid his head first on one side, and then on the other, and raised his comb. From the other side of the path, out of the grass, came a little gray Chameleon that was, like the cock himself, out on his morning reconnoitring. The cock walked straight upon it,—for the chickens eat these things,—and gave out a few clucks of satisfaction. The Chameleon stopped up dead at the sight of the cock. He was frightened, but he was at the same time very brave, he planted his feet in the ground, opened his mouth as wide as he possibly could, and, to scare his enemy, in a flash he shot out his club-shaped tongue at the cock. The cock stood for a second as if taken aback, then swiftly and determinately he struck down his beak like a hammer and plucked out the Chameleon's tongue.

She chased off the cock and killed the chameleon with a stone, for he could not get food without his tongue. She sat down and dared not look up for a long time, "such a dangerous place did the world seem".

Very slowly only, in the course of the next few days, it came upon me that I had had the most spiritual answer possible to my call. I had even been in a strange manner honoured and distinguished. The powers to which I had cried had stood on my dignity more than I had done myself, and what other answer could they then give? This was clearly not the hour for coddling, and they had chosen to connive at my invocation of it. Great powers had laughed to me, with an echo from the hills to follow the laughter, they had said among the trumpets, among the cocks and Chameleons, Ha ha![1]

She had asked Job's question and she got back the answer the Lord gives Job, when He extols His most powerful and ferocious animals. As paraphrased by the Cardinal of *Last Tales*, the Lord's reply is in effect that He never intended to create a comfortable world but a sublime one. Here she learned that the proper response to such a world is joy in its beauty, and terror—laughter among the trumpets. It is from that vantage that Isak Dinesen— having seen the unimaginable happen, having passed in Africa through that "death", which she defines as "a passage outside the range of imagination, but within the range of experience"[2]— has written her stories and reconstructed her shattered dream of Africa.

[1] New York, pp. 368-70; London, pp. 395-6. In Job, it is the warhorse who "saith among the trumpets, Ha, ha" (39: 25).
[2] New York, p. 386; London, p. 413.

The first three African reminiscences that appeared in
Shadows on the Grass (1961), twenty-four years after *Out of Africa*,
are undistinguishable in style and subject matter from the earlier
book. The last reminiscence, "Echoes from the Hills", the only
one that was expressly written for the volume, is different in
style. In writing to Isak Dinesen after I had read the proofs of
Shadows, I asked her why she had not included these episodes in
Out of Africa. She replied in a letter of November 1, 1960, that
she began writing these chapters about twenty years after her
return from Africa—that is, in the 1950's.

I have got many hundred such slight episodes and anecdotes from my
African life, which come back to me from time to time. I could go on
telling them for ages, and there would not have been room for them
in the book. It is not as easy to me to write them down now as it was
when I wrote "Out of Africa" because of the greater distance in
time, but I have tried to give them absolutely correctly.

"Farah", the first piece, was given as a radio talk on March
24, 1950, and appeared the same year as a booklet.[1] She is giving
us, she says, in describing her Somali major-domo, a "Portrait of
a Gentleman". The couple she and he made, that of Master and
Servant is, she says, perennial in literature because it is the model
of a Unity. When she explains that "a hook and an eye are a
Unity, a fastening; but with two hooks you can do nothing", she
is saying in her witty way that Master and Servant make a
society, as opposed to the modern democratic *mass* of identical
individuals. Farah was the perfect servant because he was among
his own people an aristocrat. Servant and aristocrat pay allegiance to the same code; one cannot exist without the other. It is the
point of her story, "The Invincible Slave-owners," in *Winter's Tales*.
Another way of speaking about Farah's aristocratic nature is
to say that he "was a wild animal", and that he cared not for the
thing but for the symbol. "My well-being was not his concern,
and was hardly of real importance to him, but for my good name
and prestige he did, I believe, hold himself responsible before
God." In a series of delicately comic episodes, we see how Farah
appointed himself the guardian of her prestige and how it was he
who maintained it in the end when she went bankrupt. Farah
then pulled from mysterious ancestral chests gorgeous robes she

[1] (Copenhagen: Wivels.)

had never seen before (the account here differs in certain details from the account of the same episode in *Out of Africa*[1])— robes in which, looking "like the Caliph Harun-al-Rashid's own body-guard", he "followed me, very erect, at a distance of five feet, where I walked, in my old slacks and patched shoes, up and down Nairobi streets".

Those who attended Isak Dinesen's American recitals will remember the second piece, "Barua a Soldani" (Swaheli for "Letter from a King"), in which she tells how she presented to the King of Denmark the skin of the lion she shot in company with Denys on the unforgettable New Year's morning described in *Out of Africa*. On the day she receives the king's letter of thanks, she comes upon a Kikuyu who has broken a leg. Having no morphine with which to relieve his pain, she finally lays the letter on his chest, telling him it is a *Barua a Soldani* and therefore efficacious. His pain subsides, and the letter becomes a famous talisman on the farm—sought after, according to a law the Africans tacitly legislate themselves, only for the gravest illnesses. Their restraint shows that the Africans draw upon but never violate the magic at the heart of life. The insight is tremendous because we have already had the heart of life evoked for us in superb renditions of the special rhythms and stillnesses of wild animals. Isak Dinesen sees in the king's letter "a covenant . . . between the Europeans and the Africans". In the old magical meaning of kingship they have found roots common to both continents.

"The Great Gesture", the best piece in the volume, is about Europe's violation of these roots. In this piece—which appeared in a shorter version in the Danish magazine *Alt for Damerne*, No. 51, 1957[2]—she describes her sometimes amusing, sometimes terrifying experiences doctoring the people on her farm. It is here that she speaks of the Africans' deadly fear of hospitals, as somehow violating their deep roots.

All this leads to the moving episode in which she accuses herself of violation. During the months when she was losing the farm, she took solace in treating with a new ointment the burns of a little Kikuyu boy. Distressed when Wawerru ceases to appear for treatment, she finally rides over on horseback, her dogs following her, to find out what has happened. Wawerru sees her and, "in the exact way of a mouse with its hole", slips into a hut;

[1] New York, p. 364; London, p. 390.   [2] "Den store Gestus", pp. 10-14.

she, dismounting, runs him to earth inside and sees that his bandages have been undone and that he is being treated with cow dung. Associating her failure in this matter with her failure on the farm and with all lost causes (the piece ends with Isak Dinesen's translation of a poem, by the contemporary Danish poet Otto Gelsted, on the dying Gaul as the symbol of lost causes), she clutches her riding-whip and breaks down weeping before the dimly seen Africans in the dark hut. The images of the hunt and of mastery make the breakdown impressive and suggest the violation in her good intentions.

The next morning she finds a crowd of Africans outside her house, asking to be cured of various ailments. She is "being made a fool of", but "with much generosity". They are reminding her gently that she is only human and that they are at least human. She begins to laugh, and they laugh, too.

One after another all faces round me lightened up and broke in laughter. In the faces of toothless old women a hundred delicate wrinkles screwed up cheeks and chin into a baroque, beaming mask— and they were no longer scars left by the warfare of life, but the traces of many laughters. The merriment ran along the terrace and spread to the edge of it like ripples on water. There are few things in life as sweet as this suddenly rising, clear tide of African laughter surrounding one.

That laughter, teaching her to accept failure, contains all that the book has been saying about the Africans. It is biological laughter, the laughter of endurance and survival, but it also is the ultimate in humane wisdom, the wisdom of old civilizations that have seen conquerors come and go. It is like the transcendent laughter of Yeats's consummately civilized carved Chinamen in "Lapis Lazuli": "Their eyes mid many wrinkles, their eyes,/ Their ancient, glittering eyes, are gay."

"Echoes from the Hills" takes its title from the sentence at the end of *Out of Africa* when Isak Dinesen, having learned her lesson from the cock and chameleon episode, says: "Great powers had laughed to me, with an echo from the hills to follow the laughter."[1] But here the phrase has another meaning; it points to the remoteness of the African experience, to just the sense of it that differentiates "Echoes from the Hills" from the rest of *Shadows*. It is as though Isak Dinesen were in this last reminiscence writing finis to her African story by putting a frame around

[1] New York, p. 370; London, p. 396.

it, by cutting it off from the present and the sphere of existence in which the piece itself is being written. Although Africa is treated in *Out of Africa* as a paradise lost, the experience of it is treated as continuous with the author's present experience and as the most potent force in it. But when in "Echoes from the Hills" she brings us up to date and tells us what has happened to her old servants, that Farah and Juma have died and Kamante has almost gone blind, it is like hearing what has happened to characters in a story after the story is over. The facts conveyed are somehow just facts, such as they might be in any memoir or article. They lack the extra reverberations that make literature of *Out of Africa* and the rest of *Shadows*.

Although inferior as literature, "Echoes from the Hills" contains much interesting information. We learn, for example, that Isak Dinesen did not abandon the hope of returning to Africa. After the success of *Seven Gothic Tales*, she entertained for a while a plan of running a children's hospital in the Masai Reserve and she made a special trip to London to ask advice of Dr Albert Schweitzer. She had to give up the plan for lack of funds, and it must have been shortly afterward that she wrote the letter, dated February 15, 1935, in which she asks her American publisher, Robert Haas, to help her find a job as a war correspondent in the then imminent war between Italy and Ethiopia. It was clearly another plan for getting back to Africa. She speaks further in "Echoes from the Hills" of writing in 1936 to Farah's younger brother, Abdullahi, that if the book she was then working on, *Out of Africa*, was a success, she might have the money to return to Africa. And she speaks of a plan in 1939, which was interfered with by the outbreak of war, to join Farah and his mother on a pilgrimage to Mecca.

The new thing in "Echoes from the Hills" is a realization not found in *Out of Africa* and not prominent in the rest of *Shadows*. I mean the realization that the continent of which she could write in *Out of Africa* that "the white men fill in the mind of the Natives the place that is, in the mind of the white men, filled by the idea of God"[1]—that this continent no longer exists. She says here that she realized as she listened to the then Governor of Kenya, Sir Philip Mitchell, describing on a visit to her in the early 1950's present-day conditions in Kenya, she realized that

[1] New York, p. 374; London, p. 401.

her book on Africa was "as much out of date as a papyrus from a pyramid". It is a shock for her (and the reader) to learn from a Danish journalist who saw Kamante that Kamante reported having spent a year in prison for taking the Mau Mau oath. Yet Kamante added, as he showed the journalist a letter from her, " 'Look, Msabu writes to me: "My good and faithful servant Kamante.". . . And so I am.' " Juma's son calls her, in a letter that appears in the memorial anthology "our beloved mother". And Kamante himself writes in the memorial anthology: "And the old life we stayed with her, like black & white keys of a piano how they are played and produce melodious voices."

Isak Dinesen had confirmed for her in the reports about postwar Africa what she had always understood—that a revolutionary social change is also a change in the nature of reality. Although her Africa never was the same as the journalists', it is clear from the reports brought back by other Europeans of her still legendary status in Kenya that the myth, through which she and her African servants fulfilled certain deep desires, had an objective existence. The reports in "Echoes" about her servants, all seem to be of isolated individuals exiled from a perfect society they once knew. The myth was objective because it represented a stage of civilization at which she met the Africans.

She wrote me of how she said in jest to Sir Philip Mitchell, when he visited her, that if the Government had made it possible for her to stay in Kenya, she would have saved them a million pounds. Sir Philip only half in jest agreed.[1] He was recognizing the political wisdom of the idea, stated in *Out of Africa*, that we should have brought the Africans up through all the stages of our civilization before introducing them to twentieth-century technology. Allowing

them, to catch up with us, three years to our hundred, it will now be time to send them out Saint Francis of Assisi, and in a few years Rabelais. They would love and appreciate both better than we do, of our century. They liked Aristophanes when some years ago I tried to translate to them the dialogue between the farmer and his son, out of "The Clouds". In twenty years they might be ready for the Encyclopaedists. . . . We should let them have dreamers, philosophers and poets out, to prepare the ground for Mr Ford.

She then, in a lovely irony that describes precisely what is

[1] Letter of November 1, 1960.

happening now as between the white and colored races, puts her theory of progress inside a cyclical theory of history.

Where shall they find us then? Shall we in the meantime have caught them by the tail and be hanging on to it, in our pursuit of some shade, some darkness, practising upon a tomtom? Will they be able to have our motor cars at cost price then, as they can now have the doctrine of the Transubstantiation?[1]

Will we not by that time be ourselves looking for the Dionysian virtues the Africans will have abandoned? And will we not be ready to hand over to them a material civilization in which we will have lost interest—just as we have for so long a time been all too ready to export a Christianity we ourselves had ceased to believe in.

[1] New York, p. 294; London, p. 316.

Chapter 5

CURRENTS OF DESIRE: *WINTER'S TALES*

FOLLOWING *Seven Gothic Tales* by only three years, when the success of the first book was still fresh in people's minds, *Out of Africa* solidified Isak Dinesen's reputation in the United States and Britain. It was, however, in Denmark that *Out of Africa* made the most difference; for it reassured the Danes, who had not liked the decadent, fantastic, cynical and perverse quality of *Seven Gothic Tales*, that Isak Dinesen had after all a regard for and a knowledge of reality and humanity. The Danish reviewers liked the realism of *Out of Africa* and its humanitarian sensibility, the love she shows in it for animals and simple people.

Winter's Tales, which came out five years later in 1942, may have been aimed at reconciling the Danes to her fiction, not only by giving them a great deal more of Denmark than in the earlier stories, but also by giving them the "naturalness" they had liked in *Out of Africa*. In reviewing *Winter's Tales* for *Politiken* of October 10, 1942, the Danish critic Tom Kristensen traces the development of Isak Dinesen's reputation in Denmark up to that date.

Her *Seven Gothic Tales* never became popular in Denmark because of their too aristocratic tone, verging on snobbery, and their peculiar complicated eroticism—even though they showed a sovereign imagination and a generous understanding. But after *Seven Gothic Tales* became world famous, the Danes grew more interested in it and began to understand her human loving nature behind the arabesques. To continue the form with which she had such success in *Seven Gothic Tales*, and yet show her humanity, she wrote *Winter's Tales*. If any readers are looking here for perversity, they will be disappointed. . . . Readers will be pleased to see that she has returned to Denmark with this book and also that she is still Gothic, for without that she would not be Isak Dinesen.

Since Denmark was under German occupation at the time *Winter's Tales* was completed, Isak Dinesen had to take the manuscript to Stockholm where the British Embassy—to whom she was able to give as references the names of Churchill, Eden and Duff Cooper—sent it for her to the United States.

She did not know what had happened to the book until the war ended, when suddenly appreciative letters arrived from American servicemen all over the world who had read it in the pocketsize Armed Forces Edition. Although *Winter's Tales* was considered in America and Britain to be not quite up to *Seven Gothic Tales*, it was a success. Because *Winter's Tales* showed that Isak Dinesen could sustain a remarkably high level of performance through three books, and because by that time a new generation of readers had discovered the first volume of tales which they read as a modern classic, it became clear after 1942, in the English-speaking and Scandinavian countries, that Isak Dinesen's books were not mere sensations of a season—that they were here to stay for a while, though one could not yet say for how long.

As with *Seven Gothic Tales*, the American publisher changed Isak Dinesen's arrangement of *Winter's Tales*. Her arrangement is to be found in the British and Danish editions, which give us first "The Sailor-boy's Tale" and then "The Young Man with the Carnation". In the American edition, instead, "Young Man" comes first, and it is easy to see why. Since the hero of "Young Man", the writer Charlie Despard, turns up again in the last story, "A Consolatory Tale", and since both stories deal with the problems of the writer, the two make a nice frame for the volume. When I pointed out the rationality of this arrangement to Isak Dinesen, she grew angry and said that for some instinctive reason which she could not explain she had wanted "Sailor-boy" first. Since the arrangement of her stories clearly matters, we had best follow her order.

We see on reflection that her instinct was sound. For "Sailor-boy" is a nature fable, and in placing it first she announces nature, and particularly Northern nature, as the main theme of the volume. In this way she distinguishes *Winter's Tales* from the two preceding books (which were about civilization and Southern nature, respectively), she explains its title, and connects the three books as complementary parts of a large design. "Sailor-boy" and "Young Man" both announce, however, from their different aspects, that of nature and of art, the same theme—that of rebirth. And it is this theme that connects the volume with Shakespeare's *Winter's Tale* from which it derives its title.

"The Sailor-boy's Tale" takes off from the allusion in

"Dreamers" to the falcon that tries to save itself in a storm by clinging to the mast of a ship. Here, the falcon gets "her feet entangled in some loose tackle-yarn", and her life-and-death struggle is to free herself. The little sailor-boy Simon climbs up and cuts the falcon loose. The height scares him but gives him also "a proud, steadying sensation" of unity, "as if the sea and the sky, the ship, the bird and himself were all one". The falcon hacks him in the thumb, making the blood run. This is much the best part of the story. In the rest, Simon's life is saved—after an experience of love and death that almost leads to his own death— by an old Lapp witch who turns out to have been the falcon. After mingling her blood with his and keeping him in her house all night, she pushes him out in the morning as though she were pushing him out of her womb in a second birth, a birth into manhood, the ritual of which may have been suggested by the Kikuyu initiation rites.[1] Simon is led back to the experience of unity that he had on the mast.

Standing in second place, "The Young Man with the Carnation" introduces art as a subsidiary and contrapuntal theme that makes connection with the last story of the volume. The last story also connects with the first, however, in that it deals with metamorphosis. "A Consolatory Tale", in fact, ties together the whole volume as we shall see. The young English writer, Charlie Despard, is in "Young Man" the author of a highly successful first book, who is worried that the second book, on which he is working, will not be up to the first. Critics have been tempted to see in Charlie's situation a reflection of Isak Dinesen's when she was making the change to the style of *Winter's Tales*; Hans Brix even sees in Charlie's name the initials of Christentze (her middle name) Dinesen.[2]

Certainly, Charlie's ideas about art can be connected with hers. But Charlie is the opposite kind of writer from her, the kind she was accused of not being. He had been a poor boy whose first book (a novel, one assumes, but she ought to have made this clear) treated the hard lot of poor children. His is the crisis of a writer who is moving away from a style in which he has been

[1] See Jomo Kenyatta's anthropological study of the Kikuyu, *Facing Mount Kenya* (London: Secker and Warburg, 1953), Chap. vi. Kenyatta's admiration for Isak Dinesenis is described by Peter P. Rohde in the Danish edition of the memorial anthology.

[2] *Karen Blixens Eventyr*, p. 159.

successful. He would seem to be developing in the direction of her first book; while she was apparently moving in the direction of his first book in *Winter's Tales*, in which there are four stories about poor children. Since there are also in *Winter's Tales* four stories about the aristocratic principle, it is clear that Isak Dinesen has extended her social range in this volume but has not changed her point of view.

Charlie has reached the dead end of one phase of his life and art, and must be reborn into the next phase. As so often in Isak Dinesen, life sends Charlie an answer by arranging itself like a story. Here life re-enacts, as it did in "Roads", the old tale of the substitute bride.

Charlie is to meet his wife in a hotel near the harbor in Antwerp. Arriving late, he slips into bed beside his sleeping wife, noticing with pleasure that the wallpaper is sky-blue. Someone knocks, Charlie opens the door and sees before him a tall, fair young man in evening clothes, with a pink carnation in his buttonhole, and on his face "such gentle, humble, wild, laughing rapture that Charlie had never seen the like of it". The light of the young man's "strange beatitude" remains on his face, "mingled with bewilderment", even as he murmurs apologies and departs.

Back in bed, Charlie is "seized by a tremendous agitation . . . as if a gigantic, blazing light had gone up on him, passed, and left him blinded". He feels an overwhelming pain, for he sees in the young man the image of what he might have been. "That infinite happiness which beamed on the face of the young man with the carnation was to be found somewhere in the world. . . . O God, God in Heaven, at what moment had his own road taken off from the road of the young man with the carnation?" At the moment, he decides, when he became a successful literary person, a piece of printed matter.

Deciding he must run away to sea, he walks down to the harbor, where he begins to feel reborn. At the sight of the ships, he begins to formulate his new artistic position. It is a symbolist position. "The ships were superficial, and kept to the surface. Therein lay their power. . . . They were even hollow . . . the great depths slaved for them as long as they remained hollow." The artist should not moralize life but deal with its appearances, for then the appearances operate as symbols that are profounder than any ideas about life. Life yields its depth if you treat it as though it had none.

Charlie falls in with some sailors, and engages to sail with them. Dawn breaks as he starts back to the hotel to tell his wife of his decision. He sees her in the dining-room, and when she takes him up to her room, he realizes that that is not where he went to bed. " 'Almighty God,' " he says in his heart, " 'as the heavens are higher than the earth, so are thy short stories higher than our short stories.' " As he relishes the artistic possibilities of last night's mistake, vicariously feeling the young man's longing and triumph and the lady's terror, his face takes on "an expression of rapture, laughter and delight" that corresponds to the expression of the young man with the carnation. Charlie and the young man are mirror images of each other, each lives in the gaze of the other—the young man through Charlie's appreciation of his rapturous life, Charlie through appreciating it.

There follows a rather awkward colloquy with God in which it is established that Charlie must write for God and not the critics, and that his rapture can never come from life itself but only from rendering the rapture of others. Even Charlie's wife is fitted into this new reconciliation. She is to be the lighthouse who, by keeping him from approaching and therefore from achieving satisfaction in love, keeps him on his course as a writer. Charlie is to be, as God points out, the man who, when he has beside him the lady of the sky-blue room, jumps out of bed to seek his happiness at the end of the world. Looking out the window, Charlie sees "a young woman in a blue shawl and slippers" walking away from the hotel. Associating her with the young man's mistress, he says in the final line, " 'Ah, the poor young man with the carnation' ", thinking perhaps of the young man's frustration that, like his own, helped make a good story.

"Young Man" is marred by more prolonged introspection than Isak Dinesen usually allows her characters, and also by the shadowy quality of the characters. The young man with the carnation is the most vivid character in the story. This may be intentional; for behind this story and "Consolatory Tale" lies, I think, Hans Christian Andersen's story, "The Shadow", about a learned man who sends his shadow into an open window from which wonderful music emerges. When after several weeks the shadow returns, it has become a substantial person. The shadow grows more and more substantial while the man wastes away, until they finally exchange places—the man playing the part of the shadow. Isak Dinesen obviously read the story as a parable of the artist who gives up his vitality to his creations until they become more real than he. The attempt to render such a disparity in vividness makes the artist dull in this story as he is not in "Consolatory Tale".

The best thing in "Young Man" is the "blue story" that Charlie tells the sailors. One of the three great inset stories of *Winter's Tales*, it is unique in Isak Dinesen in that it is symbolist in the distinctively modern manner. It does not take off from established symbols but sets up an aura of undefinable meanings by intensifying a real object, in this case a color. The tale may have been suggested by Mallarmé's poem, "L'Azur"; it follows Mallarmé's method. Isak Dinesen may at this point have come under the influence of French symbolism; for she makes much of Baudelaire later in the volume, and the young man with the carnation might himself have stepped out of a French painting of the period, an impressionist painting.

The "blue story" is about an English lord, who cared for nothing but collecting ancient blue china and took his daughter, Lady Helena, with him on his travels. Once in the China Sea their ship caught fire, and Lady Helena was rescued by a young English sailor with whom she spent nine days alone in a lifeboat before they were picked up. The old lord paid the sailor to sail only in the Southern Hemisphere, and Lady Helena, when she heard about this, found that she cared for nothing except to collect rare blue china. She sailed from country to country looking for a particular blue color, but none of the jars and bowls she bought was the right blue. " ' "There must be some of it left," ' " she said, " ' "from the time when all the world was blue" ' "—the time she was alone with the sailor. She had to go on sailing, she said, for

" 'there, on the other hemisphere, a ship sails, with which I have got to keep pace. We two are like the reflection of one another, in the deep sea, and the ship of which I speak is always exactly beneath my own ship, upon the opposite side of the globe. . . . I shall tell you a secret,' she said. 'In the end my ship will go down, to the centre of the globe, and at the very same hour the other ship will sink as well—for people call it sinking, although I can assure you that there is no up and down in the sea—and there, in the midst of the world, we two shall meet.' "[1]

Years passed, the old lord died, she grew old, and finally a merchant brought her a very old blue jar. " 'The moment she set eyes on it she gave a terrible shriek. "There it is!' she cried. "I have found it at last. This is the true blue. Oh, how light it makes one." ' " Now she could die, and she gave orders that her heart was to be cut out and laid in the jar. " ' " For then everything will be as it was then. All shall be blue around me. . . . Is it not a sweet thing to think that, if only you have patience, all that has ever been will come back to you?" ' " She died soon afterwards.

The "blue story" ties together all the themes of "Young Man" —the themes of the sea, love, art, and the quest for the ideal. It connects with the blue room in the hotel; the tavern where Charlie drinks with the sailors is called The Southern Cross; one of the sailors tells a story about the Southern Hemisphere, which represents in *Winter's Tales* what Africa represented in Isak Dinesen's life. The "blue story" also brings to the fore a theme latent in "Sailor-boy" and "Young Man", but important later— that of the dream or imagination as the force that resolves the story's antinomies. The imagined blue brings together the sea and blue china, nature and art, and wipes out the distinction between moral up and down, heaven and the sea. Dream or imagination is the theme in *Winter's Tales* that resolves the anti-thesis between the themes of nature and art (or civilization) announced in the first two stories.

The next three stories in Isak Dinesen's arrangement, "The Pearls", "The Invincible Slave-owners" and "The Heroine",[2] provide a refreshing change of pace. They are smart, worldly anecdotes that make wittily turned points about the aristocratic code. They are like "Old Chevalier", only crisp, without the soft blur of nostalgia. "Pearls" starts with a great stir in Copenhagen over the engagement of a rich bourgeois girl to a young aristo-

---

[1] The imagery here was probably suggested by the idea of the Somali (described in *Out of Africa*, New York, pp. 268-69; London, p. 288) that everything on earth has its replica at the bottom of the sea.

[2] The Danish titles of the first and third are: "En Historie om en Perle" ("The Story of a Pearl") and "Heloïse".

cratic officer in the guards. The time is just before the Prusso-
Danish War of 1864, and it is implied that this is one of the last
engagements of this sort that will cause a stir.

A clever old aunt warns the girl that aristocrats are not like
us, but Jensine is furious and pays no attention. The couple are
married and go for their honeymoon to the mountains of
Norway. There Jensine, who had been brought up in the honest
tradesman's world of prudence and foresight, is appalled by her
husband's lack of fear, and by his jokes about his debts and his
gambling. " 'He is really a thief, or if not that, a receiver of stolen
goods, and no better than a thief.' " She resolves to conquer his
aristocratic carelessness[1] by teaching him fear, at least on her
behalf. She puts herself in the most precipitous places, but he
only applauds her daring.

About one thing Alexander does show concern—about a pearl
necklace which he inherited from his grandmother and gave to
Jensine along with stories of this grandmother. Whenever he sees
Jensine twist the string, he warns her that she may break it, and
finally she does. She takes the pearls for restringing to the crippled
old village shoemaker, to whom she counts them out carefully.
She feels kinship with this hardworking old man as against the
carefree aristocrats. But she is wrong, as we begin to see when
she meets young Herr Ibsen, who tells her that he is collecting
children's tales—" 'pearls' ", he calls them, " 'a big store of our
old national treasures' "—from this shoemaker, who might himself have been a fine poet. The proletarian and artist, who is
steeped in folklore, will show himself closer to the aristocrat than
to the bourgeois.

The necklace is delivered as they are leaving Norway. Jensine
is about to count the pearls, but thinks better of it and puts the
necklace on. She feels she has triumphed over her husband when
he asks her if she ought not to count the pearls and she says no.
But she is sure at least one pearl is missing and that this is the
price she has paid for her triumph. Back in Copenhagen, there is
talk of war with Prussia, and the difference between herself and
her husband comes to a crisis in their different attitudes toward
the threat of war. She could not talk about it seriously with him;
"he was as convinced of Denmark's invincibility as of his own

---

[1] Isak Dinesen seems to have in mind *sprezzatura*, the word Castiglione uses in the
Renaissance *Book of the Courtier* to sum up the aristocratic attitude.

immortality". It is in the midst of this crisis with her husband that she decides to count the pearls, perhaps to see on which side the shoemaker stands. She finds an extra pearl, and learns that it is worth as much as all the rest put together. She writes to the shoemaker, and has from him a letter that is just right, that in its simplicity, dignity and charm justifies our high expectations of him. The test of an author is whether he can pull off the letter or conversation of which much is expected.

The shoemaker explains that he had accidentally left this pearl off a necklace he had restrung for an English lady; and since Jensine had counted up her pearls so carefully, he thought it would be nice to surprise her. " 'Old people, as well as young, must have a little fun at times.' " Jensine's grave image in the mirror seems to be saying to her: " 'You are really a thief, or if not that, a receiver of stolen goods.' " She realizes she will " 'never conquer these people' "—her husband, the shoemaker, the English lady who did not miss her pearl—" 'who know neither care nor fear' ". She acquires their perspective; the war seems small; all that will matter in a hundred years is continuity —the pearls. She sees a young man giving the pearls to his wife along with this very story about Jensine, just as Jensine heard from Alexander about his grandmother. The carefree people, we are to understand, are those who live by symbols. It is as a symbol of continuity that the pearls mattered to Alexander. And it was in the spirit of artistic play that the shoemaker added the pearl and so created the story that would be handed down with the necklace. The pearl he really added is the story itself.

As in "Sorrow-acre", Isak Dinesen wrote "Pearls" to answer another work—in this case Sigrid Undset's novel, *Kristin Lavrans-datter*, which takes the side of the hard-working worried wife against the insouciant aristocratic husband. As in "Sorrow-acre", she ends here with the ironic recognition that the aristocratic point of view she is defending has in any case been defeated. Alexander's conviction of Denmark's invincibility will soon be contradicted by the facts. And Jensine's bourgeois old aunt is seen in the end approaching the house with a bouquet of flowers from the villa of Jensine's bourgeois father.

The story is not quite perfect. The appearance of Ibsen among fictitious persons is disturbing, and the story is a bit heavy because too much of it goes on in Jensine's mind. Isak Dinesen is never at her best with prolonged introspection. The next two stories are perfect. They are lightly executed, yet more profound in implication than the first; the three are arranged in an order of increasing profundity.

"The Invincible Slave-owners" evokes the atmosphere of the fashionable German spa, Baden-Baden, in 1875. At the outset, an old Russian General and an old English lady vie with each other in telling stories about the devotion of an old waiter in the hotel who, according to each, would die for him. The stories are told to a sensitive and sensible young Dane, Axel Leth, who as an aristocrat himself understands that the myth of aristocracy is supported by the corollary myth of devoted servants, but who also understands that the time for such myths has passed that they now seem extravagant, if not a little mad. Axel's sympathetic, but detached and amused understanding provides the point of view necessary to make "Slave-owners" a comedy of manners.

The sensation of the hotel is a young girl who seems to epitomize the ideal of distinction the other guests are aiming at. This girl is distinguished because she is beautiful, bears a fine old name, and is dressed in a manner suitable to a girl some years younger than herself, without makeup or jewels. Her oddity of dress calls attention to the charms she is not being allowed to display, and the rich jewels at home she is not being allowed to wear. But the main source of Mizzi's distinction is an exemplary governess who, because she is always by her side, makes Mizzi seem a princess. Miss Rabe turns Mizzi into a symbol.

The young men fall in love with Mizzi, among them Axel Leth who, because he is a "dreamer", reads her symbolism more deeply than the others. He sees in her an ideal of original innocence which in our fallen world has got translated into the symbolism of social position. He quotes in connection with her Baudelaire's lines: "*D'un air placide et triomphant, | Tu passes ton chemin, majestueuse enfant.*" The lines are a kind of refrain in "Le Beau Navire" ("The Beautiful Ship"), which makes the comparison we have seen before in Isak Dinesen between the beauty of a sailboat and a woman.

Axel would like to propose to Mizzi, but he fears he could not detach her from Miss Rabe or give her the "slaves" she requires. Driving out one golden afternoon to a romantic little belvedere, Axel overhears Mizzi and Miss Rabe in the pine forest below him; and learns that Mizzi and Miss Rabe are really sisters, that they are destitute though noble, and that Mizzi is in love with Axel but dares not tell him that she is a girl who goes to market and feeds the chickens. Mizzi dresses as she does because she cannot afford to buy new clothes, and Axel gathers that the sisters take turns at playing mistress and servant in the various resorts. Axel is glad that it is he and not one of the other young men who overheard this conversation, for they might have put the sisters down as a pair of adventurers out to snare a rich husband. But Axel—who has overheard and peeped down on the sisters from above, as God might—realizes that they are like birds of passage obeying ancestral instincts in migrating to the proper watering place at the proper season and in displaying, in the place of clothes and jewels, that more impressive sign of aristocracy—the services of a distinguished slave.

Were this a love story, Axel would now propose to Mizzi. But this is an anecdote in which everything serves the point about "slave-owners". The rather mechanical reversal is followed therefore by an unexpected dénouement. Learning that Mizzi is to depart in a few days, Axel leaves town and has himself liveried and made up as an old servant wearing the colors of Mizzi's family. On the morning of Mizzi's departure, he announces himself at the hotel as Frantz, a servant of Mizzi's, come to accompany the two ladies home. The scene in which Mizzi comes downstairs to meet this unknown servant is high comedy. She must of course fall in with his pretense, and he makes her exit from the hotel a fitting climax to the sensation she has already created.

On the train, Axel sits in the third-class carriage. But when, during a stop, Mizzi takes a walk in the drizzling rain, Axel holds an umbrella over her. Now that they are close together, Mizzi lets her eyes tell him what she thinks of him. She might have struck him, even killed him, she is so furious. But she is held back by the sight of her family colors in his hat. As they walk together under the umbrella, his livery determines the relation between them; so that the figure of Axel Leth disappears and Frantz, the servant, takes his place. Axel realizes

that the slave-owner's dependency upon the slave is strong as death and cruel as the grave. The slave holds his master's life in his hand, as he holds his umbrella. Axel Leth, with whom she was in love, might

165

betray Mizzi; it would anger her, it might sadden her, but she was still, in her anger and melancholy, the same person. But her existence itself rested upon the loyalty of Frantz, her servant. . . . If she were not, at any moment, sure that Frantz would die for her, she could not live.

And if there were now to be a railway accident, Axel reflects, she would think of Frantz's safety first of all.

We see again the potency of symbols in the way pretense becomes reality. Axel has, as her servant, brought the great lady in Mizzi into full flower; just as, had he been her lover, he would have brought her womanhood to flower. Mizzi gives him—when he tactfully takes leave of the ladies in Stuttgart—an envelope containing a rose. It is the sort of token she might have given him as her lover. What she first took as a malicious trick, turns out to be a charming, creative jest (like the shoemaker's when he sent Jensine the extra pearl).

The point of the story is that the relation between master and servant is not merely external and economic but, like the sexual relation, one of those perennial unions of opposites by which each of us achieves an identity. Aristocrat and servant are two sides of the same coin—which is why the two sisters, who alternate roles as master and servant, are inseparable.

There is a psychological implication here, too, a suggestion of sexual inadequacy—of which we are given only a glimpse so as not to spoil the comedy. The scene in which Axel overhears the sisters suggests a setting in pastoral, and the dolorous sisters, locked in each other's arms, are like two complaining nymphs. Axel sees them as maidenly Laocoöns bound together in the deadly coils of a serpent. "Mizzi might twist round her indignant and affrighted young face to him for a moment, but her embrace, her bosom was for Lotti." The serpent that binds them is allegiance to a combined ideal of innocence and aristocracy that makes them want time to stand still, both historically and in their own lives.

That is what Axel means when he sends Mizzi, before leaving Baden-Baden to dress up as Frantz, Goethe's lines: "One does not desire the stars, / One enjoys their splendor." The emphasis is different but these sisters are like the sisters in "Supper at Elsinore", and it is no accident that "Slave-owners" faintly echoes "Supper" by relating through Baudelaire's lines sailboats, old-fashioned women and the aristocratic ideal. There is even the faintest suggestion that these sisters, too, symbolize twin aspects of a narcissistic personality.

The story's tragic implications are allayed in a consoling image of beauty at the end. Axel wonders sadly what will become of these sisters who have been "so honest as to give life the lie, the partisans of an ideal, ever in flight from a blunt reality, the great, gentle ladies, who were incapable of living without slaves". Then, in a waterfall, he sees the water rushing each second over the precipice and disappearing in order that the whole waterfall may be always the same; and he understands that the sisters are constantly in flight in order to achieve stillness, in order to turn their lives into an unchanging symbol. He understands further that this "static flight" is the principle of beauty that turns the waterfall into a "marble cataract" and that connects the sailboat and the woman of Baudelaire's poem.

"The Heroine" goes even farther in symbolizing the combined ideal of woman and aristocracy. It is anecdotal in the manner of Maupassant in that it leads up to a trick ending. It takes off from Maupassant's story of the Franco-Prussian War, "Boule-de-Suif" ("Ball-of-Fat"). In taking off from "Boule-de-Suif"— which is about a good-hearted prostitute who, by giving herself to a Prussian officer, saves some hard-hearted upper-class people who then despise her for her action—Isak Dinesen is once again answering a too simple liberal view.

A young Englishman, Frederick Lamond, who has been studying theology in Berlin, tries to get to France when the Franco-Prussian War breaks out, but can get no farther than a small town just inside the German border. He is stranded in the town's modest hotel along with some Frenchmen—simple people, among them an old priest and two old nuns. One day a beautiful French lady arrives, and takes charge of the anxious refugees. She restores them physically and spiritually, to the point where they eat a hearty dinner together and sing hymns. But the next day German troops enter the town, and the refugees of the hotel are arrested.

Like Mizzi, Heloïse appears as a symbol before she becomes a person. Before he meets her, Frederick sees on her trunks her family name, which seems to him to ring of heroic French history. As with Axel and Mizzi, it is in Frederick's eyes that

Heloïse takes on symbolic significance; only Frederick has not
Axel's amused condescension, for Heloïse is a far grander figure
than Mizzi and Frederick has no reservations about the thing
she symbolizes.

Frederick feels prepared for his meeting with Heloïse by his
acquaintance with great paintings. She reminds him of the
goddesses of Titian and Veronese. The preparation goes even
farther, however, for Frederick is writing a theological work on
the doctrine of the atonement—of Christ's atonement, that is,
for our sins. Frederick first became interested in art when he saw
in the great religious paintings the very ideas he was concerned
with, and he moved from the sacred to the profane work of the
great masters without apparently feeling any break in continuity.
Now he absorbs Heloïse into that continuous symbolic system.

The refugees, Frederick among them, are accused of espionage,
and Heloïse's defiance goads the youngest of the German officers
into making her an indecent proposition. He will write them all
out a passport for Luxembourg if Heloïse will come to fetch it
" 'dressed like the goddess Venus' ". Frederick hears the "distor-
tion of his own beautiful fancies about Heloïse". The officer, too,
is looking for the archetypal Heloïse.

The insult changes Heloïse "as if it had set fire to her. . . . She
seemed about to laugh in her adversary's face." Her hand goes
up to the collar of her mantilla. Then she becomes pale. "She
turned to her fellow-prisoners, and slowly let her gaze run over
their white, horrified faces." Finally, she announces that they
must decide whether they will purchase their salvation at the
officer's price. Her gestures here are important; for we interpret
them through Frederick's eyes, but understand later that they
had a different meaning. One by one the refugees make a heroic
refusal of Heloïse's sacrifice. The whole scene is as theatrical as
can be, and beautifully done.

The refugees wait in the courtyard for what they think is
certain execution. Instead, a passport to Luxembourg is sent
down to them. They return to the hotel where they take "a
hurried, spare meal of bread and wine". It has no connection
with last night's "gallant supper", for "their existence, since
then, had been set on another plane. They held one another's
hands, each of them owed his life to each of the others." The
passage carries us back to *Out of Africa*, where the African dancers

looked "as if they were really all ready to die for one another",
and forward to "Babette's Feast" in *Anecdotes of Destiny*. Heloïse,
we are told, "was still the central figure of their communion,
but in a new way, as an object infinitely precious to them all.
Her pride, her glory was theirs, since they had been ready to die
for it." After they have crossed the border and Frederick has said
goodbye to Heloïse and the others, he is left pondering the
mysteries of the heroic mind. There is in it "an unexplored, a
mysterious area" that he has still to comprehend.

His answer comes many years later when, on a visit to Paris,
he is taken by a worldly friend to see a show of scantily dressed
dancers, called *Diana's Revenge*. At the climax of the performance,
the goddess Diana herself appears with nothing on at all; and
Diana is Heloïse. Again she is the central figure of a communion.
At her appearance, "a noise like a long sigh went through the
house".

Frederick sends her a note and she comes out to see him after
the show. The scene of their reunion is *written* to the hilt, and the
conversation again is up to the occasion—for Heloïse does not,
in spite of this reversal, lose an inch of her aristocratic stature.
It would have cost her nothing to comply with the officer's
demand, and this accounts for her laughter and for the movement
of her hand to her mantilla. But she realized, she now explains to
Frederick, that the other refugees ran a terrible risk; for they
would, to save their lives, have made her do as the German
demanded, "if they had been left to themselves. And then they
would never have got over it." They were simple people for
whom "it would have been better to be shot than to live on with
a bad conscience". She knows because she is of humble origin.

Her heroism then—here is part of Frederick's answer—derived
from a piece of charlatanism designed to make heroes of the
others. Heloïse goes on to distinguish the officer and Frederick
from the others as superior beings. The officer, through his sexual
instinct, and Frederick, through his feeling for symbols, sensed
that the permanent essence of Heloïse lay in her nudity. Yet she
speaks movingly in the end of the transiency of her beauty.
Meeting one's friends again,

"one realizes how time flies. It is we who feel it, the women. From us
time takes away so much. And in the end: everything." She looked
up at Frederick, and none of the faces which the great masters paint

had ever given him such a vision of life, and of the world. "How I wish, my dear friend," she said, "that you had seen me then."

In that final vision, Frederick understands the nature of heroism and of all symbolism as a filling in of unchanging forms with transient life. The principle of incarnation is, in other words, behind the continuity he senses as he moves from Jesus to pagan goddesses to the idea of aristocracy represented by Heloïse. It is because Heloïse is not an aristocrat—if her name really is noble as Frederick thinks, she would as a widow have come by it through marriage—that she makes such an effective symbol of one, for she is aware of the impression the role makes. It is in the same way because she is not modest that she makes a symbol of modesty for which the others are ready to die. Had she been really modest, she would have been too involved in her own crisis to remember the moral needs of the others; she would, like Lady Godiva, have undressed for their sake.

There is a further implication that by a triumph of wit plays so softly around the edges of the story as not to weigh it down or make it seem, through the disproportion of cases, grotesque. The implication is that the Crucifixion was like Heloïse's sacrifice in that it meant nothing to God to die. Since Heloïse's example inspires the refugees to offer to die for her, another implication is that the Crucifixion was designed not to absolve us of our sins but to show us what we must be prepared to do for any value we cherish.

This we may understand to be Frederick's interpretation, in his book on the doctrine of the atonement. He is associated, by way of Heloïse's name, with the theologian Abelard, who taught that it is not the Crucifixion, but the effect of the Crucifixion upon us, that saves. Since the Unitarians oppose the idea of the Crucifixion as a vicarious or objective atonement, Johannes Rosendahl sees in this and other stories the influence on Isak Dinesen of her Unitarian upbringing and of Ewald's Socinianism.[1]

Subjective atonement is the one Unitarian doctrine Isak Dinesen does subscribe to. But the Unitarians also argue against the divinity of Jesus by saying that if he was God then the Crucifixion was a cheat. Here Isak Dinesen would seem to have taken over the Unitarian idea in order to refute it. It is to suggest authority for her refutation that she has Heloïse allude in the

[1] *Karen Blixen*, pp. 52-97.

end to Spinoza, who taught that the Bible is to be read as parable or metaphor. For she sees in the filling of a preordained role with human feeling and suffering, in the combination of God's comic with man's tragic view, the very essence of symbolism, which requires for its comprehension just the double vision the Unitarians reject.

We come to the heart of *Winter's Tales* in the next four stories—"The Dreaming Child", "The Fish",[1] "Alkmene" and "Peter and Rosa". These are the stories that pick up the nature theme announced in "Sailor-boy", and combine with it the ideas about art and symbolism that have been developed with increasing profundity from "Young Man" to "Heroine". These stories bring together the themes of nature and symbol, because they deal with consciousness at the point where it is barely distinguishable from unconsciousness, and with living unconsciousness at the point where it is barely distinguishable from nonliving unconsciousness. They are stories about dreams and childhood and the sea. The sea, which played a part in the first two stories, emerges here with increasing power and clarity as the symbol of desire—the desire that animates and unifies all nature. As the restless, shifting area between nonliving and living unconsciousness, the sea is the primordial desire out of which consciousness rises and to which it returns; it is the force which, when consciousness returns to it, unites our deepest desires with our biological and spiritual destiny. These are the stories that echo Shakespeare's *Winter's Tale*, where the sea is the agent that unites desire and destiny. Three of these stories are about children who, like Shakespeare's Perdita, are lost and found again; while "The Fish" is about a regressive journey toward childhood and the sea.

In "Dreaming Child", dream or desire unites not only nature and civilization, but also that social spectrum which is one of the subjects of *Winter's Tales*. The life of the little boy Jens, in a Copenhagen slum, is united with the life of the rich through an imaginative old seamstress, Mamzell Ane, who to relieve her own frustration tells tales of the great houses where she used to work. The illegitimate son of a prostitute, Jens has been brought up by a coarse, one-eyed old washerwoman, a cyclops in whose country he feels himself to be lost while his rightful parents dwell

---

[1] The Danish title is "Fra det Gamle Danmark" ("From the Old Denmark").

in the rich part of town. Jens is neither rancorous nor impatient; for in the manner of the dreamer, he takes in all facts with equal blitheness, confident of the great destiny that awaits him.

In the rich part of town, there is a childless couple, Jakob and Emilie Vandamm. It is significant that they bear the name of the couple in Isak Dinesen's early story, "The Hermits", for in that story, full of the sea, the husband was unimaginative and the wife imaginative. Here both Vandamms are unimaginative. But Emilie's unimaginativeness is different from her husband's. There is a belligerence in it which suggests that she has deliberately choked off a fine imagination, choked off access to her deepest desire—to, as we learn, the sea. Emilie's father was a great shipowner and the man she loved was a naval officer and a war hero, named Charlie Dreyer. One moonlit night before his ship was to sail, Charlie asked to spend the night with her and she, as frightened as if he had asked to cut her throat, shut on him the heavy iron gate of her garden "as if it had been the cage of an angry lion. On which side of the gate was the lion?" Charlie sailed away and died of a fever, and Emilie married her cousin Jakob and devoted herself to good works.

Emilie's character is like Jensine's in "Pearls", but there is developed in her story the sexual implication only hinted at in Jensine's—the implication that Jensine really wants to take her husband's confident manhood from him. Jensine says to herself something which is to make the subject of Emilie's story. " 'I shall never have children! As long as I must strain myself against him in this way, we will never have a child.' " Because Emilie has strained against her own deepest desires, she cannot have children.

When Jakob comes upon Jens in the street and decides to adopt him, he is struck by the child's resemblance to Emilie. This resemblance, together with the way Jens transforms his meeting with Emilie into a recognition scene, makes him figure for her as a dream child, as the offspring of her deepest desire, of her unfulfilled love for Charlie. But she dares not admit into consciousness her association of Jens with Charlie. She strains, therefore, even against Jens. She more than does her duty by the child, because she realizes that she is the only person in the house who does not love him. She feels "unsafe with him". Since Jens does not inspire in her the love which would substantiate her dream and his, he becomes more and more insubstantial, and finally pines away and dies.

While he lives, Jens takes possession of the Vandamm mansion, because he sees everything with the "rapture of recognition"—as a repetition and fulfillment of the vision communicated to him back in the slums through the tales of the imaginative old seamstress, Mamzell Ane. He gives to the house and its inmates the quality of objects seen not simply in dream but in art, for it is in the sphere of art that dream is reconciled with reality. His is the power of "the most fascinating and irresistible" person in the world: "the dreamer whose dreams come true". The last phrase, together with the whole idea, comes from Kipling's poem, "The Fairies' Siege". We are also reminded of Joseph who, because his dreams came true, rose to dominion in Egypt like Jens in the house of the Vandamms. We are reminded of Jung and Kerényi's study of the ancient myths about the Divine Child who had magical powers and was usually a foundling among humble people.[1]

When after Jens's death Emilie finally gives in to her deepest desire by creating a fable that is truer than true, when she "confesses" to Jakob that Jens was her child by Charlie Dreyer, it is a sign that she is now in the right rhythm of things that she says of Jens, without knowing she is quoting Scripture, the thing Pharaoh said of Joseph when he made him overseer of Egypt (Genesis 41: 38-39). In fulfilling desire, you unconsciously repeat the patterns of myth. We see here the influence of Mann's *Joseph and His Brothers*.

Jens's blitheness makes him an artist according to Isak Dinesen's own ideal. He makes people see themselves in their unfallen state, so that they feel "impelled to live up to an ideal" and become dependent on him for "their higher existence". Both good and evil, both happiness and unhappiness, which Emilie has all her life tried to keep separate, are welcomed by Jens "in the same spirit of gallant, debonair approval and fellowship". He is "a humorist, a comic fabulist". To Emilie, the fancies he has on his deathbed seem sacrilegious; for he makes on the theme of the rats that infested his slum house a comic and beautiful

[1] *Essays on a Science of Mythology*, trans. R. F. C. Hull (Bollingen Series XXII, New York: Pantheon, 1949; as *Introduction to a Science of Mythology*, London: Routledge and Kegan Paul, 1951).

prose poem. The great achievement of this passage, the finest in
the story, is that the terrible details are absorbed in a vision as
blithe as Jens's earlier vision of palatial splendor.

Having got his palatial splendor, Jens is still dissatisfied, and
his imagination longs back to his house in the slums. For he is,
we are told, a poet, and longing is "the essence of his nature".
He is therefore too light for this world, and we find here again
the analogy from "Dreamers" of the coffee tree with bent tap-
roots that puts forth lovely blossoms and dies. Jens's death is
described as the fulfillment of all longing, of longing for that
boundless unity which he might have found in Emilie's love but
which he finds instead in the return to unconsciousness and the
sea. "Like a small brook which falls into the ocean, Jens gave
himself up to, and was absorbed in, the boundless, final unity of
dream."

There are Shakespearean echoes in the scene of Emilie's "con-
fession" to Jakob; for it takes place in a greenwood, the scene of
regeneration in so many Shakespeare comedies. Since the scene
takes place in May, a few months after Jens's death, we are
reminded also of Jesus, who saved others by dying. Jakob
realizes that Emilie has not since Jens's death talked of him until
now—when she "confesses" that Jens is her child by Charlie
Dreyer. " 'Only in one thing,' she said slowly, 'am I wiser than
you. I know that it would be better, much better, and easier to
both you and me if you would believe me.' " There is an irony in
this, for Jakob, though unimaginative, has not been averse to
believing what he wanted to believe; whereas Emilie has scorned
such compromise with "truth". The story ends with Jakob's
nicely ambiguous play on the word *true*. " 'Yes, my dear,' he
said, 'that is true.' " That is psychologically true. Jakob, who has
a psychological reason for not wanting to believe Emilie's story,
has an even more deeply psychological reason for wanting to
believe it. For the story will bring them closer together by enabling them to express their common grief and love for Jens.

There is beyond this the very faint but endlessly suggestive
implication that we have had a parable of the origin and purpose
of myths and religions. What Emilie is saying there in the greenwood, where by giving in to her deepest desire she has become
like Jens an artist, what she is saying is: "You must believe that
Jens is my son by the Holy Ghost; for whether you believe it or

not, I shall always feel he is and shall never be able to express fully my love for him unless I can admit my intuition into consciousness through a liberating myth." Emilie's story penetrates the mother-son relation to that depth where it connects not only with Jens's intuition about his high descent, but with all myths about magical children begotten by a god upon a mortal virgin.

This last scene is the other outstanding passage in "Dreaming Child". The description of the wood is evidence of the superb nature writing that distinguishes these four stories. It is in these stories that Isak Dinesen finally turns to the uses of her mature fiction the talent for nature writing that, after appearing in her earliest stories, is so extraordinarily displayed in *Out of Africa*. These four stories are in fact best understood as nature poems in prose. For unlike the three anecdotes that precede them, they have not much "story interest". They have instead lyric intensity. Their narrative lines have life and meaning if you see the characters as moved by vast natural forces rather than by the personal motives we expect in fiction. Divorced from nature, their narratives are apt to seem as lifelessly extravagant as opera libretti divorced from music. You have the same condition in many of Wordsworth's poems, where the narrative seems insipid unless absorbed in the poet's intense vision of nature.

It is because there is less nature in "Dreaming Child" than in the others, that "Dreaming Child" is the least consistently intense and therefore, despite the many fine things in it, the least successful of these four stories. The story of Emilie and Charlie Dreyer is trite; Jens is a shadow; Emilie herself is lifeless, though her case is interesting.

There is no mistaking "The Fish" for anything but a poem—a poem that unfolds through the delicate interchange and merging of traditional and natural symbols, all of which compose a controlling vision of the continuity of consciousness with nature. The narrative line, the King's journey through the greenwood to the sea, is symbolic; and even the other two characters symbolize aspects of the King.

A medieval King of Denmark lies sleepless. A star shining through the narrow window of his castle makes him aware of his own restlessness, his unfulfilled longing. Having subdued his rebellious nobles and exhausted all the sensual pleasures, he is jaded and identifies himself with the Wandering Jew, symbol of eternally unfulfilled desire. He realizes that the single star, which in accordance with medieval symbology merges in his mind with the Virgin, symbolizes the object of his desire—that he longs for union with God, for an end of time. The realization comes to him like the ringing of a bell, its "waves of sound" enclosing him "as the sea a drowning man". He understands that his loneliness is his strength, that he must find fulfillment within himself—"for he himself was all the earth". He has still to arrive at Lady Helena's perception, in "Young Man", that the earth floats on the oceans, that the way to God is through our deepest desires. The developing imagery of the sea leads him to that perception.

The King falls asleep toward morning when "a cold current ran through the world", and wakes thinking he must visit his father's old Wendish thrall, Granze, who is a pagan and lives by the sea. Granze, once the King's best friend, "had been the beginning of his life, as he remembered it". Another boyhood friend reappears in the person of the worldly, aristocratic priest, Sune Pedersen, who is just back from the University of Paris. The King and Sune were educated together, and the King asks Sune to ride with him to Granze. "The memories that he had in common with Sune, he reflected, were all bright, as if clearly illuminated; those connected with the Wend belonged to earlier days, when he had hardly been conscious of himself or of the world. They stirred dully in the dark, and smelled of seaweeds and mussels." Sune is connected with the King's conscious self, Granze with his unconscious self; and the King wonders which of them he could best do without.

As they ride in the greenwood under a gentle rain, the King asks Sune whether it is by God's will that men cannot be happy but must be always longing for what they have not. Sune, who has referred to the spirit of Abelard at the University, replies with a parable that expresses beautifully Abelard's doctrine of subjective atonement. When God returned from His sojourn on earth, He held up a pierced hand to the Angels and said He had " ' "now reconciled the heart of man with the conditions of the earth." ' " He did this not by expiating man's sins for him, but by showing man " ' "how to get himself spat upon and scourged . . . how to get himself hung upon a cross." ' "

Sune's Christian answer would seem to counsel the denial of desire. But its real import, as we see later when Sune and Granze push the King in the same direction, is that God showed man that the ultimate object of his desire is just such a culminating experience of love and death as is symbolized in the Crucifixion. Since Sune's family fought with the rebellious lords, the King suspects Sune's motives in preaching him humility. Nevertheless, he decides that both Sune and Granze shall serve him. Since the King takes his conscious self on this journey back to the unconscious, the innocence to be regained will be different from that originally lost.

Their regress is marked by the increasing barrenness of the landscape, and finally by the seascape itself—magnificently evoked through the mixing up of air and water which in *Out of Africa* was so effective for making landscapes seem, like Jens's recognitions, the materialization of a dream.

The day was dim, but the world was filled, like a glass bell, with vague, blurred light, and with the incessant, songful murmur of the sea: a powerful, low rushing from the depths far out—strangely unreal in the still day, but a strong wind had been blowing for three or four days before—a sweet prattle near by, where the waves ran up on the stones and the gravel. It was these sounds that the King had heard in his dream.

Granze is so much a part of this seascape that it takes them time to descry his figure, wading knee-deep in the sea, dragging a heavy catch of fish. Granze, who is clairvoyant, announces that Sune has narrowly escaped poisoning by a woman with whom he has had an illicit relation. The priest has avoided his death; while the King, for whom Granze foresees a saintly apotheosis, will go forward to meet his through an illicit relation with a woman.

Granze reveals that he has been converted to Christianity, but speaks of it in terms of the rebirth symbols it shares with paganism. He establishes a communion among them in a manner both pagan and Christian, by giving them an alcoholic brew to drink and a fish to eat—the fish being an ancient fertility symbol that in Christianity symbolizes Christ. He speaks of immortality as memory, and says that the Wends pass on their knowledge in their seed, so that there is in them no distinction between individual and racial memory—they remember all that nature remembers. He makes a beautiful myth about the evolution of life out of what men now call nonliving things. He makes us understand that all things were alive before analysis killed off some things in order that others might be called living. Granze— who resembles the thrall, Finn, in the 1905 story, "Grjotgard Ålvesøn og Aud"—finds paradise at the beginning of things, as Sune at the end.

In cutting up a big fish, Granze pulls out a ring. Hailing the King to whom " 'the elements themselves swear allegiance' ", Sune puts the ring on the King's finger and recalls Herodotus's story of King Polycrates who found in a fish's belly a precious ring he had cast into the sea. When the King asks what happened to Polycrates, Sune has to admit that he was killed some time after.[1] The King, instead, has thought of the great Danish King Canute, who ordered the advancing waves to stop in order to show just such flattering courtiers as Sune that the sea would not obey him. Canute didn't want the sea to obey him, Sune says. " 'Nay,' said the King. 'But if the sea had obeyed him? If it had obeyed him, Sune?' " Rhythms such as this make the great moments in Isak Dinesen.

The point is that Canute, whom the sea did not obey, lived. When the sea obeys you, it obeys your deepest desires and carries you to your destiny—which is always death. This fish, Granze says to the King, " 'has swum a long way to meet you' ". Combining with Granze to push the King toward his destiny, Sune now recognizes the ring as belonging to his kinswoman, Lady Ingeborg, wife of the Lord High Constable, with whom Sune went sailing a week ago. She let her hand trail in the blue water, and Sune laughingly warned her she might lose the ring and would not find another blue stone so like her own eyes.

The King has a vision of the fair lady's "white fingers playing in the ripples, and underneath them the big fish swimming in the dark-blue shadow of the keel". It is, though it uses established symbols, like the "blue story" in "Young Man", a vision of desire—the lady's desire will be transmitted to him by those unifying waters that carry to all things their desire for each other. The King says he will wear the ring until he can give it back to Lady Ingeborg, and the story ends with Granze's cry that the fish

---

[1] See Herodotus's *History*, Book III, where the Egyptian King is Amasis, not Amadis as Isak Dinesen has it. Herodotus uses the story of Polycrates to illustrate the Greek idea of Hybris and Nemesis, of retribution for too much good fortune. But for Isak Dinesen, it is "good" fortune to fulfill one's destiny and move toward death.

has now only to be eaten—the King has only to move forward to his destiny. For those who have not made the identification, a postscript reminds us that King Erik V of Denmark was murdered in 1286 by a party of rebellious vassals, headed, according to tradition, by the Lord High Constable whose wife, Ingeborg, Erik had seduced.

The King has had to move backward in his life, so that he might recover desire and move forward through love to death. Like the "blue story", "The Fish" annihilates the distinction between sea and sky—between the King's sexual and spiritual desire, and his biological and spiritual destiny; between unconsciousness and consciousness; between paganism and Christianity. It gives us a sweeping vision of the continuity of mind, culture and nature. If we feel a steady deepening of statement as we move on to "Alkmene" and then to "Peter and Rosa", it is because the last two stories are increasingly tragic. The acquiescence that comes so easily to a symbolic figure like the King is achieved at a bitter cost by the more fully delineated individuals of these stories. These stories fill in the lyrical vision of the stream of things with individuals capable of standing against the stream before giving way to it.

"Alkmene" takes off from the final implication of "Dreaming Child"—that Emilie's failure as a woman causes her to conceive by the Holy Ghost. "Dreaming Child" has a happy ending, in the manner of a divine comedy. In "Alkmene", instead, it is the men who fail the women, and the ending is at least half tragic. Significantly, the myth alluded to belongs to those inventors of tragedy, the Greeks, rather than to the Christians in whose view of life tragedy has no real place.

Amphitryon failed Alkmene by accidentally killing her father, and she insisted he take revenge on her father's enemies before she would consummate their marriage. His first failure led to a second in that he was away when Zeus became interested in Alkmene. On the night of her husband's return, Zeus visited Alkmene in the form of Amphitryon; and later that night, the real Amphitryon came to her. Alkmene conceived twins. One, Amphitryon's son, was an ordinary child, but the other, Zeus's son, was the great hero Herakles. In Isak Dinesen's story, no god comes to make up for the failure of the mortal men; and her

Alkmene, who ought to have been the mother of a hero, remains barren.

Alkmene is like Jens a lost child in that she has fallen among people unworthy of her. Jens might be said to represent the modern imagination that is cut off from sensuousness and bodily vigor. But Alkmene is bold, vigorous, sensuous and imaginative. She is not a dreamer, but is dreamt of by the two men who fail her because they do not give in to their deepest desires. She epitomizes the Greek spirit in that she is at once perfectly natural, artistic and aristocratic.

Alkmene is adopted by a parson in a lonely part of Jutland. This man gave up a promising literary career in Copenhagen because he feared as sinful the egoism necessary for self-fulfillment. His wife, Gertrude, is a country girl who grew up helping her mother run a sheep farm. It is observed by the esthetical professor who plays the ironic counterpart to Zeus in this story that Gertrude has a Venus's body which is obscured, as he sees it, by her plain face and puritanical dress, but which is really obscured by lack of fulfillment. Two men are responsible for the obscuring of Gertrude's body. The first is her father who, by retreating into melancholia after he lost his money, committed his wife and children to the penurious hardship that fostered in Gertrude a worship of duty inimical to the erotic life. The second is the parson who has, it would seem, failed Gertrude sexually. She is childless, and like Rachel cries to him: " 'Give me children or else I die.' "

Playing the part of Zeus, the professor "impregnates" Gertrude (this is doubly ironical in that he may be homosexual) by offering the couple a little girl of mysterious parentage. She is apparently the illegitimate offspring of a royal personage and an actress or dancer. The professor says the child's name is Alkmene, because he knows that in the days when the parson dreamt of becoming a poet he wrote an epic called "Alkmene". Alkmene is the parson's dream child as Jens is Emilie's.

Alkmene is, like a miraculous child, brought to the parson's house out of a snowstorm, and Gertrude, after unwrapping her and remarking on her beauty, cries out to her husband: " 'Oh, Jens, she has got no shift on.' " Alkmene is superbly done; for she seems, as she grows up, a creature both wild and supernatural, a creature from before the fall who stands outside our morality.

Yet she also seems in this, as in the conflict with her parents, the quintessence of all children.

Her parents try to bind her with the bonds of love to their own fallen world. They forbid her to dance, a thing she does naturally to perfection; and they try to teach her to distinguish right from wrong and truth from untruth. It is a sign of what they are trying to do to her that they shorten her Greek name, Alkmene, symbol of creativity, to Mene, which recalls the Hebraic warning of doom, "MENE, MENE, TEKEL, UPHARSIN"— words which, as Daniel interprets them to the Babylonian King, are a prophesy of what is to happen in this story. "MENE; God hath numbered thy kingdom, and finished it. TEKEL; Thou art weighed in the balances, and art found wanting. PERES; Thy kingdom is divided" (Daniel 5: 25-28). Because the other characters do not accept the revelation Alkmene brings them, but try to cut it down to suit their own inadequate ideas, she, who might have brought them life and unity, brings them instead death through numbers and calculation, judgment for their inadequacy, and that analytic division of their perceptions that leads to division from each other, from nature and from God. It is what happens to divine revelation when, instead of being saved by it, we turn it into our own image. Alkmene becomes in the end an image of the other characters.

Twice she tries to run away from her parents, and twice she is brought back—the second time by the narrator of the story who tells her that her parents love her. " 'What about the children, Vilhelm, who do not want to be loved?' " she asks. She never runs away again after her confirmation, for it is then that her parents make themselves vulnerable by confessing, hesitantly, that they are not her real parents. Now they have won; they have tied her fast—it is what happens when you are confirmed—with the bonds of moral obligation. There are echoes here of Nietzsche and of the final pages of *Malte Laurids Brigge*, where Rilke interprets the story of the Prodigal Son as the legend of the child "who did not want to be loved".

Alkmene follows Gertrude's destiny in that two men fail her— her father and her would-be husband, the narrator. Alkmene's real father abandoned her, and her foster-father does not let her call him " 'back to Olympus' ", to his real self, as the professor intended, but leads her instead down his own self-deceiving path.

The narrator is the son of the squire on whose estate the parson has his living. Although this Vilhelm dreams of Alkmene and has, because he too is a child, the closest understanding with her, he is too trivial and conventional to give in to his deepest desire. "Even at fourteen I understood enough of the world to decide that a parson's daughter was no fit match for me." Yet he does not, in the way of squires' sons, try to seduce her either. It is because Vilhelm both understands and does not understand Alkmene that we see her, through his eyes, as both a symbol and a real girl subject to social and economic conditions.

It is significant that in his first dream of Alkmene Vilhelm meets her in a field, for their love is played out against beautifully rendered natural settings. When he first fails her by bringing her back to her parents, his action is all the less excusable because he finds her in a setting which is a materialization of his dream. The return of Vilhelm and Alkmene is one of the story's great scenes. They do not argue, they sing—ending with "an old folksong of a mother lamenting her dead child". They are in harmony with the landscape, for they are making sorrowful love to each other.

On another occasion Vilhelm has gotten a village girl with child—just the thing he refrained from doing to Alkmene—and is to be sent away to an uncle's estate. Alkmene offers to run away with him, but Vilhelm puts her off with a conventional farewell and departs dutifully for his uncle's.

His father summons him home when Alkmene suddenly inherits a mysterious fortune, so vast that " 'it becomes' ", as the parson puts it, " 'a symbol' ". Everything about Alkmene is magical, yet the magic never bears magical results. Somehow the prince is lacking to awaken the sleeping princess with a kiss. Vilhelm is, like the young man in "Chevalier", inhibited by conventional responses from reaching out and claiming his dream when it has come true. The gold therefore does not cause the lovers to live happily together forever after. Vilhelm's father has summoned him home because he wants him to propose to Alkmene. But Vilhelm is too conventionally moral to dare to propose to her now, after his previous hesitations.

He goes away again, and this time learns that the parson has died. He returns—and one ought to remember here Amphitryon's return to consummate his marriage—at a time when his father and Alkmene's mother are away. She is fifteen. It is May. All is now propitious for the consummation of their love.

But again it is Alkmene who takes the initiative. She asks him to take her on a secret journey to Copenhagen, where she reveals that she has come to see a notorious murderer have his head cut off the next day. The execution " 'is a warning to the people who may be near to doing the same thing themselves . . . for God alone knows all,' she said. 'And who can say of himself: of this deed I could never have been guilty?' " Since this last question is a thing the parson has said, we realize how thoroughly his religion of sin has taken hold of Alkmene.

Through this scene and the powerful scene of the execution, we have to fill in Alkmene's complex motives. We have to understand that the death of her father having left the responsibility for her mother squarely upon her, Alkmene has as a last desperate bid for freedom conceived the idea of killing her mother. It is to atone vicariously for this potential murder that she has come to the execution. She uses Vilhelm to bring her "home" again from this last attempt to escape.

Instead of Zeus who made love to Amphitryon's wife, Alkmene has chosen the god who is supposed to save by dying. We are told that the crowd, after the execution, "thronged round the scaffold, many of them dipping bits of cloth in the blood". When Alkmene trembles heavily at the execution, Vilhelm finally puts his arms around her: "although I was myself terrified and sad, it gave me a sweet content". This looks like the sorrowful love they made to each other when returning through the fields after Alkmene's attempted escape. But there is I think a difference. Then, the sorrow and the love went together; now, they are divided. Vilhelm and Alkmene look at death together *instead* of making love.

Like Adam and Eve, and like Boris and Athena at the end of "The Monkey", they share an experience of evil. But they are not bound together by their mutual guilt. No rebirth of love takes place in this story, even though they return to Jutland entirely by water, through a moonlit setting that makes us expect some fruition.

On the ship, Vilhelm takes it for granted that all is over between them.

"I thought that you and I might have kept together all our lives, Alkmene." "Did you think that?" said she. "It is late to speak of these things now." . . . "Have you not known that I loved you all the time?" "Love?" she said. "They all loved Alkmene. You did not help her. Did you not know, now, all the time, that they were all against her, all?" . . . "To me it was a joke," I said, "a thing of fun. Nay, I think that I did even feel sorry for them. It never occurred to me but that you were the stronger." "Yes, but it was not so," said she. "They were the strongest. It could not be otherwise when they were so good, when they were always right. Alkmene was alone. And when they died, and made her watch it, she could stand up against them no longer. She could see no way out, but she must die, too. . . . And can you not," she asked me, "not even now say: 'Poor Alkmene'?" I tried to, but it would not come to me.

Her parents " 'died' " when they confessed they were not her parents. Vilhelm's inability to pity Alkmene shows that he has not arrived at a correct, which is to say a Nietzschean, under-standing of good and evil.[1] He judges by the labels rather than by the moral reality. He doesn't see that Alkmene has been defeated by "good" people and corrupted by conscience. It is a sign of her corruption that she used the execution as a vicarious atonement and a threat of punishment. She has, as a result, repressed her murderous desire but not transformed it. All that remains inside her now is hate, which is why she and Vilhelm cannot go beyond the point where Adam and Eve turned upon each other with mutual recriminations. Vilhelm's conventional morality and her religion take them to the fall, but cannot take them forward from there to redemption. They merely part after their return.

The ending is the most powerful stroke of irony in all Isak Dinesen. Vilhelm hears that Gertrude and her daughter have bought a sheep farm in the part of the country where Gertrude's mother had her sheep farm. Sixteen years later, Vilhelm finds himself in the district and decides to visit them. He finds the farm poverty-stricken but neat. Gertrude has turned back into the peasant she originally was. She has aged, her Venus's body is now "square like a stack of firewood"; but in character she has become girlish. Although Alkmene is away—she has gone to sell wool and put money in the bank—we are skilfully made to under-stand by the change in Gertrude that the opposite change has taken place in Alkmene, that she has in character grown old and

---

[1] "I like Nietzsche very much," Isak Dinesen said to me. "People are wrong to call him a philosopher. He is an artist."

hard, that the mother and daughter have exchanged roles. We also understand that Alkmene's body must have become like Gertrude's, that she is now desexualized. Because of the failure of the men, great women like Alkmene—and like Gertrude's mother on her sheep farm—have had to take over the male role; so that Gertrude now plays not only daughter but also female to Alkmene's male.

The rich Alkmene is a legend in the neighborhood for her parsimony. And Gertrude, after complaining that Mene does not spare herself, drives home the irony by saying again in the last sentence the thing she said when Alkmene was first brought to her out of the snow. " 'Vilhelm,' she said. 'Do you know? She has got no shift on!' " The sign of Alkmene's magical innocence is now the sign of her parsimony. The fairy gold has turned destructive, and the life-giving Alkmene, who might have been a shepherdess of the pastoral tradition, has indeed become Mene —the force of vengeful judgment that has bereaved Gertrude of a daughter and the dignity of old age, and Vilhelm, who is still unmarried, of a wife. As for Alkmene herself, she has become Gertrude in order to turn her murderous desire upon herself.

It should be apparent that the conception behind "Alkmene" is tremendous. It should also be apparent that the story suffers from over-condensation. Isak Dinesen works by condensation rather than by the novelist's expansion, and achieves through it —as in this last scene—her greatest effects. But she can overdo it, and in this story the reader has to fill in too much that is important. It is one thing for meanings to be ferreted out, and another for them really to make an impression. Although "Alkmene" is even greater in conception than "The Fish", it is not so perfectly achieved.

"Peter and Rosa" is both great in conception and perfectly achieved. It ranks after "Sorrow-acre" as the second best story of the volume. I have called "Alkmene" half tragic because it is that peculiarly modern kind of tragedy, the tragedy of unfulfilled desire. Isak Dinesen has made it clear, however, in "The Fish" and elsewhere, that she considers tragedy to be fulfillment. It is in fulfilling one's destiny that one meets a completely tragic end, which is why traditional tragedy is a triumph not a failure. "Peter and Rosa" is complete tragedy. Isak Dinesen advances toward the tragic vision by showing us the stream of things in

"The Fish" and man's unique resistance to it in "Alkmene". Finally, in "Peter and Rosa", we see that tragedy is the means by which man fulfills his individuality through reconciliation with the stream of things. That imagery of the sea, which in "Alkmene" is so conspicuously muted, bursts upon us again in "Peter and Rosa". Once again we are in a world united by the moving currents of desire.

The story opens in early spring when the whole frozen world, including the ice-bound Sound between Denmark and Sweden, is beginning to turn back into water. On the night of the first spring rain, "the hard, inexorable sky over the dead landscape broke, dissolved into streaming life and became one with the ground. On all sides the incessant whisper of falling water re-echoed; it increased and grew into a song." Fifteen-year-old Peter Købke, the adopted son of a country parson, grows restless over his theology books. Opening the window, he hears through the rain the signals of the great water birds trekking north. "Such a tremendous stream of longing, on its way to its goal, passed over his head, that Peter, down on the ground, felt his limbs ache." He resolves to fulfill his desire to run away from home and become a sailor.

The illegitimate son of the parson's sister, Peter is like Alkmene being educated in a religion that violates his nature. He is preparing for the ministry, and has to contend with the parson's conviction that a prison is the safest place for human beings. This parson, too, has married a peasant woman who is more obviously neglected than is Gertrude, while the parson's mind dwells on his dead first wife who is for him an ideal like the Alkmene of the other parson's epic poem. Rosa, who is also fifteen, is the parson's spoiled and petted daughter by his first wife. The two young people inhabit their private gardens of Eden in a house where "death was zealously kept in view and lectured upon" because the parson's preoccupation with his dead wife merges with his Christian preoccupation with the life hereafter. "To grow up in the house was to the young people a problem and a struggle, as if fatal influences were dragging them the other way, into the earth, and admonishing them to give up the vain and dangerous task of living."

The great achievement of "Peter and Rosa" is that it shows how the young people are nevertheless pushed forward into the dangerous task of living by a force that they themselves are in the process of understanding through changing dreams and symbols. Again we are at the point where dream touches biology, and we see that that is where love takes place, that love is recognition —it is dream, both personal and cultural dream, come true. Falling in love is part of the process by which we gradually wake up to the external world, by which we come to know and believe in its reality because we find there fulfillment and repetition. Fulfillment is always repetition; for expectation is the product of personal memory, which shades off into cultural and biological memory. That is the vision of "Peter and Rosa", where dream is always in advance of action.

Just as in "Dreaming Child" the seamstress's memories become Jens's expectations into which Emilie steps to take on reality, so here the parson's memories of his dead wife merge in the mind of the motherless Peter with inherited memories of the sea as Great Mother to become a dream of womanhood that takes on the lineaments of Rosa. Peter does not, however, *see* Rosa's womanhood until he sees her as an archetype, in what Jung calls an anima vision, a vision of one's own soul as personified by the opposite sex. Rosa has climbed upon a windowsill and pushed open the window to let a butterfly out, when Peter comes up the garden path. He stops dead still.

Rosa, in her stockinged feet, with the skirt of her blue frock caught back by the cross-bar of the window, was so like the figurehead of a big, fine ship that for an instant he did, so to say, see his own soul face to face. . . . It seemed to him then as if she were promising him something, a great happiness; and within a sudden, mighty motion [the motion of a ship and of lovemaking] he decided to confide in her, and to tell her all.

He suggests climbing up to her room that night to tell her a great secret. She refuses until she remembers that they used to plan great enterprises in her room at night as children. And then, when they are about to take their next step forward in life, there rose "in her heart, as in his, a longing for the lost world of childhood". So she says she may leave the window open for him that night.

Rosa's characterization is more complex and interesting than Peter's. It makes us think of Eve, and it explains why Eve had the seed of the fall within her. The seed of the fall lay in the vanity, the sense of her own sexuality and power, that gave Eve her charm for Adam, and in the fact that Eve was ahead of Adam in sexual development. Two years ago at thirteen Rosa grew up taller than Peter, and it was at that time that she came into a world of which she was the sole possessor. She fell in love with herself.

Nobody could tell where her world lay; neither did the substance of it lend itself to words. The others would never understand her, were she to tell them that it was both infinite and secluded, playful and very grave, safe and dangerous. She could not explain, either, how she herself was one with it, so that through the loveliness and power of her dream-world she was now, in her old frock and botched shoes, very likely the loveliest, mightiest and most dangerous person on earth. . . . Within this mystic garden of hers she was altogether out of the reach of a clumsy boy with dirty hands and scratched knees.

But during the winter Peter grew up taller than her and became so much stronger that she was alarmed and offended. When he began to express his own fancies about the world, she feared for her dream world. "Peter might find the 'Sesame' which opened it, and encroach upon it, and she might meet him there any day." He might see her as she sees herself, and that would change everything. Rosa feels that something horrible is going to happen to her, and that it will happen through Peter. Poised between apprehension and desire, she is apt to tumble at any moment into ecstasy or "into bitter wrath against all the world". Rosa at fifteen has just the female devil in her that the gazelle Lulu has, in *Out of Africa*, when she wrathfully projects on to others her own resistance to fulfilling her biological destiny. Rosa often wishes that Peter would go to sea and die.

That night Peter lies in bed with her and tells her of his plan to run away to sea. He needs her help. There is a ship, the *Esperance*, at Elsinore, that will take him. Rosa must tell her father that she wants to visit her godmother there and wants Peter to accompany her. By playing a part in it, Rosa is to turn Peter's dream world and herself with it into a reality. " 'I have often wished that you would go to sea,' " she says, forgetting why she wished it. Without quite saying so, she agrees to help.

When Peter climbs down the ladder from Rosa's room, he is ecstatic about two apparently incompatible prospects—his future at sea and Rosa. They are reconciled, however, in a single image of boundless desire. "The sea had become a female deity, and Rosa herself as powerful, foamy, salt and universal as the sea."

Rosa is awakened toward morning by a terrible dream of desertion. She remembers that Peter is going to leave her, and conceives the idea of keeping him by betraying his secret to her father. There would then be "no ships in Peter's life, no rounding of the Horn, no drowning in the water of all the oceans. She sat in her bed, crouching on the thought, like a hen on her eggs." In the contrast between the two lines of imagery, we see the contrast between the male principle of boundless desire and the female principle which is precisely to make boundaries and establish nests. It is because this is the female principle that woman, as Isak Dinesen sees it, fears the sea and found it to her interest to bring about the fall and so establish the restrictions of civilization.

No sooner has Rosa betrayed Peter to her father than the way to redemption is pointed out by an itinerant fishwife who, in a charming little scene of old-fashioned Danish country life, brings the news that the ice is breaking up and the Sound is free. " 'I shall go down to see it,' " says Peter. " 'Come with me, Rosa,' he exclaimed in a great, happy seizure." They go scampering off like children into a scene of pastoral joy, where "to all sides they heard the sound of dripping and running water". Once again they take a step backward before taking the next step forward in their lives. Once again dream precedes action, for now Peter tells a story—the second of the three great inset stories of *Winter's Tales*—in which he unconsciously recognizes Rosa's betrayal.

A skipper named his ship after his wife and had a beautiful figurehead carved for it in her likeness. But his wife was jealous of the ship, and was not convinced when he said that he thought so highly of the figurehead " ' "because she is like you, yes, because she is you yourself" ' ". When the skipper had a pair of precious blue stones set into the figurehead as eyes, his wife wanted them. But he said, " ' "No, I cannot do that, and you would not ask me to if you understood." ' " Before he sailed for Portugal, she had the precious stones stolen out of the figurehead and two bits of blue glass put in their place. While her husband was away, she discovered she was going blind. " ' "Oh, God," the wife then cried, "that the ship was back in the harbour of Elsinore. Then I should have the glass taken out, and the jewels put back. For did he not say that they were my eyes?" ' " But the ship never came back. For the ship, too, had gone blind. It ran in broad daylight into a rock rising out of the sea, and went to the bottom with all hands.

Like a great folk tale, this story does not seem invented and could be told effectively in almost any words. It is significant that Peter breaks out with the story as a way of expressing the bliss of illumination. For now he understands why he loves both Rosa and the sea. He understands that he loves Rosa because he loves the sea, that you can only *see* the individual through the archetype. Rosa, however, hears through the story Jesus's "One of you shall betray me".

It is when she realizes that she has played Judas's role that the realization of what she has done "hit her with such awful strength that she thought she must fall headlong down the hill. . . . So now it had come, she thought, what all her life she had feared and waited for. Here, at last, was the horror which was to kill her." She was still, after she betrayed Peter to her father, a "doll". Only now is her fall completed, and only now does she fall unreservedly in love with Peter. Both falls were part of the thing she had always feared.

As in "The Fish", they journey through woods to the sea. Only here the wood is still brown, and the Sound breaks upon them suddenly, like a revelation. "It was a rare and wonderful sight. The ice was breaking up." Seizing her hand an instant, Peter communicates to her "a stream of energy and joy". He leaps out on the ice and she runs after him.

There begins now an increasingly intoxicated rush to the end of the story. The end is disastrous, yet the movement to it is one of mounting joy. It is Rosa who now takes the lead in fantasy. Like those dangerous sprites of legend that lead travellers to destruction, she dances in imagination ahead of Peter, leading him to fulfill the dream he had outlined to her the night before. Rosa sees on the Sound the breaking up of the dry, hard world of her heart.

Here all flowed and fluctuated, the whole world was fluid. Near the shore there were patches of thin white ice that broke as she trod on them, so that she had to wade through pools of clear water. Her shoes soon got soaked; as she ran the water sprinkled over her skirt, and the sense of universal moisture intoxicated her. She felt as if, within a minute or two, she herself, and Peter with her, might melt and dissolve into some unknown, salt flow of delight, and become absorbed into the infinite, swaying, wet world.

Thinking that after all she has gone to sea with Peter, she says they are going to Elsinore, that the tall packing of ice out there is her godmother's house and the one beyond is the harbor. They rush further out on the ice, leaping over deep cracks. Peter makes the next contribution to their joint fantasy and so apparently leads them to the fatal step. Pointing to a large floe of ice separated from the ice on which they stand by a long crevice, he calls it the *Esperance* and asks if they should board it. Crossing her arms on her breast like the figurehead of a ship, Rosa says yes.

Always ahead of Peter, it is Rosa who first realizes that the *Esperance* has put to sea, that the crevice has widened and six feet of water runs between them and the land ice. She wants to shriek but does not. "For within the next moment a great calm came upon her. That fate, which all her life she had dreaded, and from which today there was no escape—that, she saw now, was death. It was nothing but death." With that acceptance, she regains innocence. It does not even matter that Peter would now never know of her betrayal. She might tell him of it herself, for "she was once more Rosa, the gift to the world, and to Peter, too". Hers is the triumph of a woman who has given satisfaction to her lover, who has made it possible for him to fulfill his destiny and hers.

Peter, however, when he realizes what has happened, feels responsible. This is the moment of his fall, when he and Rosa are bound in mutual guilt. From the side of redemption, Rosa looks back at Peter's fall "beneath the long eyelashes as from an ambush". She knows his guilt is illusory, that it is she who gave him the apple to eat, but she knows too that she has done a good and a necessary thing. If Rosa led him to his fall, she also leads him to redemption. As Peter stares at her, "their danger, and his own guilt in bringing her here, vanished and came to nothing before the fact that a girl could be so glorious". Having never before "felt life to be so mighty", he realizes that, on the floe, dream and reality have become one and so have life and death.

They make love symbolically. Peter bores a hole in the ice and plants a stick in it, to which he ties a red handkerchief as a flag of distress. He wraps Rosa in his coat and muffler, and asks to take her hair down so " 'the wind will blow in it' " as it seems to do with the hair of figureheads. Then the ice breaks beneath them, as if their combined weight made it give way.

The break threw them on to their knees, and to each other. For a minute the ice still bore them, a foot below the surface of the water. They might have saved themselves, then, if they had separated and struggled on to the two sides of the crack, but the idea did not occur to either of them. Peter, as he felt himself flung off his balance, and the ice-cold water round his feet, in one great movement clasped his arms round Rosa and held her to him. And at this last moment the fantastic, unknown feeling of having no ground under him in his consciousness was mingled with the unknown sense of softness, of her body against his. Rosa squeezed her face into his collar-bone, and shut her eyes. The current was strong; they were swept down, in each other's arms, in a few seconds.

Only Rosa would seem fully to understand the moral complexity with which their dream has been realized, and that is perhaps a flaw in the story. But sexual and spiritual consummation, love and death—the whole course of adult life is telescoped in their drowning together. To show their life as lived out in pieces over the years would be to make its meaning less obvious.

In the American edition of *Winter's Tales*, "Sorrow-acre" has been placed second in order to draw readers into the volume. But in the editions that follow Isak Dinesen's arrangement, it comes after "Peter and Rosa" and thus makes the climax to the ever-deepening tragic vision of the volume. "Sorrow-acre" fills in the vision of man's tragic position in the natural order with the vision of his tragic position in the social order, where men are set over each other and are under the cruel necessity of acting as destinies to each other. "A sad tale's best for winter," says Shakespeare in *Winter's Tale* (II, 1, 25). The line might serve as motto to this volume. The title of the last story, "A Consolatory Tale", refers not only to the problem within the story but is, I think, a direct answer to the title "Sorrow-acre", and an answer to the sadness of the whole volume.

"Consolatory Tale" brings back the writer, Charlie Despard. The book he was worrying about in "Young Man" has been a success, but none of his other problems has been solved. Charlie

finds in a Paris café an old friend, Aeneas Snell, to whom he
expresses his old worries about his public. He is disturbed
because a book can be beautiful only if the public sees its beauty.
This is the problem Aeneas's consolatory tale is addressed to.

We are told of Aeneas that he has practised many professions
in many lands, and that "no great events, either fortunate or sad,
seemed ever to have come to him personally but it had been his
fate to have strange happenings, dramas and catastrophes take
place where he was". He is therefore "a skilful raconteur".
Aeneas, who looks like Charlie, is Charlie's double. But in looking
into his face across the table, Charlie is looking at the opposite
image of himself from the one he saw in "Young Man". The
young man with the carnation was more vital than Charlie;
Aeneas is less vital. In the radiant face of the young man, Charlie
saw life, the artist's subject-matter which he can never quite
get hold of. In the neatly made, expressionless face of Aeneas,
Charlie does not quite know he is seeing the artist, the perfect
storyteller whom he can only hope to approximate. The young
man and Aeneas have in common a debonair composure; while
Charlie, who oscillates between these opposite ideals, is ill at ease.

Aeneas takes on character enough as he steps into the role of
storyteller. The frame of "Consolatory Tale" is not very interesting, but Aeneas's tale is the best of the three great inset stories of
Winter's Tales and the best *tale* in Isak Dinesen. It comes closest
to seeming an age-old thing through the perfect economy of its
fable, the stateliness of its wit and its apparently bottomless
wisdom. Although it derives the theme of the double from "The
Tale of the False Caliph" in *The Thousand and One Nights* (286th
Night), its wit and wisdom are its own, and it gives to the theme
of the double a philosophical meaning that is entirely lacking in
the Arabian story.

Aeneas was physician to the Shah of Persia at a time when the
young Crown Prince, Nasrud-Din Mirza, took it into his head to
imitate the Caliph Haroun of Bagdad by wandering through the
streets of Teheran disguised as a beggar. The old Councillors
thought it might "upset the whole ancient system of the country"
for a Prince to know so much about his people; so they often
"pre-instructed" the beggars and prostitutes with whom the
Prince talked. One day, the old High Minister informed the
Prince that a man who looked just like him was walking the

streets of Teheran in a beggar's disguise similar to the Prince's.

Determined to meet his *"doppelgänger"* or double, the Prince takes Aeneas, and both of them, disguised as beggars, spend several beautiful blue spring evenings, searching for this man. They finally find him in a vile quarter, sitting on the ground beneath a crooked old fig tree close to the oldest gate of the town. There is an atmosphere of dignity around him. Passersby slacken their pace, half avert their gaze and conduct themselves with reverence. Because the people of the quarter take him to be the Prince in disguise—an incarnation—he becomes a symbol magically capable of creating order in a disorderly part of town. The Prince and Aeneas seat themselves on the ground near the beggar.

A poor old woman beseeches the beggar to accept a loaf of bread, since he has eaten nothing for two days. But he refuses. " 'For I know of a beggar, my brother in mendicancy, who sat by the town wall for three full days, and was given nothing. I will experience myself what he did then feel and think.' " When the woman departs, the Prince says the beggar's story must be wrong; for he himself has never been refused alms even the length of a day.

The beggar asks if he is the Prince, and the Prince accuses the beggar of counterfeiting him. " 'Might not I as justly charge you yourself,' " the beggar replies, " 'with having, in your greatness, mimicked my humble countenance, and embezzled my beggar's appearance?' " It is true, he says, " 'that I have made use of the likeness that God deigned to create between you and me. I have profited by it to be proud, and grateful to God, where before I was cast down. Will a Prince blame his servant for that?' " No courtier could be more adroit. The other man, who reveals himself to be a beggar born and bred named Fath, wins all the wit combats. And the wit here is the wit of parables, in which words are measured out like pearls because nothing less than souls are at stake. When the Prince finally asks him who this beggar was who was so cruelly treated, Fath says it was he himself before he had taken to suggesting that he was the Prince in disguise.

The Prince is amused to think that " 'a beggar of Teheran has harnessed me to his wagon' ", that all the Prince's accomplishments in love, war and the hunt will redound " 'to the greater

glory of Fath' ". Fath suggests that the Prince created him by
turning him into a symbolic beggar, by giving to his beggarliness
magical value. Just as every person, to the extent that he is a
symbol, has the Holy Ghost in him, so every symbolic beggar is a
Prince in disguise. As for the Prince, it would be no great thing
for him to be disguised as a Duke, and it is no great thing that
Aeneas is disguised as a beggar. It is because it is remarkable for
a Prince to be disguised as a begger that the princely title has
symbolic power. The principle of identity is thus connected with
the social principle that binds men and classes together precisely
by differentiating them.

The Prince decides that he will walk no more in disguise; for
Fath is there to keep up his end of the dualistic symbol from
which both derive identity. Fath refuses an offer of gold which
would dilute his beggarly " 'grandeur' ", but asks instead a favor
designed to enhance it. He wants the finest regiment of the
Prince's horsemen to ride up to where he is seated on the ground,
to pull up " 'in great surprise and dread' " when they see him,
and finally to ride over him—but in such a way as not to hurt
him. When the Prince objects that his horsemen never ride over
people in the streets, " 'In that way,' " says Fath, " 'my mother
was killed.' "

The Prince accedes to Fath, but with one reservation. If Fath
is to wear the beggar's mask the Prince fashioned, he must not
frequent any longer a certain woman who gives performances
with a donkey. " 'You are taking a great liberty with our person
when you make us tread, so to say, in the footsteps of an ass.' "
Aeneas apologizes for the Prince, who has yet to understand that
there is nothing so low as to be irreconcilable with the highest.
But Fath has the victory again as he gazes down humbly and
wrings his hands. " 'Oh, my lord,' he cried, 'this command of
yours comes hard on me. The woman is my wife. It is by the
gains of her craft that I live.' "

" 'Fath,' " says the Prince "in a very gentle and royal manner"
—*royal* in this connection suggests that, though the strength of the
Prince and the beggar is exerted from opposite directions, it has
the same quality—

"when, in the matter between you and me, I give in to you in everything, I cannot myself say whether it be from weakness, or from some
kind of strength. Tell me, my beggar of Teheran, what in your heart

you hold it to be." "My master," said Fath, "you and I, the rich and the poor of this world, are two locked caskets, of which each contains the key to the other."

That last sentence—the metaphor is applied by Fath to all the polarities of life—is the consolatory point of the tale. For it shows Charlie that the opposition and interdependence of himself and his public is in the nature of things. We are reminded in the end that Charlie and Aeneas are counterparts like the Prince and Fath. "The two small gentlemen, each at his side of the table, smoked on in peace, and gazed at the faint blue tobacco smoke."

It is amazing how many of the themes of *Winter's Tales* are resolved through being combined in Aeneas's tale. Even the "blue" motif is alluded to through the color of the tobacco smoke and the blue evenings through which the Prince searches for Fath. The tale offers the archetype of the many mirror images in the volume. The most obvious are the two sisters of "Slave-owners", and Charlie and the young man with the carnation. But there are others—the sailor boy and the falcon, Sune and Granze as opposite images of the King, the old nobleman and the old peasant woman of "Sorrow-acre", Peter and Rosa, Peter and the sea, and Rosa herself and the sea. The fable of the Prince and the beggar offers as an object of contemplation all that Isak Dinesen has been saying about symbols, about their relation to the principle of incarnation, and about God's Incarnation in Jesus. Like God when He played at being a man, the Prince does not suffer the beggar's existence as Fath does; nor does he "absolve" Fath of his beggar's condition. But the Prince does through his disguise turn the beggar's existence into a symbol, and he therefore makes it possible for Fath to contemplate and endure and even rejoice in his condition.

Chapter 6

DIAGRAMS OF SPIRIT: *LAST TALES*

IN 1944, while Denmark was still under German occupation, there appeared in Copenhagen a novel called *Gengældelsens Veje* (*Ways of Retribution*) by a Frenchman, Pierre Andrézel, who was acknowledged on the jacket to be a mysterious figure. It was an open secret that the author was Isak Dinesen. Not only was the publisher hers, but the person who had allegedly translated the novel into Danish was her secretary, Clara Svendsen.

When the newspaper *Politiken* named her as the author, Isak Dinesen sent in a reply saying that even if she were the author she would not admit it, for a pseudonym is a game readers ought to play along with. It was clear, she said, that the novel had been written for entertainment and that Andrézel might not want to take responsibility for it. " 'In an exceptional time, he has written an exception to his own work.' " She pointed out the remark of one of the characters, which appears as epigraph to the novel: " 'You serious people must not be too hard on human beings for what they choose to amuse themselves with when they are shut up as in a prison, and are not even allowed to say that they are prisoners. If I do not soon get a little bit of fun, I shall die.' "[1] The prison was occupied Denmark. In her fashion, Isak Dinesen was publicly separating this novel from her serious work.

Andrézel's novel appeared in Britain in 1946, and in America in 1947, under the title *The Angelic Avengers*. Isak Dinesen was annoyed when it was taken in America by The Book-of-the-Month-Club, for she did not think it fit to stand with her other work. In a *Paris Review* interview of 1956, she finally acknowledged the novel as her "illegitimate child", and explained how, finding herself bored under the German occupation and in want of money, she asked her publisher for an advance and a stenographer, and dictated the novel, improvising it as she went along.[2]

[1] Isak Dinesen's article is reprinted in Brix, *Karen Blixens Eventyr*, pp. 254-57.
[2] Autumn, pp. 47-48.

Angelic Avengers, as we shall call it, has no literary value and
need not detain us. As a melodramatic thriller, however, written
in the style of certain early Victorian English novels, it makes
good reading. Set in the England of the 1840's, the opening
chapters, in which the beautiful, pure and orphaned young
governess flees the improper advances of her employer, might be
a parody of *Jane Eyre*. Lucan flees to her beautiful and pure
young friend Zosine, who has at that point to leave her own
home. The two girls fall in with a puritanical old Scottish couple,
the Reverend and Mrs Pennhallow, who take them to a country
house in France for the apparently philanthropic purpose of
educating them. The girls discover that the Pennhallows are
monsters who use their mask of holiness to ensnare young girls
and sell them into white slavery. Lucan and Zosine, however,
are not to be sold; they are to be well treated in order to throw
the police off the scent. In the most exciting part of the book, the
girls try to keep the Pennhallows from knowing that they know,
and come to realize that the Pennhallows do know and are trying
to do away with them. After all possible tricks of plot have been
pulled, Pennhallow hangs himself and the girls marry highly
desirable young men.

Even such light work gives evidence of Isak Dinesen's skill and
intelligence. The sense of horrifying discovery is beautifully
rendered, as is the full impact of the Pennhallows' wickedness.
Pennhallow comes off as another one of Isak Dinesen's extraordinarily intelligent characters. The ingenious morality by
which he justifies his crimes and binds his wife and his male
accomplice to him through their idealism is the negative statement of Isak Dinesen's moral monism. Pennhallow recalls the
puritanical clergymen of the stories, who come as close to being
villains as anyone does in Isak Dinesen's serious work. The
comparison should make us realize that the poles of good and
evil, that are separated among the different characters of *Angelic
Avengers*, are combined within the same characters in the stories—
that there are no villains in Isak Dinesen's serious work.

In his review of *Angelic Avengers* for *The New York Times*, Robert
Gorham Davis pointed out a possible allegory of Denmark under
the occupation. He suggested that Pennhallow might, with his
remarkable eyes and curious voice, represent Hitler; and that
the well-treated Lucan and Zosine would be in the position of

Denmark, which received special privileges from the Nazis because they wanted to make it a showcase of the New Order. The Danish title would bear, therefore, on the question of retribution for Germany, and the novel might be an answer to the revanchist play, *Niels Ebbesen*, written by the Danish resistance fighter Kaj Munk in 1943. Zosine wants justice, which means the worst possible punishment, for Pennhallow. But Lucan, who speaks for Isak Dinesen, wants mercy.[1] Isak Dinesen intimated to me that she had some such allegorical intention as this. But the novel is less interesting, especially now, as political allegory than as plain melodrama.

After the war, Isak Dinesen became a public figure in Denmark, writing and speaking on questions of the day. When the outbreak of the war interfered with her plan to join Farah on a pilgrimage to Mecca, she, to relieve her frustration, marched into the office of the newspaper *Politiken* and asked for a job as a correspondent anywhere outside Denmark. *Politiken*, together with a Norwegian and a Swedish newspaper, assigned her to spend a month in London, Paris and Berlin, respectively, and to send back four articles from each belligerent capital. She went to Berlin first, on March 1, 1940, and returned to Denmark on April 2 to write her articles on Berlin. The Germans occupied Denmark on April 9, so she was not able to publish her articles or go on to London and Paris. In 1948, she published her four Berlin articles in the magazine *Heretica*, under the title, "Breve fra et Land i Krig" ("Letters from a Country at War").

Her criticism of Nazi totalitarianism shows that her own political ideas are in the tradition that has produced modern liberalism—that she is really in her political thinking recalling liberals to their true tradition and their true ideals. The thing that appals her about Nazi society is that it glorifies will power, that its achievement is not a growth but a mechanical *tour de force* that suppresses the human and natural desire out of which, for her, all good things come. She opposes to Germanic will power the English quality—"that particular kind of confidence in God's grace that is called humor".[2]

She wrote in 1952 against vivisection; and spoke, at a Women's Rights Congress in 1953, for the right of women to develop as

[1] *New York Times Book Review*, January 5, 1947, pp. 9, 22.
[2] *Heretica*, nos. 4, 5, 1948, p. 337.

women not men.[1] Her talks on the Danish radio became famous. In *Daguerreotypier* (*Daguerreotypes*), two charming talks of January 1, 7, 1951, published as a booklet, Isak Dinesen cuts through the difference between the aristocratic past and the democratic present by suggesting that the real change is in the thing valued. Taking her cue from Aldous Huxley's essay "Comfort", she says that the past valued prestige, which cannot be shared, while the present values comfort, which is easily shared. The epoch of prestige could have used Voltaire's motto: *"C'est le superflu qui est le nécessaire"*, because superfluity turned the material thing into a symbol of grandeur. In a brilliant piece of social analysis that explains her preoccupation in the stories with the change in women's fashions, she sees the change during World War I to the vertical line and the hungry look as a reassertion in the epoch of comfort of the aristocratic spirit. "Hunger became the symbol of the élite. The *superflu* here threw the *nécessaire* completely away."[2]

She paid a certain price during this period for fame and for using pseudonyms, in that two Danish writers published under pseudonyms and gave out the impression that these were still other pseudonyms for Karen Blixen. One was Poul Sørensen, who may have intended a friendly hoax in publishing a short story under the name of Joachim Stenzelius.[3] But the other was Isak Dinesen's friend, Kelvin Lindemann, who under the pseudonym of Alexis Hareng published in 1953 a novel in her style, called *En Aften i Kolera-Aaret* (*An Evening in the Cholera Year*), that in the United States and Britain appeared in Lindemann's name as *The Red Umbrellas*.[4] Isak Dinesen sued Lindemann's Danish publisher, Carit Andersen, but without success. She never got over the bitterness of this affair, and referred to it often in her conversation.

Although her health had not been good since her return from Africa, bad health became the over-riding problem of her life in the 1950's. In 1946, she underwent an operation on her spine that was designed to cut off certain nerves and thus relieve her of

---

[1] *Omkring den Nye Lov om Dyreforsøg* (*Concerning the New Vivisection Law*) (Copenhagen: Politiken, 1952). *En Baaltale med 14 Aars Forsinkelse* (*Bonfire Speech 14 Years Too Late*) (Copenhagen: Berlingske Forlag, 1953).

[2] *Daguerreotypier* (Copenhagen: Gyldendal, 1951), p. 65.

[3] "Enkelegen" ("Widow's Games"), in the Swedish magazine, *All Världens Berättare* (March 3, 1953) and in a collection of Danish ghost stories edited by Sørensen (*Gys og Genfærd: Danske Spøgelseshistorier*, Copenhagen: Borgen, 1952).

[4] New York: Appleton-Century-Croft, 1955; London; Methuen, 1956.

painful attacks that she had been suffering since her return from Africa. In 1955, these attacks had returned, her weight was reduced to 85 pounds, and she had to undergo in August a second, very serious spinal operation. This time the doctors found something besides what they had been looking for. This other thing, an ulcer, led in 1956 to a third operation in which most of her stomach was cut away; so that she could hardly from that time eat anything, and her weight remained under 70 pounds. It was characteristic of her that she managed to turn even this disability into an elegant joke, by letting it be known that she lived on oysters, asparagus and champagne.

By 1955, she had in preparation both *Last Tales* and *Anecdotes of Destiny*. Impressed by the prices paid by American mass-circulation magazines, she talked as early as 1948 of collecting the stories she would publish in American magazines into a volume to be called *Anecdotes of Destiny*. "Babette's Feast" and "The Ring", both collected in *Anecdotes*, appeared respectively in June and July 1950 in *Ladies' Home Journal*. "Babette's Feast" was translated into Danish by Jorgen Claudi for radio perform-ances on November 24, 1950, and February 8, 1952; Claudi's translation appeared in 1952 in book form.[1] Isak Dinesen translated "Babette" herself for the Danish edition of *Anecdotes*.

She had by 1950 started work on her big novel *Albondocani*. A chapter of it, "The Cardinal's Third Tale", appeared as a deluxe book in Denmark in 1952.[2] Writing on December 19, 1952, to Robert Haas of Random House, Isak Dinesen proposed a plan for three volumes—*The Cardinal's Third Tale*, which she would translate into English; a collection of short stories she was work-ing on, to be called *New Winter's Tales*; and "my collection of short stories published in American magazines, *Anecdotes of Destiny*. . . . I very much want to have these three books published at the same time. Perhaps you will not agree or even understand, but I should not like to reappear to my readers as the author of any of these particular books *singly*. I think it might be an amus-ing thing to have them appear hand in hand!"

Random House decided against publishing "The Cardinal's

---

[1] *Babettes Gæstebud* (Copenhagen: Fremad), under the name of Isak Dinesen since the story first appeared in the United States. The title page mentions Swedish radio performances on April 18 and 19, 1951.

[2] *Kardinalens Tredie Historie* (Copenhagen: Gyldendal), illus. Erik Clemmesen.

Third Tale" as a separate volume. But that, together with the other chapters from *Albondocani*, combined with *New Winter's Tales* to make up *Last Tales*. Isak Dinesen had an idea of publishing *Last Tales* and *Anecdotes* in a single volume, and then she proposed publishing them as two volumes simultaneously. Her publishers turned down both proposals. They preferred to publish the volumes separately and with an interval between them. Judging by the titles of the volumes, Haas assumed in a letter of August 13, 1956, that the Baroness was planning to bring out *Anecdotes* f.rst and then *Last Tales*. But Isak Dinesen wrote back very emphatically, on September 25, that if the books could not be published simultaneously, then she wanted as short an interval as possible between them and she definitely wanted *Last Tales* to be published first. "I hope you will understand my view: that I do not want after such a long silence to reappear to my readers with *Anecdotes of Destiny*,—the which, although I do not really consider this book to be of a lower literary quality than *Last Tales*, to me myself is played on a different kind of instrument to *Last Tales*, and does carry less weight."

It is clear from all this that Isak Dinesen felt that her reappearance after fifteen years (*Angelic Avengers* did not count) would have to be something of a sensation if it was not to be an anticlimax. She did not trust any one part of her work to create such a sensation, but she thought that in the bulk, and with a replay of her whole repertoire of styles, she might succeed. She was right, for the appearance so close together of two successful volumes brought her very vividly back to mind—especially in America and England where she had not, as in Denmark, her existence as a public figure, so that even the people who went on reading her first three books had little idea what had become of her. With the publication of these volumes of 1957 and 1958, a number of literary people in this country, myself included, came to feel that Isak Dinesen had now produced an *œuvre* and was ripe for serious critical consideration.[2]

After the dark year of 1955—the year when, thinking she "had got but a short time left to me in this earth",[1] she conceived the title *Last Tales*—her life brightened. The operation of 1956

[1] Letter to Haas, September 25, 1956.
[2] *Last Tales* was taken by the highbrow American book club, The Reader's Subscription; Lionel Trilling reviewed it for them (see *The Griffin*, January 1958).

relieved much of her pain, and she was able to return to work with new hope and vigor. She made a very happy trip that summer to Rome, where Eugene Walter interviewed her for *The Paris Review*. When she returned to Rome for the week of November 3, 1957, Eugene Walter arranged in her honor a *Festival of the Two Monkeys*, which lasted three evenings and drew its guests from the worlds of high society, diplomacy and the arts. The first evening was devoted to painters; the third was an evening of musical performances. On the second evening, there was presented in the apartment of the John Beckers in Palazzo Caetani a marionette comedy, published in the memorial anthology, that Walter wrote about her for the occasion. After the play, the Beckers' little daughter appeared dressed in golden leaves and led her to a room filled with tiny gifts for her—such things as cups and saucers painted with butterflies, a crystal pendant from a dwelling of George Sand, candied violets in a cloisonné box. The festival was a wittily appropriate tribute to her.

In 1957, even before *Last Tales* came out in November, she was elected to Honorary Membership in The American Academy and National Institute of Arts and Letters and was talked of for the Nobel Prize. She was a leading contender for the Nobel Prize every year after that. The first four months of 1959 she spent in America at the invitation of the Ford Foundation's Fund for the Advancement of Education, and of the Institute of Contemporary Arts. She told on film for the Encyclopedia Britannica Films, and in recitals in New York, Washington and Boston, "The Wine of the Tetrarch" from "Deluge" and the African reminiscence, "Barua a Soldani", that was later collected in *Shadows*. She gave three recitals to packed houses at the YMHA Poetry Center in New York, and added as an encore in her last recital the story of the blue eyes from "Peter and Rosa".[1]

Her American visit, undertaken at great risk to her health, was a triumph for her; for she always felt she was most appreciated here. She was widely feted and publicized, appeared on television shows, and was guest of honor at a dinner of The American Academy and National Institute of Arts and Letters. The strain of all this activity was in fact too much for her, and she had to be hospitalized before returning. She returned to

---

[1] A cartoon in the *New York Times Book Review* (March 8, 1959, p. 2) showed two beatniks in an expresso house—one asking, "Did you catch Isak Dinesen at the Y?"

Denmark, however, in a state of exhilaration that carried her through the production of *Shadows on the Grass*. Her old marion-ette play *Revenge of Truth* was performed on television on October 3, 1960, and appeared as a booklet the same year. Just before *Shadows* came out, she was hospitalized again, in the fall of 1960, and she declined from that time until her death at the age of seventy-seven on September 7, 1962.

I have the following account from her secretary, Clara Svendsen, of her last year of life.

After the hospital she had a quiet time at home, and she had one of her oldest friends here on Christmas evening. But in the beginning of the New Year things were bad again, and from sheer exhaustion and malnutrition she had a fall in her bathroom and broke a rib. Then some friends of mine made me buy a kitchen machine for making fresh vegetable juice, and she drank several big glasses of that daily for three months. . . . This really gave her sufficient strength to spend a happy spring and summer, with house guests and small parties, walks in the nearest part of the garden, many sunny hours on the veranda looking out on the sea. But when the winter vegetables began to get dreary, we slackened the efforts with the juice ration, and when the brief asparagus season was past, she ate practically no proper food either. . . . During August, she developed some nasty new symptoms . . . which the doctors said were a result of malnutrition. Still on September 5, playing bezique with her and listening to a new record-player in the evening, the idea never entered my mind that when I had supported her upstairs to her bedroom she would never come down again alive. But that is how it was.

On September 6, she seemed very sleepy. About half past one, she had difficulty in speaking. I thought she was just exhausted. But the housekeeper, whom I summoned to get some consommé and lemon juice, was less optimistic and very soon gravely alarmed. Thanks to her, the Baroness's brother Thomas and his wife arrived in time for her to recognize them. After an injection, she fell asleep and never woke up again. She died at 5 p.m. on Friday the 7th.

Right to the end, however, her life was full of plans and activity. In order to keep Rungstedlund intact, she had, before coming to America, concluded, together with her sister and brother who were co-owners, an arrangement by which they gave the estate to Denmark for a bird sanctuary to be open to the public. She was to put all her earnings into a fund to maintain the estate, and was to have the use of the house and the right to draw on the fund while she lived. She had made a radio talk in which she asked her listeners to contribute to the fund a krone

(1/7 of a dollar) and no more than a krone ("for that would spoil the fun"), and she had been gratified by the deluge of 90,000 coins that poured in. Just before her death, she wrote an article for *Vogue*, that appeared posthumously, in which she made a similar appeal to the American public.[1] The house is now being used for meetings of the Danish Academy, which she helped to found. It tickled her fancy to show visitors to Rungstedlund the site of her grave; and it is there she is buried, under an old beech tree, at the foot of "Ewald's Hill", beside a favorite dog.

On the days she felt well, she thought she might just finish *Albondocani* before she died; when she felt bad, she was sure she would not. But she talked to me in September 1961 of bringing out very soon a volume of five stories to be called, like Dumas' novel, which she admired, *Twenty Years After*. The title story would be a sequel to "Copenhagen Season" (*LT*); it would follow the fortunes of Ib's sister Drude. The volume would also include two stories not finished in time for *Anecdotes*, "The Bear and the Kiss" and "The Loyal Mistress"; a story about a boy who catches an eagle; and a story called "Second Meeting" about a conversation between Byron and Pino Pizzuti, the philosophical marionette master of the *Albondocani* stories in *Last Tales*.

"Second Meeting", which I have since read in typescript, would have been, had Isak Dinesen lived to perfect it, a very powerful story. It takes place just before Byron sails to his death in Greece; and the point is that Byron's final defeat was necessary to give his life the artistic shape that makes it, rather than his poems, his greatest work. Pino, who looks like Byron, was able by the resemblance to save Byron's life fourteen years earlier in Malta. Now Pino returns to provide Byron with that sight of his double that portends death. Every story, says Pino, requires a second meeting to complete it; the story lies between the first and second meeting.

The view here is tragic. But the last story that Isak Dinesen completed to her satisfaction before her death (she sent the story to Random House, but did not live to translate it herself into Danish) is the comic masterpiece, *Ehrengard*, that appeared as a posthumous volume in the United States, Britain and Denmark in 1963.

[1] November 1, 1962, pp. 132-34, 170.

In the British and Danish editions, which follow Isak Dinesen's arrangement, *Last Tales* (1957) is divided into three sections. The first seven stories, from "The Cardinal's First Tale" through "The Blank Page", appear under the heading, "Chapters from the Novel *Albondocani*". "The Caryatids" and "Echoes" appear under the heading, "New Gothic Tales"; and "A Country Tale", "Copenhagen Season" and "Converse at Night in Copenhagen" appear under the heading, "New Winter's Tales".

We have already discussed "The Cardinal's First Tale". The next three chapters from *Albondocani*, "The Cloak", "Night Walk" and "Of Secret Thoughts and of Heaven", show what Isak Dinesen meant when she said that each chapter of *Albondocani*—which takes place in the Kingdom of Naples in the 1830's—was to be a complete story in itself and at the same time—like Jules Romains' *Les Hommes de Bonne Volonté*—part of a connected story.[1]

In "The Cloak", the great old sculptor and revolutionary, Leonidas Allori, the Lion of the Mountains, is arrested and condemned to death for high treason.

His pupils wept and stormed. For to them he had been spiritual father, archangel and immortal. They assembled in Pierino's hostelry outside the town, in a studio or in an attic, where they could sob, two or three, in each other's arms, or—like a big tree in a gale with its bare branches reaching upward—crowded in a cluster could shake ten pairs of clenched fists to the sky, in a cry for rescue of their beloved, and for revenge on tyranny.

The pupils are arranged like sculpture, and the arrangement helps establish that elevation and nobility of style which is the great achievement of *Albondocani*.

Because the characters are larger than life in the manner of sculpture—of the sculptural tradition that runs from Michelangelo through Bernini to the early nineteenth-century Danish sculptor, Thorvaldsen—we find ourselves, without any sense of disproportion, reading a divine story behind the human one. When we learn that Angelo Santasilia, Allori's most beloved disciple whom he calls son, does not grieve because his heart is filled with passion for the master's beautiful young wife, Lucrezia, we see in the eternal triangle with which the story deals the

[1] An Italian Prince Albondocani—whose name derives from *The Arabian Nights*, probably from that of the Sultan Al-Bundukdari in the *Supplemental Nights*—was to appear and reappear throughout the novel.

Oedipal situation, and the recurring situation in which the disciple and son both inherits from and plunders the master and father. But we see also Adam and Eve with God in the Garden, the Holy Family, and Christ's betrayal by Judas (with love, or the mystery of Judas's motivation, the third force); and all these human and divine stories seem to be related as aspects of a single story. The plot, for all its ramifications, is simple and definite in outline. It is itself conceived like sculpture in that it is static. It works through the balance of masses rather than movement; and it ties together master and disciple, father and son, through a visible object, the cloak, as a sculptor might—in the way the serpents tie together the Laocoön group. The effect is to make the plot seem as tangible and non-discursive as sculpture.

Angelo's love of Lucrezia proceeds from his love of Leonidas. Leonidas had dwelt upon Lucrezia's beauty to Angelo, and, when she posed for him, had made Angelo sit beside him and carve her, too—even interrupting his own work "to point out the beauties in the living, breathing and blushing body before them, enraptured and inspired as in front of a classic work of art". Leonidas was in the position of the master and father who, even to his own cost, must pass on the tradition. He was also in the position of God when He gave Adam the woman who was to cause Adam's rebellion against God.

After trying to resist their passion, the young people finally gave themselves up to their destiny and planned a rendezvous for a Saturday night two weeks hence that turned out to be the night before Leonidas's execution. Expecting trouble, Leonidas had a week before his arrest decided to send Lucrezia to a friend's house in the country, and she told Angelo how he was to throw pebbles at her window as a signal for her to open it. It is a sign of the inextricably triangular relationships of this story that these plans were made in a room next to the studio where the master was working and that the door to the studio was open. The extent to which Leonidas knows of the affair is the enigma of the story.

Leonidas was arrested on a Sunday morning and condemned to die on the following Sunday morning. He asks for a twelve-hour parole to take leave of his wife, and is granted this request on the condition that his favorite disciple, Angelo, take his place as hostage. Angelo rushes to the prison as passionately as he would have rushed to Lucrezia. When Leonidas speaks passionately of his coming night with Lucrezia, Angelo realizes that this is the Saturday night of his rendezvous with her.

Leonidas may have overheard Angelo tell Lucrezia of the "large and fine cloak of violet goat's wool with brown embroidery" that he had bought for his nocturnal journey. Leonidas now asks to borrow the cloak for his own nocturnal journey. " 'In my native parish,' " he says, " 'a bridegroom wears a cloak like this on his wedding day.' " And he recalls the time Angelo collapsed of cold and exhaustion in the mountains and Leonidas wrapped his own cloak around them both. Angelo hears in all this a bitter reprimand. Since Leonidas tells how he will throw a pebble against Lucrezia's window, Angelo is sure that Lucrezia will call out his name to the man in the violet cloak and that their treachery will then be known.

This is an example of the balance of masses I have mentioned. It is developed with steadily increasing irony. Leonidas saved Angelo's life with a cloak, and now a cloak symbolizes both Angelo's repayment and his treachery. There is also the developing implication that, by putting on Angelo's cloak, Leonidas is saving Angelo's life a second time—saving this time his spiritual life by preventing him from committing the sin he plans. Leonidas delivers a beautiful sermon on faithfulness, which can be understood as both a reprimand to Angelo and a justification of his unfaithfulness. Leonidas declares his own faithfulness to this earth, and faithfulness to the earth would justify Angelo and Lucrezia in giving themselves up to the destiny their passion dictates.

Leonidas's creed is not only appropriate to the artist; it also sets forth the paradox of the moral life, which is lived between opposite imperatives. We must be faithful to others and to ourselves. The son must obey and revere his father, yet he must psychologically overthrow him and biologically replace him. It is in God's scheme that we rebel even against Him in the course of our moral development. In the enigma for Angelo of the intention behind Leonidas's words and actions, we see the enigma of the moral life, which must be lived without certain knowledge of God's intention and judgment.

Leonidas says he will return the next morning with his eyes closed in order to preserve, before his eyes are finally bandaged for the execution, the vision of the best earth has to offer—his final sight of Lucrezia at daybreak. Only once will he open his eyes, " 'to see your face, which has been so dear to me' ".

During that Saturday night in prison, Angelo lives through the whole Christian scheme of moral experience. He has three dreams, each worse than the last. He dreams, finally, of murdering Leonidas and Lucrezia in the midst of their lovemaking. But when at daybreak the turnkey wakes him and suggests that Leonidas is not coming back and that Angelo will have to die in his place, Angelo's heart is filled with joy that God has granted him "this happy, easy way out". As he thinks it is for Leonidas he will die, he feels himself pardoned.

Leonidas's closed eyes, when he enters between two gendarmes who hold his arms, recall the blank unseeing eyes of the greatest statues. Sensing where Angelo is standing, he unhooks the cloak from his own shoulders and lays it around the young man's shoulders even as the young man had laid it around him. Again the cloak brings them together, making them two aspects of one person. Angelo thinks Leonidas will perhaps not open his eyes and look at him after all. He dreads that gaze; yet if Leonidas does not open his eyes, it will mean he does not want to spoil his final vision of earth with the face of his faithless disciple.

But whenever had Allori not kept a given word? The hand which—as it put the cloak round him—rested against Angelo's neck forced his head a little forward, the large eyelids trembled and lifted, and the master looked into the eyes of the disciple. But the disciple could never afterward remember or recall the look. A moment later he felt Allori's lips on his cheek.

Leonidas's look is enigmatic as the absolute always is.

This last scene cannot be understood in simple naturalistic terms. We cannot simply ask whether Leonidas found out about the treachery of his wife and his disciple, what he felt about it, and why he acted toward Angelo as he did. For Isak Dinesen has, through her simple fable, telescoped different levels of action and motive and even different delineations of these three characters as persons separate from each other. There are things we know on one level of consciousness that we do not know on another (the sort of things Angelo came to know through his three dreams); so that Leonidas could know and not know, in the way every father knows and does not know about his son's betrayal of him.

Inasmuch as Leonidas and Angelo are separate egos locked in the boundaries of their own bodies, Leonidas would resent Angelo as a rival. But as a father, and even more deeply as an agent of the biological and spiritual tradition, Leonidas can only give Angelo his blessing and lay the mantle on his shoulders, passing on to him his woman and his craft—for Angelo is himself reborn. The man who was to have gone, and the man who in fact did go, to Lucrezia in that cloak were the same archetypal husband; just as Lucrezia is the archetypal wife who is for every man his mother reborn.

As always in her work, Isak Dinesen is dealing with the way in which relative or human motives are unconsciously at the service of absolute or divine intention. She has, however, in *Last Tales* and *Anecdotes*, gone farther than before toward saying all that she has to say through plot. Her plots have become more diagrammatic, with even less disparity than before between the mechanics of the story and symbolic meaning. Her last two volumes of stories represent an advance in that the best stories come closest to being perfect fables or myths or parables. Certain other virtues have been sacrificed to this effect, but it is the effect toward which she worked all through her career.

In explaining to me the difference between the novel and the *story* as she conceived it, she said that in the novel all kinds of details are there simply to give a sense of reality, but in a story every detail—a letter, a handkerchief (a cloak, we might add)—must bear directly on the action and meaning. In *Anna Karenina*, Anna fumbles with her handbag before committing suicide; that, she said, would never happen in the story. Her remarks explain the method of "The Cloak". For the fumbling with the handbag is in *Anna* for its lifelike irrelevance and as the patently inadequate sign of internal agitation. But in the *story*, where the internal has been completely externalized, there is no place for the kind of detail that we call "realistic" just because it reminds us that the external world is different from the internal.

Leonidas's simulation of blindness was probably suggested by Mann's brilliant interpretation, in *Joseph and His Brothers*, of Isaac's blindness. Isaac, who *thought* he preferred Esau to Jacob, became blind, Mann tells us, because only so could he be betrayed into following his own deepest desire, and therefore the will of God, by conferring the blessing upon Jacob.[1] Leonidas returns with his eyes closed as a sign that he is completely the agent of destiny, that he takes God's rather than his own view of Angelo's treachery, that he knows *who Angelo is*—himself reborn —and must therefore bless him. It is because Leonidas sees that the thing has happened which must happen that the gaze he turns for a moment upon Angelo is Godlike.

Angelo's references to his own "blindness" are connected with Leonidas's "blindness" in that Angelo, too, as he discovers his deepest desire, is in the process of discovering *who he is* and is therefore moving along his appointed path. So far, Angelo's sin and redemption are only potential. Like all Christians, he is condemned and absolved in advance; Leonidas's gaze and kiss are like Christian revelation. The next two stories, "Night Walk" and "Of Secret Thoughts and of Heaven", are not nearly so good as "The Cloak", because they have little plot—they are largely discursive. They retain symbolic power, however, because they take off from the fable of "The Cloak"; they draw out its implications in a language which, for all its discursiveness, is the nobly allusive language of parable.

Smitten by guilt after Leonidas's death, Angelo, in "Night Walk", descends spiritually into hell, where he learns in a surrealistic nightmare experience that he is Judas. He also learns, however, that only the great sinner has a spiritual intensity equal to that of the saint and is therefore ready for salvation.

The same point is made in "Of Secret Thoughts and of Heaven", which takes place seven years later. Angelo is a famous sculptor and the owner of a fine villa. He has married Lucrezia, and they have reproduced by means of their three children, two boys and a girl, the triangle of the first story. Significantly, Lucrezia is expecting a fourth child.

Angelo speaks of his happiness, which is marred only by the secret Lucrezia keeps from him. " 'For I do not know what happened on the night when I was hostage for Leonidas Allori in prison.' " The setting of this story is purgatory or the fallen but beautiful world of the successful middle-aged man, which is imperfect only in that the absolute remains disturbingly enigmatic. Angelo is talking to Pino Pizzuti, the puppeteer of the

[1] Trans. H. T. Lowe-Porter, New York: Knopf, 1934, pp. 214-16; London: Martin Secker, 1934, pp. 189-91.

previous story who has lost the use of three fingers of his right hand. Pino is no longer sure it is necessary to go to heaven; and, to make his point, he tells a story, reminiscent in its sweetness of Dante or early Italian painting, in which even in heaven Christ's blessed grandmother, Saint Anne, looks back for an example of miracle to the simplest domestic detail on earth.

When asked if he expects to go to heaven, Angelo, who has been modelling tiny figures of clay, says that " 'a man is more than one man' " and his life " 'is more than one life' ". He sets one of his small clay figures on a balustrade. This young, unfallen Angelo, who aspired to be a great artist and possess his master's wife, " 'will not go to heaven' ", he says, for he did not yet know he would have to pay a moral price for these things. He sets another figure on the balustrade, at some distance from the first and to the right of it. This Angelo, the famous sculptor and husband of Lucrezia, " 'will not go to heaven either . . . because he is not at all eager to go there' ". He sets the third figure between and behind the other two.

"Do you see, Pino?" he said softly. "These three tiny toy figures are placed to mark three corners of a rectangle, in which the width is to the length as the length to the sum of the two. These, you know, are the proportions of the golden section."

But, he concludes, the young man of the second story who was in hell, suffering the torments of guilt—that young man will go to heaven.

The passage finally explains Leonidas's admonition to " 'keep always in your heart the divine law of proportion, the golden section' ". The reference is to *De Divina Proportione* (1496), the treatise of Leonardo's friend, Luca Pacioli, which sets forth, in the proportion of the segment of a line to the whole line, a relation among three points that determines the fourth point of a perfect rectangle. Leonidas's admonition explains the diagrammatic structure of these three stories around the number *three*; for Leonidas, Pino and Angelo refer to the divine proportion as a principle of life as well as art. One recalls Jung's theory that the ideas of threefoldness and fourfoldness are a "spontaneous product" of the collective unconscious—that *three* represents the relative and *four* the absolute.[1]

Isak Dinesen has in this new diagram moved beyond the

---

[1] *Science of Mythology* pp. 22-23.

diagram in *Winter's Tales* of the " 'two locked caskets, of which each contains the key to the other' ". There she reconciled us to polarities (life and death, man and woman), but here she seems to have realized that simple polarities produce a stasis, that it is the third or complicating force—the young man in hell, the sinner—that accounts for development and the divine art of the story. It is because the rectangle is already determined by the three points of it visible on earth that Angelo and Pino do not feel the need to go to heaven. The fact that Lucrezia is expecting her fourth child is a sign that the absolute is potential in earthly events.

Between the solid masses of "The Cardinal's First Tale" and the "Cloak" stories on the one hand, and "The Cardinal's Third Tale" on the other, Isak Dinesen interposes a charming little *jeu d'esprit*, which she hesitated at first to include in the volume for fear that it was, as she wrote to Robert Haas on September 25, 1956, "too nonsensical". If "Tales of Two Old Gentlemen" is nonsense, it is the kind that only the finest mind could have produced. For it deals most cogently with the irrationality of women, which is, as the first old gentleman suggests in his tale, in tune with the irrationality of the universe. The Sibylla of Babylon gives Alexander the Great just such a nonsensical answer as the universe returns to questions that exceed the limits of rational inquiry. The second old gentleman's tale suggests that the apparent irrationality of women may be a superior rationality.

" 'I, too, can tell a tale which may somehow illuminate our theme,' " says Cardinal Salviati, of "The Cardinal's First Tale", in the opening lines of "The Cardinal's Third Tale". Since we do not know what theme the Cardinal is referring to, our minds move back to "Tales of Two Old Gentlemen", the theme of which is in fact illuminated by what follows. For Lady Flora Gordon, the heroine of "The Cardinal's Third Tale", is just what the first old gentleman said no real woman could be. She is an atheist and rationalist, alienated from God and nature, who considers her individuality as a thing really delineated by the confines of her body. She loathes the flesh and all physical contact, recoils from love, and despises men, setting herself up in rivalry to them. Everything we need to know about Lady Flora is condensed in the fabulous circumstance that she is a giantess, a beautiful, aristocratic, Scottish giantess—a circumstance that externalizes completely a psychological, spiritual, social, cultural and historical condition.

Her size brings back the theme of sculpture. She is often compared to the statue of a goddess, and in this aspect she is to be understood as too grand in body and soul, as well as in the style of her beauty, for mortal men or at least for puny modern men. Isak Dinesen is redoing, far more successfully this time, the kind of woman she attempted to portray in Athena Hopballehus in "The Monkey". But the figure of the giantess has in this story a new significance. Isak Dinesen directs our attention to the Second Book of *Gulliver's Travels*, where Swift uses the size of his giantesses to reveal the grossness of the human body. An admirer of Swift, Lady Flora feels as he does about her own body; so that her size is, in this opposite aspect, the externalization of her feeling that she has too much body.

Since the Scots are notoriously Protestant and puritan, the Scotswoman stands out in almost comic contrast to the intensely Catholic world of Rome, where the narrated events mainly take place. The Protestants, who do not make a virtue of celibacy and asceticism as the Catholics do, are nevertheless hostile to the senses as the Catholics are not. Although she has long since ceased to be religious, Lady Flora is a kind of nun, as a psychological condition—not because she wants to submit to God's will and become His bride, but " 'to corroborate' ", as the Cardinal says, " 'her essential suspicion of both Creator and creation' ".

In the attempt of the humble and saintly Father Jacopo to convert Lady Flora, and in the friendship between them, we see again the contrast and attraction between North and South. Father Jacopo's failure to convert or even understand Lady Flora Gordon has to do with still another set of allusions that derive from her Scottish and aristocratic connections—the allusions to Byron. Byron's mother was a Gordon and a descendant of Scotland's kings. His father was a rake who mistreated her; just as Lady Flora's rakish father betrayed and mistreated her mother, who was like herself a giantess. Lady Flora's frigidity is to be understood as a reaction to her parents' unhappy marriage. Byron's reaction, instead, took the form of sexual promiscuity. What Isak Dinesen seems to be saying in comparing Lady Flora to Swift and Byron is that frigidity and promiscuity are two sides of the puritan coin, and she seems to be contrasting the Protestant division of flesh and spirit with the Catholic view of their harmonious relation.

Lady Flora solves her problem by moving from frigidity to at least symbolic promiscuity, from Swift to Byron. It is a sign that Catholicism is not the solution for her that she leaves Rome to go to Greece where, we are reminded, Byron died. In Missolonghi, the Greek town where Byron died, she discovers the syphilitic sore on her lip that is the sign of her salvation. Father Jacopo fails to understand Lady Flora, because he is provincial and plebeian and cannot therefore understand the Protestant and aristocratic soul. Father Jacopo can only think of altering Lady Flora's nature, of making her humble and obedient in accordance with the Catholic idea of virtue. It takes the saintly but worldly and aristocratic Cardinal Salviati to realize that heaven saves the great individualist through his own nature. " ' "She is a noblewoman, and it is she who will transform the things that touch or strike her—not the outside things that will ever transform her." ' " This is the essence of Byronism.

It is to add to the Catholic position her own qualification of it that Isak Dinesen tells the story from two points of view, Father Jacopo's and the Cardinal's. The Cardinal has had most of the story he is telling from Father Jacopo. He himself witnessed only the dénouement, which Father Jacopo would not have been equipped to understand. The bulk of the story is devoted to conversations between Father Jacopo and Lady Flora that set forth the contrast between Catholicism and a certain quintessential Protestant position. These conversations are the story's main artistic achievement. Although they are not witty—wit would not be appropriate to Father Jacopo—they have the profundity and sweetness, the quality of an amorous exchange between souls, that is characteristic of Isak Dinesen's greatest conversations. Father Jacopo realizes in the course of his conversations with Lady Flora " 'to what extent his own soul was the lover of the woman's soul' ".

The harmonious Catholic view is based on an idea of degree, an idea that each thing achieves perfection within its degree, that is lacking in Protestantism. That is why Protestantism leads to the opposite heresies of revolutionary egalitarianism and Lady

Flora's kind of antiseptic exclusiveness. Both heresies are based on the idea of the individual as a self-contained atom with only tangential or contractual relations to other legally identical individuals. Confusing the doctrine of the brotherhood of man with Jacobinism, Lady Flora sees it as a threat to her individuality; just as she says in regard to the doctrine of Christ's atonement: " ' "Never in my life have I asked any human being—much less any god—to die for me.... What I have neither ordered nor paid for will I not receive." ' " The commercial terminology is significant; for—as we shall see later in "The Immortal Story" (*Anecdotes of Destiny*)—the bookkeeping view of life follows, just as desexualization follows, from the Protestant position.

That is because the fundamental failing of Protestantism is the failing already identified in Isak Dinesen's criticism of the Unitarians. In trying to rationalize Christianity, Protestantism cut fact off from myth and thus lost double vision or the ability to understand symbols. When Father Jacopo speaks of " ' "the oneness of all creation" ' ", Lady Flora says she wants " ' "to be one, and alone in my skin" ' ". She thinks her statement contradicts his, because she thinks an identity can, like an object in physics, occupy only one place at the same time. But Father Jacopo points out that the " ' "likeness between all things" ' " is a metaphorical resemblance that can only be found between dissimilar things. The individuality of each thing is enhanced through the comparison. " ' "I do not," ' " he says, " ' "comment on the likeness of one button of my cassock to another, but I may well allow myself to hold forth on the likeness between the diamond in your ring, which measures not half an inch, and the clear star in the sky, which according to the astronomers is a sun, if not a whole solar system!" ' "

Since Lady Flora compares by measuring, she thinks the size of a thing and its moral highness or lowness are as fixed as its identity. But in metaphorical comparison, it is because things are different that the likeness between them reveals the signature of God's workmanship and therefore wipes out the distinction between big and small, high and low, good and bad. Lady Flora, who does not like metaphors, is shocked by the inappropriateness of the sexual imagery that is used in The Song of Songs to prophesy on the relation between Christ and His Church. It is because she cannot reconcile the "purity" of religion with the "impurity" of sex that she is both irreligious and asexual. The dénouement is shocking, because Lady Flora learns in it to reconcile what she herself considered to be shockingly irreconcilable opposites.

Father Jacopo's most efficacious act is to take her to St Peter's, in the vast spaces of which she finally feels at home. She stands a long time before that bronze seated statue of St Peter, the foot of which has been worn away by pious kisses, as though here at last she had found a man big enough for her. In her attraction to the statue of the holy fisherman, she has found a mythical analogue to her human situation—her attraction to the plebeian Father Jacopo. She returns alone many times afterward to stand before the statue. But she does not stoop to kiss its foot until she "stoops" to awareness of the erotic element in her attraction to her plebeian opposite. This happens on her last evening in Rome. She tells the story of that evening to Cardinal Salviati when they meet, apparently a year later, after her return from Greece. The cathedral was empty and half dark, she says, and in the flickering candlelight St Peter's face seemed to change,

" 'as if his lips moved faintly, and parted. A young man in a brown cloak came into the church, went by me and kissed the foot of the statue. As he passed me I felt a smell of sweat and stable, a smell of the people. I first paid real attention to him after he had passed me, because he stood still so long with his mouth against St Peter's foot. . . . I had thought that the bronze would be ice-cold, but it was warm from the young man's mouth, slightly moist—and that surprised me. Like him, I held my lips against it for a long time.' "

Having got fact and sexuality into connection with religious symbol she has made contact with the external world and is "saved". She had, as Father Jacopo foresaw, to do penance; but she had by sinning to do penance for having been entirely too "pure". When four weeks later she discovered the syphilitic sore on her lip, she remembered Father Jacopo and wondered, she says in the end, whether the sore bore a likeness to a rose or a seal. The answer is to both—to the rose that has always symbolized both sexual and divine love and to the red seal that is reminiscent of covenants sealed in blood. The question shows that Lady Flora now understands the symbolic connection of all things.

The Cardinal meets Lady Flora by chance in a mountain spa resorted to by people with venereal disease, who, because they have learned the worst about themselves, have the " 'fine, gay equipoise' " that Isak Dinesen prescribes for navigating through life's ambiguities. The Cardinal's wittily periphrastic description of the spa exemplifies its spirit; he describes the mercury treatment it offers by quoting the old Latin saying: " 'For one hour with Venus, ten years with Mercury.' " The Latin saying suggests that the spa, with its regenerative waters and pure mountain air, is a station on the mountain of purgatory.

Lady Flora has not, as Father Jacopo expected, abandoned her pride; she has transformed it. Before, she displayed the pride of the outsider. Now, she is at the center of the spa's society and " ' "displays the pride of one initiated" ' "—of one who knows the hundredth name of Allah, a name we may understand to be the name of the devil.

Isak Dinesen wrote of "The Cardinal's Third Tale", when sending it to Robert Haas on April 11, 1952: "Here it seems to shock people a little, but it is not meant to be frivolous, and I hope you will read it in the spirit in which it is written." The story is among her most serious statements on the nature of the spiritual life. But since her statement requires that she reconcile the most disparate things, that she pull salvation out of syphilis, she inevitably runs the risk of seeming merely incongruous. She overcomes, but just overcomes, the danger by an effect of sublimity that is itself a triumph of wit because maintained against incongruity.

But why, we may still ask, does Lady Flora have to contract syphilis vicariously? The situation would have been less repellent had she kissed the man on his own lips. It was important, for one thing, for Isak Dinesen to continue her theme of vicariousness in order to show that sin and redemption take place in the imagination. A woman might sleep with many men and never sin if she did not imagine her action as such; while another might suffer the torments of hell for a sin she had—like Angelo in "The Cloak" trilogy—only desired to commit.

This idea, that moral significance lies in what is thought rather than in what is done, is distinctively modern. It is the criterion by which Kierkegaard distinguishes ancient from modern tragedy.[1] To externalize, however, a spirituality that is by definition incongruent with external conditions would seem to

[1] "The Ancient Tragical Motif as Reflected in the Modern", *Either/Or*, Vol. 1.

be a contradiction in terms, and we would expect the resulting fables to be full of uneasy conjunctions and to be, therefore, ironical and exaggerated, to verge even on grotesqueness and absurdity.

A good example of the problem and the solution is the fact that Lady Flora kisses the man by way of the statue. This shows both the modern disconnection between the individual and the archetype and the need to force the two together to make a most uneasy and therefore distinctively modern solution.[1] Kierkegaard's brilliant analysis of what he calls modern isolation would seem to have influenced the characterization of Lady Flora. "The isolationist idea," says Kierkegaard,

is always in evidence where men assert themselves numerically. When one man will assert himself as one, then this is isolation; in this, all friends of association [i.e. socialism] will concur, even if unable or unwilling to see that there is quite the same isolation when hundreds stress themselves simply and solely as hundreds. . . . This spirit of association is, therefore, in principle just as revolutionary as the spirit it would counteract.[2]

Both socialism and capitalistic individualism are revolutionary because both consider individuals to be self-contained identities rather than incarnations of an archetypal identity. Isak Dinesen's art is designed to represent modern fragmentation in a fable that can overcome it.

"The Blank Page", which closes the *Albondocani* section, brings back briefly the theme of the story introduced in "The Cardinal's First Tale". It offers a diagram of the perfect story as the exceptional and enigmatic case, as the story written upon the blank page.

"The Caryatids", which begins the section called "New Gothic Tales", was originally written for the 1934 volume of *Gothic Tales*. "Caryatids" is subtitled "An Unfinished Gothic Tale", and Isak Dinesen may have withheld it in the hope of one day finishing it. It was first published in the Swedish *Bonnier's Magasin* (March 1938) with an interesting headnote in which the editor, who suggests that the story may have been left

---

[1] Yeats makes similar use of a statue when he speaks of "boys and girls, pale from the imagined love / Of solitary beds", who "pressed at midnight in some public place / Live lips upon a plummet-measured face" ("The Statues").

[2] "Ancient Tragical Motif", New York, p. 139; London, p. 114.

unfinished on purpose, quotes Isak Dinesen's reply to his question on this point. " 'It is best that the story ends where it does. Best for the characters and best for us. I did not dare to continue.' "[1]

Certainly, the story reaches a climax of horror that it would be difficult to top. Except for *Angelic Avengers*, "Caryatids" is Isak Dinesen's only attempt at the horror story. While she showed in "Caryatids" how well she could do the horror story, she also showed by not finishing "Caryatids" that she did not like to do it. She modeled her own fiction, she said, after dream not nightmare, and she objected to Kafka's nightmare quality. Even as a horror story, however, "Caryatids" is in a class, not with *Angelic Avengers*, but with Isak Dinesen's serious work. For it is a story about psychological and moral ambivalence, a story in which the polarities of identity and moral quality are to be found—it is the whole point of the story—within the same characters. In drawing out, as a matter of fact, the nightmare implications of ambivalence, "Caryatids" should remind us that this is what Isak Dinesen generally does not do, that she generally turns ambivalence into a blessing, the sign of our spiritual nature.

"Caryatids" is also unusual in that it begins very slowly with an involved exposition that makes it difficult to get into. The case makes us realize how little exposition there generally is in Isak Dinesen, how little background information is required for her characters to swing into action. That is because their inner reality is defined by appearance, which is why style and gesture have to be exaggerated—to make the inner reality manifest. This is the essence of *story* in Isak Dinesen's sense.

The novelist, on the other hand, preserves the naturalistic appearance of things, but at the price of separating appearance from reality. In "Caryatids", Isak Dinesen operates—until she gets to the most powerful scene, the mill scene—like a novelist. Her handsome young French aristocrats of the 1840's seem perfectly fortunate. But then we are shown through a multitude of details that the reality contradicts the appearance. Philippe and Childerique, who call themselves husband and wife, are really brother and sister; while the emotion that unites Childerique with the young man she calls brother is really the emotion of lovers.

We learn that Philippe's father had a love affair with Child-

[1] P. 269.

erique's mother, the lady of the neighboring estate. When Childerique was born of this union, Philippe's father, who was a widower, moved with Philippe to Canada. Childerique's mother died soon afterward; the man she called father remarried, and the man she called brother was born of this second marriage. Childerique's ostensible father had died by the time Philippe returned to France after his father's death. Shortly after Philippe married Childerique, he discovered the truth in a packet of old letters. He decided not to tell her, because she was so virtuous that the truth, he told himself, would destroy her. But he knew that his real motive was sexual. For he had felt sexual excitement at the discovery that Childerique was his sister, and "he would not suffer her to think with horror of his embrace".

She, Philippe feels, seems to have some instinctive knowledge of the truth; for she acts toward him like a sister, and toward her brother like "a passionate and jealous mistress". Watching sister and brother on the terrace together, Philippe has a momentary vision of his wife as a witch. Philippe does not know that Childerique's brother is announcing to her his decision to marry the miller's widow, a gypsy reputed to be a witch. Childerique tries to dissuade her brother in two opposite ways. She cites the family honor, and asks bitterly why it is the women's task to maintain the purity of the noble houses, " 'to hold up the houses, like those stone figures which they call caryatids?' " On the other hand, she offers to compete with the gypsy woman, without consciously understanding the sexual implications of her offer. When she touches him, the boy turns deadly white, saying " 'No, do not do that. Simkie has held me, holds me, like that.' " At that point, Childerique has a vision of herself like Philippe's vision of her. It adumbrates the thing she is to learn about herself.

The gypsies in this story represent the forces of nature. In themselves, they are neither good nor bad; but they seem bad to those who fear them and would drive them off the estate. The gypsies see as nature sees. They seem sinister for the reason that snakes, with which the gypsies are associated in this story, seem sinister—that they remind us of forces in ourselves of which we are afraid.

In trying to explain his decision to marry a gypsy, Childerique's brother says that he wants to be with people who are at home among the dangerous forces of life. The dangerous force he fears is his apparently incestuous love of Childerique. Because he idealizes Childerique, Simkie's mill figures in his imagination as the bad, low place where he goes for the satisfaction he cannot get from his caryatid sister. The mill, he tells Childerique, is, when he dreams of it, the one place in his dreams she never enters.

When Childerique goes next day to the mill, it is to drive the low gypsy woman off from her brother. But she has another unconscious motive—to obtrude herself in the bad, low place from which her brother has excluded her. Philippe's conscious knowledge of their incestuous relation, and of his own deepest desire, is the condition Childerique must achieve. The gypsy's witchcraft—and here appearance begins to symbolize an inner reality—is the means of bringing the buried truth to light. With her mill wheel, the gypsy churns up the bottommost water, making manifest scenes reflected there in the past. She makes Childerique see with the eye of the pond. The pond is the image of that point where the personal subconscious meets the mindless mind of nature, and Childerique is to move downward and backward into that mind. Her journey into the self is not, however, going to be liberating. It is going to be a nightmare.

In *Out of Africa*, Isak Dinesen defines nightmare as the thing that happens when the idea of necessity enters the free world of dream; so that in this world without purpose or cause and effect, you have the anxious sense that there is a train to catch, yet no way of putting yourself on the road to catching it.[1] The web of necessity is such in "Caryatids" that the knowledge Simkie offers is clearly going to be bought at the price of destruction. Another way of putting it is to say that the world of appearance has up to this point been so solid in its distinction from the inner reality, that the inner reality cannot become objective without destroying existing objective arrangements.

When Simkie asks what Childerique wants the Devil of the water to do for her, Childerique asks " 'that the lord of Haut-Mesnil [her brother] turn entirely . . .' " " 'To me,' " she is going to say; but the gypsy places a finger on her lips, saying names must never be spoken in witchcraft. Witchcraft deals with the mysteries of identity. The gypsy suggests a formula and asks Childerique to approve it. " 'This shall be a charm to turn the

[1] New York, p. 88; London, p. 96.

heart of your brother, your father's son, entirely away from the woman whom he now loves, and thinks of as his wife.' " Thinking the formula refers to the lord of Haut-Mesnil and Simkie, Childerique approves it. But she is, of course, placing a curse upon her own marriage. In expressing her deepest desire, she is destroying existing objective arrangements. Her children, for example, are going to pay the price of her knowledge.

This kind of conflict between desire and necessity does not occur in Isak Dinesen's other stories. Even in her tragic stories— in "The Fish" and "Peter and Rosa", even in "Sorrow-acre"— the self-discovery and self-fulfillment of the heroes do not destroy or even threaten the objective order. Necessity falls away before desire, and the objective world of the story changes— King Erik and Peter and Rosa change location—to indicate an internal change. In "Sorrow-acre", Anne-Marie's death is not simply forced upon her by the external world; it is the fulfillment of desire. In "Alkmene", it is true, desire is not fulfilled, but the obstacle is not external necessity.

All this is to say that Isak Dinesen's talent is comic, romantic, pastoral; so that she writes, when dealing with tragic material, tragicomic romance. In "Caryatids", however, she is trying her hand at the material of pure tragedy—of that classic tragedy of the conflict between desire and necessity, *Oedipus Rex*. The irony of Simkie's charm is like the irony of the oracle that said Oedipus would kill his father and marry his mother. Like Childerique with her brother-husband, Oedipus fulfilled his desire because he was deceived—or let himself, psychologically speaking, be deceived—about who his father and mother were. The catastrophe does not occur, however, until, by learning he has fulfilled his desire, Oedipus makes the dream or inner reality objective and thus destroys existing objective arrangements.

The horror we feel as Oedipus approaches his discovery is the model for the horror we feel as Childerique approaches hers. The horror is in both cases the horror of the nightmare come true. But it belongs to only one side of Sophocles' play—the Dionysian side that makes it a story about desire. Tragedy has also an Apollonian side—an idea of order large enough to meet the Dionysian threat and reconstitute the objective world after the Dionysian work of destruction.

There is no such idea in "Caryatids". The responses of Philippe and Childerique to the discovery are, in their opposite ways, nontragic and characteristically modern. Philippe recognizes the truth scientifically, as one might in psychoanalysis, without turning upon himself, as Oedipus does, the judgment deriving from its full moral implication. Childerique, on the other hand, is not going to be able to reconcile the truth with her inadequate modern morality, her puritanism. She is either going to throw morality away and become the "bad" woman she thinks Simkie is; or else disintegrate, if she tries to hold on to the truth and her morality, into madness. Neither outcome is satisfactory for the story.

An unendurable irony is being prepared for her as the fragment ends. Like Philippe after he has read the letters, Childerique is overcome, as she walks home from the mill, with sexual desire. Philippe, whose knowledge is complete, knows he desires his sister, Childerique. But Childerique, who has only begun the process of discovery, feels the presence "in the darkness of the forest path" of a nameless lover. She thinks of her husband: "for the first time in her life she felt an overwhelming longing for his embrace". But when she gets home, the sight of him is disappointing—as though the real world "were pale and cold in comparison with the world of witchcraft". "She took his hand, eager to prove to herself that he was, after all, the lover of the forest path." She wants to prove to herself that her sexual desire has finally turned in a legitimate direction. Yet it is Philippe's appearance in his aspect of husband that disappoints her.

The discovery simply that Philippe is her brother would not account for the witch's curse—that the discovery is to turn her brother's heart away from her. Nor would such a discovery be unequivocally horrible, since it would show that her instincts had been right all along. One has of course only hints to go on, but I think Childerique is heading toward the discovery that the nameless lover of the forest path, the real object of her desire, is her *brother*—the archetype not the individual who fills it. The lord of Haut-Mesnil is given no Christian name, in order to suggest that he has attracted her as an archetype. Childerique begins to desire Philippe as she is about to learn that *he* is her brother. And he will turn from her with disgust when he sees that the woman, whom he has held up as an ideal of purity, has become sexually interested in him just when she discovered that their relation was incestuous. It would require a talent different from Isak Dinesen's, a talent for either the horror story or tragedy, to know what to do with Childerique from that point on.

"Echoes", the other story of "New Gothic Tales", relates also to *Seven Gothic Tales* in that it picks up again the story of Pellegrina Leoni, the diva who lost her voice. "Echoes" takes place just after Pellegrina has fled from Rome and her lover Lincoln Forsner. It deals with a time when she thought she might resurrect Pellegrina Leoni, the great diva, and it shows how the crushing of that hope led her to resume the career of nameless wandering dealt with in "Dreamers".

We can learn from "Echoes" how Isak Dinesen turns life into art, because the story is based—she was anxious to have me know this—on an incident in her life. According to her account, she grew interested in the early 1950's in a young Danish poet of the circle that published *Heretica*, a literary magazine of which she was a patron. The young poet became her protégé and friend, and would come for long periods to work at Rungstedlund. But then, fearful that she was gaining too much influence over him, the young man turned against her with a suddenness and violence that shattered her. The break between them, which occurred in 1954, is the experience behind "Echoes".

The story suggests that in her soul-searching Isak Dinesen pointed the finger of accusation against herself. For "Echoes" is about cannibalism—literal, psychological and ritual cannibalism. Pellegrina comes to realize that her love of the twelve-year-old boy, Emanuele, to whom she has been giving singing lessons, has been cannibalistic—that she has been feeding on him in order to restore her own youth and resurrect the Pellegrina Leoni whom she buried in Milan twelve years ago. She can come to this realization, because she meets at the beginning of the story an old man, Niccolo, who, when shipwrecked as a boy, committed an act of physical cannibalism upon a dead man whom he had loved. After her break with Emanuele, Pellegrina sees at Mass a very old woman, the counterpart of herself, whose "wrinkled lips and toothless gums were still moving and munching a little with the consummation of the Host". She understands in the end that you can feed on God but not on men—that religion is a sublimation of cannibalism and that the love of God is a means of sublimating the cannibalistic element in human love.

Emanuele turns against Pellegrina when, to teach him courage, she pricks three of his fingertips with a needle. She wipes the three drops of blood off on her handkerchief and lifts the handkerchief to her lips. Emanuele returns only once after that for a lesson and then disappears. They come upon each other in town, and he flees up "a steep side street ending, high up, in a flight of stone steps". She runs after him, pausing on the stairs. He calls down to her: " 'You are a witch. You are a vampire. You are wanting to drink my blood. . . . Witches live on forever by drinking children's blood." To stop her from advancing, he hurls a stone down upon her, drawing blood from her forehead. If we think of this scene as transmuting the Danish poet's accusations, we see how Isak Dinesen exploits the psychological significance of witches and vampires.

The scene is operatic—played on a kind of stage setting, with big voices. In renouncing their love, Emanuele's voice rings out "as it should ring when at last she had made it what it was meant to be. It was Dido's lament, Alceste's heroic sacrifice, in Pellegrina Leoni's voice." She tries to respond with the same voice, but "what should have been the roar of a lioness was the hissing of a gander". They have exchanged voices.

Their mutual drawing of blood is another such symbol of the bond between them; as is the theme of echoes from which the story takes its name. Isak Dinesen spoke to me about the motto of Denys Finch-Hatton's family, which she liked so much that she had made it her own. The motto is, in the Old French spelling, "*Je responderay*", I will answer. "It is a rare and a wonderful thing to answer," she told me. "Most people cannot answer. Most conversations are double monologues. From most people you do not get so much echo [she rapped upon the arm of her chair] as that. But to really answer some one, that is rare and wonderful."

Now when Pellegrina first hears Emanuele's voice in the church choir of the little mountain town to which she has wandered, she hears in it the echo of her own voice, the voice of the young, untrained Pellegrina Leoni. And when he comes for the one lesson that follows the drawing of his blood, she tells him he is now singing with the voice of the great Pellegrina Leoni and that " 'Pellegrina Leoni herself till now did not know how beautiful it was' ". As he is about to leave her apartment for the last time, Emanuele says he has been happier here " 'than in other places. I think that here I have heard my own voice coming to me from somewhere else, I know not from where.' " They have mingled identities, each has found his own soul in the other. When in the end Pellegrina understands the meaning of her relation with the young boy, it is because the words come echoing back to her that she and the old man, Niccolo, spoke to each other at the beginning of the story. Niccolo, too, though the episode with him is dull, enters into the mingling of identities as an aspect of both herself and Emanuele.

Especially beautiful is Pellegrina's experience of resurrection as an experience of music, of Emanuele's voice. When she learns that Emanuele was saved from a fire twelve years ago, she feels her voice must have been reborn in him at the very moment she lost it in the fire in Milan. It is, in other words, the mythical identity which by way of the singing voice the two share—and not their separate naturalistic identities—that is immortal.

Although its symbols evolve beautifully and intelligently, "Echoes" does not generate the power its subject matter would lead one to expect. Perhaps Isak Dinesen was working too close to her source in personal experience to generate the power that comes from sources unknown to the author. Even the climactic scene of accusation is not as powerful as the mill scene in "Caryatids". "Echoes" is a fine story, but not one of Isak Dinesen's best. It is certainly not up to "Dreamers".

The final section, called "New Winter's Tales", contains the two best stories of the volume—"A Country Tale" and "Copenhagen Season". They rank in their different ways with the best Isak Dinesen has written. The subject matter of the section is, as we would expect, Danish. In "Country Tale", Isak Dinesen returns to the subject of "Sorrow-acre"—the old manorial culture that embraced both lords and peasants. The Danish title, "En Herregaardshistorie" ("Tale of a Manor") is more descriptive than the English "Country Tale".

Isak Dinesen takes up in "Country Tale" the question she felt she had treated inadequately in "Sorrow-acre"—the question of the justice of the old order, the question whether the boy, for whose sake the peasant woman undergoes her ordeal in "Sorrow-acre", was or was not guilty. The first time we talked about "Sorrow-acre", Isak Dinesen told me she wished she had not left the question of the boy's guilt ambiguous, because readers assumed his innocence and had attacked her for writing an immoral story. But on another occasion, she said you must not be told whether the boy is innocent or guilty. She meant, I think, that the question of the justice of the old order is so complex— as complex as the question of the justice of life itself—as to render the legal definition of guilt or innocence almost irrelevant. The legal question is more effectively minimized, however, if the writer takes a stand on it and then shows its unimportance. In "Sorrow-acre", the boy ought to be guilty; Anne-Marie's suffering is gratuitous enough even after that.

The legal question is more effectively managed in "Country Tale", where the peasant, Linnert, is unequivocally innocent and the man who passes as his grandson is unequivocally guilty. In neither case does the legal judgment have much bearing on the moral judgment. For the point, only suggested in "Sorrow-acre" but dramatized here, is this—that guilt is inherited and inherent in the appointed roles of the manorial culture. The question of individual responsibility becomes therefore a question of identity, of who is filling the appointed role.

Isak Dinesen's idea about the manorial culture is that lords and peasants are so intertwined in it as to derive their identity and their guilt or innocence from each other. This idea, which is suggested as a justification for the lord in "Sorrow-acre", is dramatized here through the old motif of the changelings. As the man who passes for her son is to be executed for murder, Linnert's daughter tells the present lord of the manor that he is her son. She tells a story of having, to avenge her father's death, exchanged her infant son for the son of the lord who caused her father's death. If her story is true, then the wrong people have inherited the categories of lord and peasant, guilt and innocence. Even if her story is not true, it still objectifies the guilt the present lord feels toward Linnert's grandson.

In its concern with inherited guilt, "Country Tale" has the quality of Greek tragedy. It follows Kierkegaard's statement that individual responsibility is in ancient tragedy only half emerged into consciousness—only half emerged, that is, from the guilt inherited through family and race and passively accepted.[1] The story might be understood as a conflict between the characters who represent the half that is emerged, those who care for justice, and those who represent the unemerged half, who accept life as it is.

"Country Tale" is also like Greek tragedy in that it says everything it has to say through plot. Its plot is the best in all Isak Dinesen. "Country Tale" thus epitomizes the special achievement of *Last Tales*. Its plot, which is both ingenious and connected with mythical patterns, is always absorbing in itself and not simply—as is often the case in "Cloak" or the story of Lady Flora—because of what it means. "Sorrow-acre" is still the greater story of the two because it is so actually painful and the old lord is such a magnificent character. But "Country Tale" is the more nearly perfect of the two, and it achieves its relative perfection by sacrificing interest in character and in immediacy of emotion.

Although "Country Tale" seems to take place in the same period as "Sorrow-acre", the late eighteenth century, the emphasis here is on a guilt that is in the nature of things rather than, as in "Sorrow-acre", the product of a particular historical moment. The guilt of the young lord, Eitel, comes mainly from his deepest instinct about who he really is. The passion for justice is a characteristic of the peasant, Linnert, and his family, while the old lord and the man in prison, who may be his son, are conspicuously without it. Eitel's mistress, Ulrikke, who is married to the neighboring squire, is also without it. All through the story we see the contrast between, on the one hand, the tangled skein of human relationships and, on the other, moral responsibility and the too simple idea of justice. It is the people who seek justice who cause all the trouble that follows upon the old lord's original arbitrary crime, and even that crime was partly brought about by the peasant Linnert's arbitrary insistence upon justice for its own sake.

Ulrikke is like Eitel a victim of parental injustice. Her mother, a famous beauty, married her off to an old man when she saw in the budding girl a rival to be got out of the way. Ulrikke thinks of her misfortune, however, as a question not of justice or

[1] "Ancient Tragical Motif", *Either/Or*, Vol. i, New York pp. 141-42; London, pp. 116-17.

injustice but of the way things are. Her view is opposed to the reforming view and is identified with the blithe acceptance that is the human counterpart to nature's view.

In the opening scene, Eitel tells Ulrikke the story of his father's crime. He tells it as an old tale in which motives are inexplicable. The trouble started when a small bull-calf of Linnert's got mixed up in the herd of Eitel's father. When Linnert came for the calf, Eitel's father, as a jest, had a calf much bigger and finer than Linnert's sent out to him. But the peasant would not accept it and stood by the barn all day waiting for his calf. The next morning Eitel's father sent a fat young bullock down to Linnert's lot, but Linnert led it back, saying, " ' "There shall be justice on earth." ' "

Then Eitel's father sent his prize bull, known for its ferocity, down to Linnert's barn (it took three men to lead the bull down) with a message that Linnert was to keep the bull if it was his. " ' "But if it is not yours, and if you yourself are such a great man as to know that there shall be justice on earth, surely you will be great enough to bring it back to me on Sunday evening." ' " There were to be guests Sunday evening and Eitel's father wanted to show off the prowess of Linnert, who used to be his playmate.

But Linnert would not play. He appeared Saturday morning, riding on the bull. Excited by the feat, Eitel's father cried out, " ' "This is like one of our earliest games, and I shall drink a cup of wine with you, Linnert, and have you take home the silver cup filled with rigsdalers." "And one of our last games, I think," ' " said Linnert as he rode the bull into the barn. An hour later came news that the bull had died; and when Eitel's father asked why Linnert had not come to drink with him, he was told that Linnert was again waiting by the barn for his calf.

Since Linnert would not receive more than his due, Eitel's father said he must pay his due; he summoned Linnert and said he must pay for the bull unless he acknowledged it to be his. Linnert said it was not his and that he had not come " ' "to get a bull, but to have justice" ' ". You refuse the things I can give you, said Eitel's father, yet " ' "go on asking me for what I cannot give you, seeing that it is not to be found on earth" ' ". He decreed that to pay for the bull Linnert should ride the timbermare. This was a punishment used on Danish manors, in which the culprit had to sit astride a high wooden beam with weights attached to his legs. The exposure was painful and humiliating, and the Danish peasants have never forgiven the lords this punishment.

When toward the end of the day, Linnert said he had had enough, Eitel's father had him taken down. " ' "Are you then," he asked him, "going down on your knees to kiss my hand and thank me for my mercy?" ' " Linnert refused and Eitel's father had him put back up, but at dusk ordered him taken down. He was told Linnert had died. Linnert had, it was found, been gored by the bull.

The gratuitousness of the action suggests that the conflict between the two men was fundamental. It was a conflict between the unpredictable spirit of play or imagination, which is passionate in its generosity and its wrath, and the rationalizing moral spirit which is just as passionate in its insistence that things make sense. Here and elsewhere, Isak Dinesen identifies the former spirit with the aristocracy, and the latter with the middle class. Linnert is a harbinger of the new middle-class order. His daughter, Lone, joins through her second marriage the *petite bourgeoisie*.

The epilogue to the story is even crueler than the story. Eitel says he heard that morning that Linnert's grandson was on the following day to have his head cut off for murdering a keeper and his boy who caught him poaching. Eitel feels responsible for the death of this second Linnert, too. For when, after his father's death, Eitel was born, his mother, to do a kindness to Linnert's daughter, who also had just lost a husband and given birth to a boy, took her on as Eitel's wet nurse. To better fulfill her duties, Lone sent her own baby away, and the neglect, Eitel feels, led the boy to the executioner's block. Since Lone is the only person other than Ulrikke whom Eitel has ever loved, since he appropriated her as in a psychological sense his mother, there seems no limit to his family's usurpation of Linnert's.

" 'There may be,' " says Ulrikke, " 'another justice than ours, which in the end will set all things right.' " She now realizes that she once knew this boy, that he had been apprenticed to their keeper, and that as a girl of thirteen she bestowed upon him her first kiss. Young Linnert, we learn at the end, has remained faithful to Ulrikke. Has Eitel then taken from young Linnert his girl too? The question as to which of them is the real possessor of

Ulrikke's heart is connected with the question as to which of them is the real lord of the manor.

That evening Lone is announced. Eitel has not seen her since she went with her new husband to the island of Funen (the story takes place on the island of Lolland). As their eyes meet, he is seized with terror. "It was the dark old ages, eternity, destiny itself entering his room." It is his fears come true. For as they embrace and he feels himself a child again in her arms, he understands his terror; he remembers that it was she who long ago told him that story of his father's crime that has been ever since the objectification of his fears. As they play at mother and son by recapitulating their old times together, he wonders why she does not mention the son for whose life she has come to plead. When he says he will take her the next morning to see her son, she says Eitel is her son, that to avenge her father's death she put her baby in place of the master's and sent the master's away.

" 'It is an ancient nursery tale that you are telling me here, Lone,' " Eitel exclaims. " 'The tale of the changelings, so old that one smiles at it.' " When later she tells how she switched the babies,[1] using *you* for her baby, Eitel says she must not speak the word *you*. " 'If you will tell me your story, tell it like any other nursery tale.' " In "Caryatids", the gypsy said names must not be used in witchcraft. Lone's tales from the dark old ages are, like the magic formulas of witchcraft, manifestations of that buried stratum of our existence where it makes no difference whether the guilt inherent in our identities stems from crimes that are actual or potential.

No one in the whole world knows Lone's story. She will not even tell it to the parson on her deathbed.

"But now I have come to tell you how it all happened." "Nay, you shall tell me nothing," he said. "All this is but what you have dreamt, my poor Lone." She stood up straight before him. "I have got no one in the whole world," she said, "to tell it to except you, I have been waiting to do so for twenty-three years. If my tale is not told now, it will never be told."

The scene is the high point of the story. It recalls Kierkegaard's description of a modern *Antigone*, which would be a tragedy of the buried life; for Kierkegaard's Antigone would be the only one in the world, not excepting Oedipus himself, who knows the secret

[1] The details recall the switching of the babies in the affair of Kaspar Hauser.

of Oedipus's birth.[1] When Eitel tells Lone he does not believe
her—" 'I could not believe you if I wanted to' "—we see in
Lone's lack of preparation for such a response Isak Dinesen's
criticism of Kierkegaard. For Kierkegaard did not see the real
tragedy of his Antigone—that even if she had told her story, no
one, not even Oedipus, would have believed her. " 'This is the
one thing that I had never thought of,' " Lone says dully, " 'that
when I told you my tale you were not to believe it.' "

She understands, therefore, her tragedy—that the aristocrats
have taken her son along with everything else, that Eitel shrinks
from the thought of her as his mother. " 'Justice, with you and
me, cannot mean,' " Lone wails,

"that when I did carry you up to the house, in danger of my life, so
as to give it all to you, it was the house and the people up here who
took you over and made you one of theirs! Justice," she wailed on
lowly, her body doubling up as in great pain, "cannot mean that I
am never once to call you my son, and never once to hear you call
me mother!"

But this is what justice does mean, the justice other than ours that
Ulrikke spoke of.

Eitel's attitude toward Lone is completely ambivalent. He
holds her dear, he says, as if she were indeed his mother, and he
shrinks from her as if she were a witch " 'gloating over a crime
against nature, as one mad with wickedness, wishing to drive me
mad with her' ". But as the two stand face to face, and to her
question, " 'And shall there be no justice on earth?' " he answers,
" 'Yes, there shall be justice on earth' "—we see that they are
mother and son, descendants of Linnert. Eitel both knows and
dares not know this. The most awesome passage in the story is
Lone's description of the christening where hearing, amid
aristocratic pomp, " 'my son christened Eitel after the master's
father, and Johan August after the master himself, in the name
of the Father and of the Son and of the Holy Ghost, I said to
myself: "Now that is done which cannot be undone." ' " Nowhere else in her work does Isak Dinesen convey so powerfully
her sense of the importance of names, and nowhere else in the
story does Lone's crime seem so frightening.

Isak Dinesen said to me of "Country Tale" that she began it

[1] "Ancient Tragical Motif", *Either/Or*, Vol. 1, New York, pp. 152-62; London,
pp. 124-32.

233

with the idea that the boys were not changed but that the story itself seemed to tell her, as she wrote it, that the boys were changed. "You can tell they have been changed," she said, "by comparing their characters to the characters of the fathers." It was a nice stroke of art to have taken ambiguity out of the facts while retaining psychological and moral ambivalence—the ambivalence in Eitel's mind. Because we know what really happened, we can see in the end, as God would, a justice other than the characters understand, even as we participate in Eitel's limited human view.

No sooner has Lone retired, presumably to go to bed, than the housekeeper enters, says Lone has left the house, and discredits her story, casting doubt on Lone's sanity. Eitel is faced with two absolutely contradictory stories, but the perceptive reader will have noticed that the valet brought in the evening wine at the moment when Lone made her revelation. The housekeeper might, while the door was open, have heard Lone and have come in deliberately to refute her.

Eitel, for whom the truth is now completely ambiguous, finds the same tragic irony in both possibilities. For when he is told he is the lord's son, he feels himself to be secretly Lone's; but he feels himself the lord's son when Lone claims him. We have here, as with the twins of "The Cardinal's First Tale", a fable of the double identity that is reflected in different and conflicting ties to father and mother. But the conflict here is the tragic conflict around which is organized not only the individual personality but society itself. " 'We ourselves, my father,' " says Eitel to the old lord's smiling portrait, " 'and these people of ours have got the roots too tightly intertwined, deep down in the ground, ever to be able to free ourselves of one another.' "

Who then has wronged whom, and where in this tangle does justice lie? From a tale he now reads in an old storybook, Eitel learns that there is no objective counterpart to the thirst for justice in the human heart, that an external vindication cannot relieve the tragic loneliness of the guilty human condition. He decides he will go the next morning to see the prisoner who " 'is as lonely as I' ". The decision enables him to sleep that night, for he is laying himself open to the possibility of once again exchanging places with his double.

The story resolves itself unexpectedly; for the prisoner turns the scene of their confrontation, which Eitel views tragically, into comedy. Eitel is disgusted at the filth of the cell and the prisoner's bad odor. But the prisoner is beautifully built and in his "collectedness", "grace" and "obstinate joy of life", reminds Eitel of a wild animal. In acknowledging that he knows Eitel as the owner of the land on which he has spent his life poaching, the prisoner shows no resentment.

Eitel tells the prisoner about his mother's " 'curious tale' ". " 'It was not true,' " says Eitel. " 'Nay, it was not true,' Linnert repeated. Then, suddenly, with the same kind of fox-joviality as before: 'But if it had been true?' 'If it had been true,' Eitel said slowly, 'then thou, Linnert, wouldst today have been in my place. And I, who knows, in thine.' " The *thou* form indicates they are speaking dialect, which is all that Linnert speaks.

Linnert rises with a noiseless movement, "so extraordinarily vigorous that it had all the character of an assault". Equal in height, the two young men face each other "meaningfully, conscious of a trial of strength". All this is done to surprise us when Linnert, thinking only that Eitel would then owe to him the hunting he will be doing in a fortnight, asks not for restitution and retribution but only to be thanked. " 'Wilt thou then,' " he asks, repeating the demand the old lord made of the other Linnert, " 'go down on thy knees to kiss my hand, and thank me for my mercy?' " Eitel goes down on one knee, "in the straw where Linnert had spat", and touches his lips to the outstretched hand the smell of which nauseates him.

Just before Linnert makes his demand, Eitel thinks he recognizes on his face an expression he has looked on a short time ago. In identifying it, however, with "the hard glint of triumph in Lone's face", Eitel shows he does not understand Linnert. For Linnert does not make of his victory what Lone would. The expression Eitel recognizes is the smile in the old lord's portrait, the comic spirit that is allied to the spirit of the absolute. The aristocrat, like nature and God, likes to bestow gifts and wants only to be thanked. The bourgeois, on the other hand, wants to receive only his due because he does not want to bend the knee. "My medieval knees lack health until they bend," says Yeats, referring, in "Municipal Gallery Revisited", to the same conflict in world-views that divided the old lord and the other Linnert.

It is, given his circumstances, as a sublime jest and a sublime act of courtesy (again pulled out of a grotesque situation), that Linnert raises his hand from Eitel's lips to his own head to scratch deep down in his long hair as he smiles or grins. " 'They are biting,' " he says in the last line of the story. " 'It was well that thou didst set me loose.' " In thanking Eitel for enabling him to scratch his lice, Linnert is in effect raising Eitel from his knees with lordly graciousness.

Because we know who these two young men really are, we see beyond the tragic lesson Eitel learned from the tale he read in the storybook. We see, as the young men cannot, that justice has after all been done. The son of the lord is to die to atone for Linnert's death; while Linnert's grandson atones for Linnert's refusal to receive, by paying Linnert's debt of thanks. We see a divine comedy where Eitel sees a tragedy both for young Linnert and himself, since he must go on suffering the loneliness of guilt. Nowhere else does Isak Dinesen so successfully show us through a single action both the world as we see it, the world of experience, and the world as it is, the world of pattern.

"Copenhagen Season"[1] is the story in *Last Tales* of which Isak Dinesen was proudest, for here she felt she had finally done the novel. She spoke of it to me as a "short novel", and to indicate its novelistic quality wanted it known that the story was a history —that it was about her father and his family and about the manners of Danish aristocratic society during her father's youth. "It is different to my other tales," she wrote when sending the story to Robert Haas on May 8, 1957, "and I do not know if you will like it. It has amused me to write down what I myself have been told as a child about conditions, individuals and happenings of my father's generation—before knowledge of these things has been altogether lost. To write, too, somehow in the way of that past age itself."

We have had all along, to be sure, the social notation we get here, but not so explicitly. We have found ourselves in the other stories inside the past, and have had mainly to infer the modern point of view toward it. Here, instead, Isak Dinesen does the novelist's job of giving us an outright history lesson. The story takes place in 1870, just before the Franco-Prussian War, and we are told what is implied in "Old Chevalier" and all the stories

[1] The Danish title is "Ib og Adelaide" ("Ib and Adelaide").

about the 1870's—that the old aristocratic order already had, without knowing it, "one foot in the grave", but brought forth in its "eleventh hour . . . an abundant flowering, equal to that of its rise." The gaudy Second Empire was the sign in France of that flowering, while in Denmark "life in country houses sprang into a luxury unknown for three hundred years". But the Indian summer betokened the coming death. For the source of the new aristocratic prosperity was the prosperity of the new bourgeois order that made profitable the recent changeover "from grain production to cattle breeding". And in those who bore ancient names, the stark grandeur of the aristocratic soul had given way, in that period when "the art of upholstery . . . had been brought almost to perfection", to the bourgeois love of comfort. This contradiction, at a particular moment of history, between social appearance and social and spiritual reality is the appropriately novelistic subject of "Copenhagen Season". Its treatment combines affectionate irony with the style of the melodramatic novels of the period—novels which used the aristocratic milieu as an ornamental setting for bourgeois emotions.

The story turns upon two related families, the Angels (pronounced *Ahnjel*), who are the Dinesens, and the Counts von Galen, who are the Frijses, a noble family to whom the Dinesens are related. Ib Angel is Isak Dinesen's father; Ib's sister, Drude, is her godmother and a favorite aunt. Like Ib, Wilhelm Dinesen loved in his youth a Frijs cousin whom, as a mere army officer, he could not marry. But it is not certain that this unhappy love affair was Dinesen's reason, as it is Ib's, for joining the French army in the Franco-Prussian War.

The Angels are the product of a rashly romantic marriage between a young half-sister of Count Hannibal von Galen and a big Jutland horsedealer. Although shocked by the marriage, the aristocratic world had come to accept the horsedealer as, with his feeling for soil and animals and his Jutland brogue, someone out of "the historic and heraldic age to which they themselves belonged". The horsedealer's estate, Ballegaard, where the soil is poor, gives an impression of "sparsity and grandeur". The spirit of aristocracy corresponds there to the appearance of it.[1]

---

[1] The hero of Kleist's "Michael Kohlhaas", a story Isak Dinesen admired, is a horsedealer, who shows more aristocratic spirit than the people who bear the titles. The theme of justice in "Michael Kohlhaas" bears, as in "Country Tale", on the

After their mother's death, the Angel children are taken over by the von Galens. They are introduced into society, where they are an enormous success but are treated also "like fresh and clean carriers of some grim social bacillus". For they have the qualities of artisocracy without the name and property. Ib becomes the inseparable companion of his cousin, Leopold von Galen, and Drude of Adelaide von Galen. We see in each couple the contrast between internal and external legitimacy—between "the children of love" and "of the law". Kasparson of "Deluge" externalizes his spiritual legitimacy, when he plays the Cardinal's role and is finally acknowledged by Miss Nat-og-Dag to be a true son of St Louis. But we never see the action in which Ib and Drude externalize their spiritual legitimacy. We follow instead, as a novel should, the fortunes of Adelaide in whom the contradiction between appearance and reality is to become complete.

In the fact that Ib falls in love with Adelaide and Leopold with Drude, we see why the Angels carry a bacillus—provided we understand that aristocratic world, the brilliant surface of which Isak Dinesen describes in loving detail. That whole world is summed up as "the world of the name". To a nobleman, his name was his immortal essence. Individual deaths were easily accepted, but

the extinction of an old name was a mournful, somehow inexplicable event . . . namelessness was annihilation. A later generation will not easily conceive to what extent, to the eyes of the aristocratic classes of the past, they themselves were the one reality of the universe. . . . The vast gray masses of humanity, individuals without a name, washing beneath them and around them, remained imperceptible.

We have to understand all this to understand why it is out of the question for Ib to marry Adelaide. Ib himself, who understands the symbolism of aristocracy better than his titled kinsmen—for Ballegaard is also a place where the spirit of poetry merges with the spirit of aristocracy—would not want Adelaide to occupy a position in the world inferior to the position she occupies·in his imagination.

The most memorable scene in the story is the reception in a

---

question of the old order versus the new; only there it is Kohlhaas, the untitled man of aristocratic spirit, who becomes a destroyer through his passion for justice. Elishama, in "Immortal Story" (*AD*), is also—it is a thing in his favor—descended from a horsedealer.

great house in Copenhagen, where we see the world of the name gathered together in all its late-flowering splendor. It is at this reception that a famous old painter of the time, in the witty discourse I quoted at the beginning of the book, connects the world of the name with big noses and the capacity for tragedy. Our great-grandchildren, he says, " 'will be able to fly to the moon. But not one of them, to save his life, will be able to write a tragedy.' " That is because they will by then have rid themselves of a most absurd and troublesome idea, the idea of honor.

The joke, and also the point, is that the painter—who is modelled after a painter and art teacher of Isak Dinesen's youth, Kristian Zahrtmann—has himself hardly any nose or hair or expression, has a face so "like the posterior of an infant" that his admiring pupils can only suppose him to have "an eminently expressive face in the other place". The painter says he himself has not got, nor would he want to have, the idea of honor he admires in others. As an artist, he does not have to be anything in himself; he is " 'the nose of society' ". Since his aristocratic listeners half understand and half laugh off such talk, we see already the time when the artist will be the sole repository of the aristocratic ideal.

Ib and Drude appear at the party as slightly obsolete types, and as therefore more truly aristocratic than the others and more tragic. Ib creates a stir at the party, because he has the night before fought a duel—a feat which is received with laughter and admiration as an anachronism. He has made up his mind to resign his Danish commission and join the French army as the honorable solution to his hopeless love of Adelaide.

When the next day Ib comes upon Adelaide and his sister in Adelaide's boudoir, Adelaide shows herself to be a spoiled, frivolous girl, who takes for granted the homage paid to her name and beauty, without understanding the price that must be paid for these privileges. Ib says she is known everywhere, even on shipboard.

"People who did not know who I was?" Adelaide said thoughtfully. "They must be very queer people, and silly. An old ship's captain who did not know who I was—what on earth would I do with him?"
"You would make him find out soon, you mean?" Ib asked.
"No," said she. "No. And I should never try to find out who he was

either. He could remain for me among the people of his own kind, undisturbed."

She taunts Ib for not loving her as " 'all the others love me' ". If she were Ib, she would be in love with Adelaide. " 'At the end of the season,' " she says, " 'I should make up my mind to die. I should resolve to join the army of the French, now that they are going to have a war down there.' " Pleased with herself for making up a romantic tale, she sketches out the scene in which she as Ib would take leave of Adelaide and declare his love.

Like the painter's aristocratic auditors, Adelaide has through art a link with old values she does not really understand. The tragic surface of the scene she sketches out turns, therefore, into melodrama. As Ib repeats the words she prescribes for him and even gives her the farewell kiss she prescribes, we see him play out his tragedy as melodrama. From this point on, we see the same events as both tragedy and melodrama. The ironic contrast is the finest stroke in the story.[1] Once again, Isak Dinesen shows herself to be an excellent critic of the literary tradition, making the meaning of the different literary forms part of her meaning. She makes, through the contrast between melodrama and tragedy, the transition to that novelistic kind of tragedy in the end, which is opposite to the kind of tragedy the painter had in mind. I wish she had offered a few more signposts to the transition. For the unwary reader, expecting the story to fulfill the painter's words, may miss the irony in the end and think Isak Dinesen has failed where she has most brilliantly succeeded.

One such signpost is Ib's relation with his low-class mistress, Petra. Ib is devoted to Petra because her unhappy love of him resembles his unhappy love of Adelaide. Although he cannot return it, Ib appreciates Petra's passion as Adelaide cannot appreciate his. Another signpost is the advancing spring, beautifully described, that prepares us for the rising of passion, for the end of the Copenhagen season and, like the Petra episode, for the tragedy that does and does not come off.

After Ib has left the boudoir, Drude tells Adelaide that Ib has loved her all his life, that he is indeed going away to join the French army and that he came to say goodbye to her. Smitten with remorse, Adelaide devises a scheme that smacks again of the

---

[1] It distinguishes Adelaide's lack of fulfillment from Miss Nat-og-Dag's in " Deluge" or Fanny De Coninck's in " Supper ".

theater. Drude is to write Ib to meet her in the house of the maiden aunt with whom she is staying. But instead of Drude, Adelaide will arrive disguised in the clothes of her maid. Since no one will be home that afternoon, Adelaide will be compromising herself.

While waiting in the aunt's house, Ib's eye falls upon a letter from Adelaide's brother, Leopold, to Drude, setting forth plans for their elopement that afternoon. Since it is clear to Ib that Leopold's intentions are not honorable, his first impulse is to kill Leopold. But then, filled with awe by the intensity of a passion for which Drude is willing to risk so much, a passion like his own for Adelaide, he asks himself what he will have done for his sister if he leaves her for the remaining years of her life "the one remembrance: that there was nothing to remember". Ib realizes he almost sinned against a higher law than the moral law Leopold broke. This higher law, which he obeys without naming or formulating it, is the law of tragedy that says each person must fulfill his destiny and pay the price of fulfillment.

Adelaide, when she arrives, asks Ib to speak his own words of love to her. He does, and she offers herself to him without quite understanding what she is offering. Ib knows that orthodox morality requires him not to take advantage of her innocence. He acts, however, not for a moral reason, but in instinctive obedience to the law of tragedy that "will allow its young maiden to sacrifice her honor to her love" but "forbids its young man to do the same thing". Acting, in other words, on the idea of honor, he casts himself rather than Adelaide in the tragic role.

He makes up his mind when he sees the similarity between this scene of Adelaide's devising and the climactic scene of Victor Hugo's tragedy, *Ruy Blas*. In Hugo's play, Don Salluste, to take revenge on the Queen of Spain, disguises his lackey, Ruy Blas, as a nobleman and has him make love to her. Ruy Blas and the Queen fall in love, and Don Salluste tricks them into meeting alone in an empty house. Don Salluste appears and, announcing to the Queen that she has been compromised, says she must renounce her throne and flee with this nobleman who is worthy of her. Not wanting to take advantage of the Queen's ignorance, Ruy Blas announces he is a lackey, kills Don Salluste and, after begging the Queen's forgiveness, poisons himself. Although the ranks are reversed, the aristocratic values are maintained. For

Ruy Blas shows himself to have the soul of a nobleman, while his master has the soul of a lackey. Ruy Blas manifests his soul and fulfills his love through the tragic ending.

Our story does not end that way, for we follow the girl who has precisely not been cast in the tragic role. We see a novelistic tragedy of unfulfilled desire when, after Ib has said he would rather die than take advantage of her, Adelaide, feeling there is one move more she might make, does not make it. She would rather die emotionally than assume the tragic role. Ib's future, it is suggested, will be rich with the sorrow of this parting, but Adelaide will never in later life be seen to shed a tear.

She feels as she leaves the house that she is "storming forth in a wild and mad flight". But she is walking very slowly, "like an old woman"; for this is a tragedy in reverse, a "*Liebesflucht*" or flight from love. Her strength goes not into passion, but into suppressing the unrestrained cry of passion, the words of which come to her from Goethe's *Wilhelm Meister*: "My head swims, / My bowels are burning."[1] She realizes with horror that she has lost her sense of smell. And the painter's voice is now brought back to us to explain that in grieving for her lost sense of smell Adelaide is really grieving because tragedy has gone out of her life, because she has been handed over to those forms into which she has all along managed to turn the scenes of her devising— " 'to comedy, to the drawing-room play or possibly to the operetta' ". The recapitulation of the theme of smell would be more convincing had Isak Dinesen made Adelaide overhear the painter's words at the party. The painter's voice is brought back to solve the problem of the novelist, who in describing the inner life from the character's point of view must somehow express meanings beyond what the character understands. We see here the advantage of the story that externalizes the inner life and its meanings.

In her inability to shed the tears she wants to shed, Adelaide feels there is no place in all Copenhagen where a human being can weep. Finally, she comes to a churchyard—a distinctively bourgeois preserve ("her relations had their family vaults near their houses"). It is the one place in the new order—as we see by the mourners there—where the bourgeois proprieties allow one, indeed require one, to weep. She sits down by an abandoned

[1] Book IV, Chap. XI.

grave and weeps for the last time in her life. Having finished, and feeling a certain happiness in having avowed to the world that she "had lost all", she turns to the headstone to see on whose bosom she has been weeping. The story ends with the inscription: "Here lie the remains of JONAS ANDERSEN TODE, Sea Captain. . . . Faithful in friendship, a helper of the afflicted, steadfast in adversity."

This is the old ship's captain of whom she had said she would " 'never try to find out who he was' ". His last name means death in German. She has had to find out about the one reality that binds all social classes together and that gives life a tragic quality no historical changes can erase. The captain has also the best bourgeois virtues (ship captains always do in Isak Dinesen); so in losing tragedy and in weeping at the bosom of this exemplary bourgeois, Adelaide has ironically fulfilled her destiny by manifesting her essentially bourgeois soul. She is therefore quite properly the subject of a novel.[1]

The final story, however, "Converse at Night in Copenhagen", returns to the theme, with which *Last Tales* begins, of the kind of story that is antithetical to the novel. It is called *mythos* here, and is discussed in a room that is a refuge from the commonsense world of affairs, by characters who are another version of the trinity of the "Cloak" stories—the father, the son and the woman they share. They are the mad King Christian VII of Denmark, the drunken poet Ewald, and the prostitute Lise whose room it is. Ewald calls the King Orosmane after the sultan in Voltaire's tragedy *Zaïre*; the two passages of French verse quoted by the King are from *Zaïre*. Since Voltaire's Orosmane is a king and lover who is driven mad and destroyed by the moralizing force of Christianity, Ewald is saying in effect that a king and especially a Mohammedan king—it is the thing Isak Dinesen liked in Mohammedanism—symbolizes the kind of spirituality that has its source in the erotic instinct. This is what the king and the poet have in common. They agree about the innocence of Lise and the holiness of the sensual life.

As buffoon and sentimentalist, Ewald takes the name of

[1] The resemblance, in theme and in the final scene in the graveyard, to Henry James's *Beast in the Jungle* suggests that both writers understood all the implications of the appropriately novelistic subject. Although Isak Dinesen read some James, I have no evidence that she knew *Beast in the Jungle*.

Yorick, after the fool in *Hamlet* and the sentimental traveller in Sterne's *Sentimental Journey*. Even in heaven, he says, he would want " 'the earthly reflection of my heavenly existence' ", that is called *mythos*. The poet's function is to give back to the Father as speech the Word by which He created the world. The King, we are to understand, symbolizes the perfection that is the Word or Logos; while Lise, who says not one word, is the earth on which takes place the intellectual dance of Logos and speech, and which the poet unites with God through the sensual imagery of his speech. Yorick departs and leaves Lise to the King.

The "Cloak" stories, where the father hands the woman over to the son, deal with art as revelation downward from heaven. Here, where the son offers the woman to the father, we have art in its opposite aspect as the mythos that shows heaven its earthly reflection. Thus, Isak Dinesen rounds out her discussion of the story as absolute vision. In what it says about art and life, this brilliant little conversation is Isak Dinesen's most succinct statement—it is a kind of diagram—of her credo.

Chapter 7

THE REDEMPTION OF ARIEL:
ANECDOTES OF DESTINY AND *EHRENGARD*

ISAK DINESEN said of *Anecdotes of Destiny* (1958) that it "is played on a lighter instrument" than *Last Tales*. "You might say it was played on a flute," she told Curtis Cate, "where the others were played on a violin or a cello."[1] She did not mean—as she made clear in her letter to Haas of September 25, 1956—that *Anecdotes* was inferior in literary quality to *Last Tales*, but that it was more purely comic and fanciful, that it was intended to be evanescently light. It was, I suspect, because she had in mind the comedy and fantasy of Shakespeare's last play that she wanted *Anecdotes* to follow *Last Tales* as her final statement. The central and most ambitious story of the volume is called "Tempests" and deals with Shakespeare's Ariel. The whole volume might be said to be about Ariel as the representative of our disembodied ideals. In no other book has Isak Dinesen dealt with such airy essences or made the ideal seem so glitteringly inhuman. *Anecdotes* is Isak Dinesen's most mystical book.

Although *Anecdotes* was designed as a catch-all for the stories that Isak Dinesen began in 1949 to publish in American magazines, her standards for the book were high. Of eleven stories originally planned for it, she had dropped by 1956 four—"The Ghost Horses", "The Bells", "Uncle Seneca" and "The Fat Man"—as not good enough; and she later dropped two others—"Ehrengard" and "The Loyal Mistress"—as not sufficiently in shape. "Ghost Horses"—which appeared in the *Ladies' Home Journal* of October 1951, and in book form in Denmark in 1955[2] —is far inferior to the published *Ehrengard* and to the stories in *Anecdotes*. "Ghost Horses" is, however, related in theme to

---

[1] "Isak Dinesen", *Atlantic Monthly*, December 1959, p. 153; *Cornhill*, Winter 1959-60, p. 127.

[2] *Spøgelseshestene* (Copenhagen: Fremad), under the name Isak Dinesen.

Anecdotes, in that it locates the force of instinct, memory and imagination in two children who rightly connect the family jewels—which for the twentieth-century adults have just so much cash value—with horses and the regal processions of the old regime. Isak Dinesen must have had a certain unity in mind for the stories she was to publish in American magazines; since she already had, at least a year before the first story was published, a title for the volume in which she was to collect her American stories.[1] The title suggests that she had in mind stories which were to be both light and profound. The stories would, in the manner of anecdotes, make their witty points, but the points were to be about the strange ways in which destiny works out its own patterns.

As for the literary quality of *Anecdotes*, the three main stories are as good as "Country Tale" and "Copenhagen Season", the two best of *Last Tales*, and rank with them among the best Isak Dinesen has written. Since the two other stories in *Anecdotes* are very short and serve successfully—the first, brilliantly—as prologue and epilogue to the volume, *Anecdotes* is more evenly successful than *Last Tales*, though it has not the richness, variety and power of the earlier book.

The first story, "The Diver", states the theme of the volume. For the young Mohammedan theology student, Saufe, fails to reach the absolute when he tries to fly, but reaches it instead when he becomes a diver. He loves the dancing girl Thusmu as long as he thinks her an angel. But he abandons her when, falling in love with him, she confesses that she has only pretended to be an angel. She is better than an angel, for she can dance and love. Hers is human love with its rich admixture of guilt. But he cannot absorb guilt into his love. He abandons his art of flying, too; for he has no longer any hope, and " 'without hope,' " he says, " 'you cannot fly' ".

This much makes a story; for it is about the human world of disequilibrium, where innocence is lost and aspiration exceeds realization. It is presented to us as a story told by Mira Jama, who in the second part meets Saufe as a real person who has stepped outside Mira's story. Saufe has become a pearl-fisher, and is now fat, rich and contented; for by diving, he has at last achieved

[1] The title is mentioned as early as July 9, 1948, in a letter of Haas to Erik Petri of Copenhagen.

absolute knowledge. " 'But that,' " he says, " 'makes no story.' "

We see why when we hear that he has learned, from an old cowfish with horn-rimmed spectacles, a doctrine which, if it were actualized, would make stories impossible. The cowfish proclaims, in a nice parody of theological reasoning, that the fish must be made in God's image for " ' "all things work together for the good of her" ' ". While men and even birds labor to move in their elements, " ' "We fish are upheld and supported on all sides. . . . And the pattern of the universe we read with ease, because we see it from below." ' " The fish never did and never will fall, for where would they fall to. We fish know " ' "one may quite well float without hope" ' ".

The absolute negates the distinction between up and down. Diving is as "spiritual" as flying. "The Diver" prepares us for Ariel, who is a spirit of sea and air, and for the contrast that runs through the book between the fluid world of biology and spirit and the rationalist dry land that is most completely represented by Mr Clay of "The Immortal Story".

We can understand by reference to Kierkegaard that the Saufe who dives has, in fact, made an advance over the Saufe who aspired to fly. For the diver has made what in *Fear and Trembling* Kierkegaard calls "the first movement of faith", the movement of "infinite resignation". "After having made the movements of infinity", faith, says Kierkegaard, ". . . makes those of finiteness". Speaking of himself as at the stage of resignation, Kierkegaard says, in a sentence that may have suggested the central metaphor of Isak Dinesen's story: "I can swim in existence, but for this mystical soaring I am too heavy."[1] In the three stories that follow, we see how for human beings the mystical "soaring" is achieved by a movement downward and backward to the finite. The character who, in "Tempests", cannot come to terms with the finite is the incompletely human Ariel of the story.

The first of the three main stories, "Babette's Feast", originated in a bet. The English writer, Geoffrey Gorer, bet Isak Dinesen that she could not sell a story to *The Saturday Evening Post*. When out of a batch of stories she sent the *Post*, they chose one she considered "idiotic"—"Uncle Seneca", published as "The

[1] *Fear and Trembling and The Sickness Unto Death*, translated with introductions and notes by Walter Lowrie (Garden City, N.Y.: Anchor Books, 1954), pp. 48, 60; trans. Robert Payne (London: Oxford University Press, 1939), pp. 47, 68.

Uncertain Heiress", December 10, 1949—she turned to the *Ladies' Home Journal* which had, through arrangement with Random House, published "Sorrow-acre" during the war. Hearing that Americans were now going in for *food*, she wrote "Babette's Feast", which appeared in *Ladies' Home Journal*, June 1950. It is right that so high a comedy should have been written in a spirit of fun.

"Babette's Feast" deals in the simple symmetries and contrasts appropriate to comedy. The main contrast is between the ethical and the esthetic life, with the ethical represented by the puritan North and the esthetic by the Catholic, sensuous South. Two elderly Norwegian spinsters, daughters of the dead leader of one of those radically puritanical private sects that are the last result of Protestantism, have, of all outlandish things for their isolated little fjord town, a French maid, Babette. Babette came to them twelve years ago as a legacy from the one period in their youth when they were exposed to that other, esthetic and sensuous life.

Each sister had her exposure, and their exposures are dealt with in separate, symmetrical chapters. In 1854, when the elder sister Martine was eighteen, a young officer of noble family, Lorens Loewenhielm, exchanged glances with her in the market-place. The effect of that exchange on Martine is implied through its effect on Lorens. There was a legend in the Loewenhielm family that "a gentleman of the name had married a Huldre, a female mountain spirit of Norway, who is so fair that the air round her shines and quivers. Since then, from time to time, members of the family had been second-sighted". Young Lorens saw behind the figure of Martine "a sudden, mighty vision of a higher and purer life". He began to frequent the house of the Dean, Martine's father, but he was so obsessed by the cold, glittering purity of his vision, so unable to reconcile with it his senses and feelings, that he went away without expressing his love. Back in garrison, he decided to renounce second-sightedness and concentrate on career and pleasure. His choice of the sensuous life implies Martine's choice of the ethical life.

A year later, the great singer Achille Papin of the Paris Opera passed through the town and, hearing the younger sister Philippa sing in church, had like Lorens a vision. Only his vision was of a great prima donna. He asked the Dean if he might give Philippa singing lessons and the Dean, who grew pale at his first sight of a live Roman Catholic, gave his permission, saying: " 'God's paths run across the sea and the snowy mountains, where man's eye sees no track' "—words borne out by this anecdote of destiny.

One day Achille and Philippa sang together the seduction duet from *Don Giovanni*, which ends with a kiss, and Achille, who did not in his rapture distinguish his own from Don Giovanni's emotion, kissed Philippa. She asked her father to write Monsieur Papin that she wanted no more singing lessons—which the Dean did, saying: " 'God's paths run across the rivers' ", meaning the rivers that separate people.

The impersonality of Achille's kiss suggests that it might have led Philippa back to the innocence she thought she was losing. It also suggests that Lorens's sensuous life may lead him back to the vision of purity he thought he was escaping. It introduces the third force in the story, the mystical, that resolves the antithesis of sensuous-esthetic and ethical. The vision that impels Lorens and Achille is larger than the sensuous-esthetic life they pursue; just as the Dean's words suggest that his vision is larger than the ethical life to which it impels his daughters and disciples.

It was Achille who in 1871 sent Babette to the sisters. She carried a letter from him, informing them that Babette had fought with the Communards in Paris and had to flee when the Commune was put down. The letter also said Babette could cook. Dismayed by "the idea of French luxury and extravagance" and the knowledge that French people ate frogs, the sisters showed Babette—"during the demonstration the French-woman's face became absolutely expressionless"—how to prepare a split cod and an ale-and-bread soup. The comedy turns on the contrast between the elaborations of French high cuisine and the puritan pride in not knowing what one is eating. Babette, too, moves toward the mystical on a path that seems to lead away from it; for at this point she made miraculous ale-and-bread soup and miraculously reduced the household costs, so that the sisters became entirely dependent on her in all practical matters.

Now, twelve years later, the Dean's hundredth anniversary is approaching, and the sisters are worried because the communion he founded seems to be breaking up; the Brothers and Sisters are returning to the sinful ways they had before he redeemed them. The sisters are also worried because Babette has won ten thousand francs in of all things a French lottery (another incongruous import into that austere territory), and they are sure she will use the money to return to France. But God's paths do indeed run "across the salt sea". Because she has won the lottery, Babette begs to be allowed to cook for the Dean's birthday on December 15th "a real French dinner" and to pay for it. Fearfully, the sisters assent to the first request, having "no arguments wherewith to meet the proposition of cooking a real French dinner". They assent finally even to the second; for Babette, they reason, is now richer than they and how much can a dinner cost.

The high comedy begins as, through the startled uncomprehending eyes of the sisters, we watch Babette's month-and-a-half-long preparations for the dinner. When the sisters learn that the goods for the dinner are coming all the way from Paris, they see "the French dinner coming upon them" as "a thing of incalculable nature and range". Martine, who watches the goods being brought in wheelbarrows, sees an object "like some greenish-black stone", which "suddenly shot out a snake-like head". Realizing she is beholding a large and terrible tortoise, she backs "out of the kitchen without a word".

Not daring to tell her sister what she has seen, Martine goes contritely the next morning from house to house to warn the old Brothers and Sisters that she could not tell what they would be given at her father's birthday dinner. The old people console her by promising to be silent on the great day "upon all matters of food and drink. Nothing that might be set before them, be it even frogs or snails, should wring a word from their lips. . . . 'On the day of our master,' " a white-bearded Brother assures her, " 'we will cleanse our tongues of all taste and purify them of all delight or disgust of the senses, keeping and preserving them for the higher things of praise and thanksgiving.' " The resolution prepares us for a delightfully comic dinner scene.

We are prepared from another side as well, when on the Sunday morning of the dinner old Mrs Loewenhielm writes to ask if she may bring her nephew Lorens, now General Loewenhielm, who has come unexpectedly on a visit. Her remark that the General lived several years in Paris prepares us for someone at table who will know what is being set before them. This is important for the comedy. We follow the dinner through the comprehending eyes of the General, who measures for us the incongruity of finding such food and wine in such a place as well as the comic obliviousness of the others.

Lorens's return also brings together all the elements of the story. The snowy day outside glitters like the cold ideal of purity the congregation serves and Lorens escaped from. The Brothers and Sisters, when they gather, break into a hymn—" 'Take no thought for food or raiment' "—the third verse of which— " 'Wouldst thou give a stone, a reptile / to thy pleading child for food?' "—inspires Martine with hope for the dinner. Directly after this charmingly apposite hymn—which is used, like the hymn in "Converse", to show the sensual and spiritual life as reflections of each other—the General arrives to represent the sensuous-esthetic as against the ethical life. The imagery of witchcraft used for Babette's activities in the kitchen suggests the third or mystical force that reconciles the other two.

Just as the congregation has been losing impetus in its ethical life; so the General, having renounced second sight, finds himself wishing "one little dream would come his way". He wants to go to dinner at the Dean's house to convince himself that his choice of success and pleasure, thirty-one years ago, was right. "The low rooms, the haddock and the glass of water on the table before him should all be called in to bear evidence that in their milieu the existence of Lorens Loewenhielm would very soon have become sheer misery."

Instead, the General sees wine before him and is bewildered to find that it is " 'Amontillado! And the finest Amontillado that I have ever tasted.' " To test his senses, he takes some soup and has the distinct impression that he is tasting " 'turtle-soup—and what turtle-soup!' " " 'Incredible!' " he tells himself as the next course appears. " 'It is Blinis Demidoff!' " He looks round to see how his fellow-diners are taking it. "They were all quietly eating their Blinis Demidoff, without any sign of either surprise or approval, as if they had been doing so every day for thirty years." The provincials conduct themselves like consummate men of the world; while the man of the world gasps and splutters like a yokel. The sensuous man "cannot trust his senses"; while the ascetics consider their growing intoxication to be spiritual. All are experiencing miracle, which is the same experience whether it seems to be coming through the senses or the spirit. There follows a sublimely comic counterpoint in which the old Brothers and Sisters, elated by the wine and by food of such refinement that it makes them feel lighter rather than heavier, discourse on the Dean's miracles; while the General exclaims over the culinary miracles before him.

The General remembers a great dinner in Paris at which it was said of the chef that " 'this woman is now turning a dinner at the Café Anglais into a kind of love affair—into a love affair of the noble and romantic category in which one no longer distinguishes between bodily and spiritual appetite or satiety!' " This was said when the woman's specialty, Cailles en Sarcophage, was served. And here is that dish again.

We are reminded that Christianity began with a Supper which it renews in its ritual (the date of the Dean's birthday connects him with Jesus). We are reminded of the two suppers in "Heroine" (*WT*); only here the fleshly and spiritual suppers are combined into a single meal and a single experience. It is to hail the singleness of the experience that the General rises to speak; and he hails it in words taken from the Dean, words the General has only now come to understand. " 'Mercy and truth, my friends, have met together,' " says the General. " 'Righteousness and bliss shall kiss one another.' " Having seen only coarse drunkenness, never having seen the effect on a noble nature of noble wine, the congregation do not realize the General is drunk. But how distinguish such drunkenness as his from spiritual ecstasy? That is the meaning of his words, that morality and pleasure come together in the mystical experience.

" 'We tremble,' " the General continues, " 'before making our choice in life, and after having made it again tremble in fear of having chosen wrong. But . . . that which we have chosen is given us, and that which we have refused is, also and at the same time, granted us.' " Having chosen pleasure, the General is getting that and through it the spirituality he rejected. Having chosen spirituality, the congregation are getting that and along with it the pleasure they rejected.

None of the guests could later remember exactly what happened the rest of the evening.

They only knew that the rooms had been filled with a heavenly light, as if a number of small halos had blended into one glorious radiance. Taciturn old people received the gift of tongues; ears that for years had been almost deaf were opened to it. Time itself had merged into eternity. Long after midnight the windows of the house shone like gold, and golden song flowed out into the winter air.

It is a beatific orgy; and since the old people have been waiting for it all their lives, they are not surprised. As the company breaks up, the General takes Martine's hand and says he has been with her every day of his life and will in the future sit down every evening, " 'if not in the flesh, which means nothing, in spirit, which is all, to dine with you, just like tonight. For tonight I have learned, dear sister, that in this world anything is possible.' "

In this world, note—and Martine repeats his words—not the next. The General has joined the congregation, but the congregation has, in finding the millennium through the senses, joined him too. Every step the General took away from Martine was, it turns out, a step toward her. As the old people caper home in the snow, they are finally at one with the glittering ideal they and the General have been pursuing. They

wavered on their feet, staggered, sat down abruptly or fell forward on their knees and hands and were covered with snow, as if they had indeed had their sins washed white as wool, and in this regained innocent attire were gamboling like little lambs. It was, to each of them, blissful to have become as a small child; it was also a blessed joke to watch old Brothers and Sisters, who had been taking themselves so seriously, in this kind of celestial second childhood. They stumbled and got up, walked on or stood still, bodily as well as spiritually hand in hand, at moments performing the great chain of a beatified *lanciers*.[1] "Bless you, bless you, bless you," like an echo of the harmony of the spheres rang on all sides.

The dinner scene concludes with the most ineffable epiphany in all Isak Dinesen.

The General's speech about " 'making our choice in life' " reminds us of *Either/Or*, in which the choice is as here between the sensuous-esthetic and the ethical ways of life. But Isak Dinesen seems to be taking issue with Kierkegaard. For Kierkegaard insists that you must make a choice; whereas the General suggests that it doesn't much matter what choice you make, that all paths can lead to salvation. Isak Dinesen also reinterprets Kierkegaard's alternatives. He shows the inadequacy of both the esthetic and ethical life in order to recommend the life of religious faith. She shows the inadequacy of two kinds of bookkeeping approaches to life, that which seeks its advantage in this world

---

[1] *Le quadrille des lanciers*, a dance.

and that which seeks its advantage in the next, in order to recommend the imaginative apprehension of life—to equate the magical art of Achille Papin and Babette with the mystical vision of the Dean. The General differs from Achille and Babette, for the same reason that the congregation differs from the Dean.

Isak Dinesen does follow Kierkegaard, however, in her understanding of the mystical way as the triumph of the absurd—in the General's realization that we are granted both what we have chosen and what we have refused. "But the next thing astonishes me," says Kierkegaard in describing the movement from resignation to faith, "it makes my head swim, for after having made the movement of resignation, then by virtue of the absurd to get everything, to get the wish whole and uncurtailed—that is beyond human power, it is a prodigy."[1]

In the end, Babette informs the sisters that she was cook at the Café Anglais and that she cannot go back to Paris because she has spent all ten thousand francs on the dinner. " 'I am a great artist,' " she says. She had, for reasons opposite to the bookkeeping approach to life, to do her best even though no one at the dinner—she did not foresee the General's appearance—would understand what she had accomplished.

All this is rather prosaically explicit after so high a flight of poetry and wit. But the story ends well with Philippa's fulfillment, matching Martine's. Philippa's understanding grows along with a growing tenderness for Babette. When Babette quotes Achille Papin as saying it is terrible to an artist to be applauded for doing his second best, Philippa "put her arms round her. She felt the cook's body like a marble monument against her own, but she herself shook and trembled from head to foot." As marble monument, Babette symbolizes Achille and art. She symbolizes Philippa as well; for Babette will never cook another great dinner, just as Philippa will never be the great singer she might have been. Because she sees Babette as a symbol—as belonging to a sphere where to have and have not mean something other than in this bookkeeping sphere (this is what General Loewenhielm said in effect to Martine)—Philippa can console Babette and herself. " 'In Paradise,' " Philippa whispers in the final paragraph, " 'you will be the great artist that God meant you to be! Ah!' she added, the tears streaming down her cheeks.

---

[1] *Fear and Trembling*, New York; p. 58; London, p. 64.

'Ah, how you will enchant the angels!' " Now she understands what food it is that is symbolized by Babette's food. She understands how art unites heaven and earth.

The artist's life is explored still further in "Tempests", where the point about the great old actor and theater director, Herr Soerensen, is that he does not confuse life and art. Like Babette, Herr Soerensen is an extravagant visionary. He has thrown up a good post at the Royal Theater of Copenhagen to travel by steamer with his small company, playing all the small towns on the fjords. He has done this because Norway and the sea appeal to his imagination and because an inner voice impelled him to carry the Word to barbarous places. But just as Babette excelled in the economical management of the sisters' household and in the management of her elaborate dinner, so Herr Soerensen is severely practical in executing his vision. Herr Soerensen is thoroughly acquainted with the facts of life. But he also knows that if you put the facts of life into verse, they become something else. They achieve, we may understand, the innocence of the diners' drunkenness and Achille Papin's kiss.

To realize the culminating vision of his life, Herr Soerensen decides to produce Shakespeare's *The Tempest* with himself as Prospero. His problem is to find a suitable Ariel. It is as a revelation that he finally finds " 'the most exquisite Ariel the world has ever known' " in a girl of his company whom no one but a man of genius would have recognized as Ariel. So moved is he, we are told, that he forgets Ariel is male. But that is the point. It is because the girl Malli is still all potentiality, because she has not yet discovered her body, has not yet been born as a woman,[1] that she is right for an epicene spirit like Ariel.

Norway figures here and in "Babette" as fairy-tale country, and the story of Malli's birth is a kind of fairy tale. For her father, a Scottish sea captain, came out of the sea one summer, when his ship had to lay up for repairs, married the town's prettiest girl and left at the end of summer, promising to return. He never returned. But he had, in courting her, whispered, " 'It's the sea

---

[1] "A young girl . . . does not grow," says Kierkegaard, "she is born. . . . Therein lies her infinite richness; at the moment she is born she is full-grown" ("Diary of the Seducer", *Either/Or*, Vol. I, New York, p. 327; London, p. 274).

that brought me, little heart of mine. Stop wave-beat, stop heart-beat.' " And his wife, after she watched him sail away, had, as a symbol of the happiness he had given her, a pile of gold coins and a new life in her belly. She knew, when he did not return, that his ship had gone down; and though the town said he had deceived her, Malli's mother never felt deceived. That is because Malli's father came out of the sea; he was an agent of the life force, a god, and gods do not deceive—they bring to fruition.

Out of the gold pieces the captain left her, Malli's mother set aside for her child a single sovereign as "an heirloom of pure gold from its father", token of an inheritance uniting nature, desire and imagination. As the girl grew up by the sea, she "dizzily felt that the swell in her own heart was like that in the water". She began to understand the swell when she learned her father's tongue, and began to read and love Shakespeare because he rendered for her her sense of her father. Shakespeare turned—we may understand from "Converse"—her apprehension of Logos into speech.

When Herr Soerensen's company played Shakespeare in the town, she knew she wanted to become an actress and follow this man who had come out of the sea and spoke her father's Shake-spearean speech. We see here how Isak Dinesen opens unexpec-ted psychological depths by exploring all the implications of the imagery she has set in motion. For as Prospero, Herr Soerensen makes himself into the father-god figure Malli is seeking; while her identification with her father is the properly psychological background of feminine idealism and explains the epicene quality that makes her suitable for Ariel.

The company is sailing into Christianssand, where *The Tempest* is to open, when there is a terrible storm offshore and the steamship is abandoned by all except Malli and ten crew members. In their panic the crew would have brought the ship to destruction, but Malli inspires them with the courage to keep full steam up all night; so the ship is brought safely into port next morning. A young seaman, named Ferdinand, stands by Malli, "and through the stormy night carried out each of her orders. Above the weather's roaring din the girl could often be heard calling him aloud by name." Although there is no passage just like this in Shakespeare, we understand that Malli, finding herself in the tempest of Shakespeare's opening scene, proceeded to play Ariel and bring the ship home as Ariel brings Prince Ferdinand's ship to safety.

When Malli alights from the ship to be greeted by a heroine's welcome, she finds herself in the arms not of the seaman, Ferdinand, who has been carried off by a crowd, but of Arndt Hosewinckel, the son of the rich shipowner whose ship she saved. Arndt carries her off to the Hosewinckel mansion where she is to stay. The town, who foresee the marriage of the heroine to the prince and therefore the fulfillment of the fairy tale Malli set in motion, think she may be a sea spirit and that the waves, having rolled her in, may roll her out again. Like her father, she has come out of the sea to bring the lives of others to fruition. Herr Soerensen, however, loses his voice. We are to understand by this not only his grief at the prospect of losing Malli but his fear for her future and also, perhaps, that as Prospero he has not the speech for this new situation; for Malli has stepped out of the play, she is confusing life and art.

Malli feels, when she first sees Arndt, what Miranda feels when she first sees Prince Ferdinand: "I might call him / A thing divine; for nothing natural / I ever saw so noble" (I, ii, 420-22). Miranda is seeing the first man other than her father whom she can love; and so is Malli, with Herr Soerensen standing here for her father. In stepping into life, Malli is Ariel trying to play Miranda and failing because she remains, in a psychological sense, Ariel.

Arndt looks like another Ariel and started out as one, but he has, we learn, fallen. At fifteen, he had an affair with one of the maids in the house. He was too young to feel guilt over what he took to be a sweetly secret game. But one spring night, the girl cried out, " 'I am a lost creature because I have met you and have looked at you, Arndt!' " and two days later her body was found floating in the fjord. It turned out she was pregnant, and for three days the boy thought he was responsible. That was his fall, his descent into hell. But then he learned that he might not be responsible after all, because the girl had been seeing a sweetheart from her home town. Arndt has learned about guilt and has learned to live with it. Malli, who will do the same thing to Arndt and Ferdinand that Arndt did to Guro, will not be able to live with her guilt.

Since Malli's engagement to Arndt fulfills the fairy tale, it

257

confirms for Malli her sense of herself as Ariel, the spirit who makes desire and imagination come true. Feeling himself restored to innocence, Arndt thinks Malli " 'has power to wake the dead' ", and he understands now that "the sea had taken Guro in a mighty embrace wherein there was power and love, forgiveness and forgetfulness"—that even his sin is transformed by connection with the Ariel force into innocence. " 'It is not happiness that you are, Malli,' " he says. " 'It is life.' " And she says, " 'Yes. "I am the resurrection and the life." ' " It is a very special kind of fiction in which characters can talk that way. Isak Dinesen is invoking not only the traditional conventions of poetic drama, but also the modern symbolist conventions that have accustomed us to characters who speak with the voice of cultural memory.

When Arndt goes away on a business trip, Malli fears he may never come back, like her father. But it is she who will repeat her father's role and go away. During Arndt's absence, she learns that the seaman Ferdinand has suddenly died of injuries incurred during the storm. Now she knows guilt. Earlier, Herr Soerensen wondered whether the tempest could have been brought about "by the will of that forceful, fearless, formidable child". She is disturbed by the same thought; for the tempest that killed Ferdinand fulfilled her desire—it enabled her to play Ariel, to become her father, a male and a spirit. She feels responsible for the tempest as people do for the subconscious desires that come true.

The cry that she had as Ariel addressed to Prince Ferdinand was harkened to by the seaman, who fell mortally in love—for we are to understand that he really died of unrequited love— with an epicene spirit in a play. Ferdinand is in Malli's life what Guro is in Arndt's. Ferdinand and Guro are the real or fallen human beings who respond with human or tragic passion to what Malli and Arndt take to be a play or game. The real human beings are brought to fruition by the experience, and the innocents fall.

We have seen how Arndt recovered from his fall. The question now is whether Malli will be able to absorb guilt into her love of Arndt and become a woman. Shakespeare's Prince Ferdinand has in this story been split up between the Prince (Arndt, the ideal) and the Ferdinand who was really with Malli in the storm.

If Malli can in Arndt love two men, both the Prince she called to in the storm and the real man she overlooked, she will love Arndt in spirit and flesh and win her way through to existence.

Malli wakes the next morning to find that she has like Herr Soerensen lost her voice. It is a sign that she grieves like him over loss of the ideal. It is a sign she is at an impasse, that she has stepped out of her role of Ariel and is waiting to learn what role she is to play. The answer comes to her from memory and art. It originates in of all places the memory and imagination of the rich businessman, Arndt's father. Arndt's father was growing old in a way different from the people of his family. He did not like them "grow stiff or petrified, but the whole world, and he himself with it, day by day seemed to be losing in weight and dissolving". We see here the contrast, introduced in "The Diver", between the stiff world of categories, of double-entry bookkeeping, and the fluid world of nature and imagination. Old Hosewinckel tells Malli the story of his grandmother's grandfather who, like Herr Soerensen, had a foot in both worlds.

As a hint to Malli in her despair, old Hosewinckel says that this ancestor, who knew how to make the forces of nature and God serve human life, bequeathed to the family a Bible with this quality—that if anyone in the house is at an impasse and lets the Bible fall open where it chooses, he will get from it the answer to his problem. Malli is found in a dead faint before this Bible. We do not learn until the end to what passage it fell open for her.

Malli goes the next morning to Herr Soerensen and tells him that Ferdinand is dead and that Arndt loves her. They quote to each other Oehlenschläger's *Væringerne i Miklagard* (*The Vikings in Byzantium*) to indicate that Malli has now stepped into a tragedy. For she has learned that she, who thought herself angelic, is diabolic, and that her father, with whom she identifies herself, must therefore be diabolic. " 'I betray them all, as Father betrayed Mother!' " she cries. She realizes she must go away before she brings misfortune on Arndt. " 'I speak,' " she says, paraphrasing the passage to which the Bible fell open, " 'as one that has a familiar spirit, out of the ground.' "

Herr Soerensen reveals that he once was married and that he deserted his wife for the same reason Malli is deserting Arndt. We are the same, he says in effect; and Malli, when they sit down together, lets "her fingers run through his wig" in a caress. It is a sign that, unable to reconcile spirit and flesh, she will remain faithful to her father who, whether angelic or diabolic, is spirit. This is unlike Miranda, who conspires with Prince Ferdinand against her father. The epicene sexuality by which Herr Soerensen and Malli pay allegiance to art is also Malli's way of paying allegiance to her father, who had the sexual potency of which art is a sublimation. All are operating along the single line of the Ariel force.

If Malli were Miranda, her decision would be tragic; and Herr Soerensen thinks for a moment that he is Lear with Cordelia. But then he remembers that Malli wants him to play Prospero, to solve her problem and turn the play into a comedy. Addressing to her Prospero's words to Miranda: " 'Sit still, and hear the last of our sea-sorrow,' " he says he will cancel the Christianssand performances, which would have been an enormous financial success, and move on to Bergen.

When Malli learns they cannot sail for two days, she expresses Ariel's disappointment when he learns he must wait two days for his freedom. Having tried to be Miranda, she turns back into Ariel as—coming toward Herr Soerensen "tardily but with great strength, like a wave running toward the coast"—she recites Ariel's speeches—and we are to understand that she has become a greater actress, that she recites them as never before—ending with the song by which Ariel leads Prince Ferdinand to Miranda. She says, however, " 'Full fathom five my body [instead of " 'thy father' "] lies,' " thus identifying herself with her own drowned father and suggesting that her " 'sea-change' " is from Miranda, the materialization of Prince Ferdinand's ideal, back to Ariel, the ideal itself.

In her letter to Arndt, which concludes the story, Malli shows that she has become a genuine artist; for she now knows the difference between life and art. She knows, as she did not before Ferdinand's death, that she deceived Arndt in the way she deceived Ferdinand—in that she was looking through Arndt to Prince Ferdinand, her father, herself, to a dream of innocence. Ferdinand's death taught her there was a real Arndt to whom she would have to give herself. But since she could not, without losing innocence, accomplish this surrender in life, she chose to simulate it through the renunciation of self required by art. She knows now what she is renouncing and what she is choosing.

She has returned to art with a knowledge of life, of the human passions and virtues she is to simulate. Her action in the storm was not heroic, she writes; for heroism is the conquest of fear, and she was not afraid since she thought she was in Shakespeare's comedy. Should she run into another storm, she will this time "clearly understand that it is not a play in the theatre, but it is death. And it seems to me that then, in the last moment before we go down, I can in all truth be yours. And I am thinking that it will be fine and great to let," she writes, reversing the phrase by which her father won her mother, "wave-beat cover heart-beat". She will say, reversing what Guro said of Arndt, " 'I have been saved, because I have met you and have looked at you, Arndt!' " Guro was destroyed by the inhuman innocence of Arndt; the inhumanly innocent Malli will be saved by Arndt's humanity. She will be his because she will genuinely share a human experience, that of death, but she will share it at the point where human experience returns to the Ariel force. The moment of drowning is the moment when life has the innocence of art.

The passage to which the Bible fell open was, she reveals, Isaiah 29, which begins: " 'Woe to Ariel, to Ariel! . . . And thou shalt be brought down, and thou shalt speak out of the ground, . . . and thy voice shall be as of one that hath a familiar spirit, out of the ground, and thy speech shall whisper out of the dust!' " The passage, which takes its meaning here not from the Biblical context but from Malli's application of it to her own case, told Malli what had happened to her. The angel, Ariel, speaks with the voice of a devil; his purity has turned diabolical. The eighth verse told her what would happen to Arndt if she did not leave him. " 'It shall even be as when an hungry man dreameth, and behold, he eateth; but he awaketh, and his soul is empty.' " Arndt would be embracing thin air. Malli offers Arndt the consolation General Loewenhielm offers Martine, that his unfulfilled desire will pass into memory and imagination to become, in Wordsworth's phrase, the master-light of all his seeing. As a token of what remains to him, she sends with the letter the gold coin her father left her mother.

We see again how destiny leads across the seas. "Tempests" is not only an anecdote of destiny; it is also a great winter's tale, in that it is a nature poem, taking up again the imagery of *Winter's Tales*. "Tempests" has in common with *Winter's Tales* the imagery that connects Shakespeare's last two plays. For in passing back and forth across the seas, the characters of Shakespeare's *Winter's Tale* and *Tempest* fulfill their desires and thus reconcile nature with art, with in other words memory and imagination.

It is hard to rank the three main stories of *Anecdotes*, since each excels in a different way. "Babette" is the lightest, and "Tempests" is the most intense, the most nearly tragic. "The Immortal Story" has the best plot, and was Isak Dinesen's favorite in the volume. We start with Mr Clay, an immensely rich old English tea-trader of Canton in the 1860's, who stands for all that is opposite to the sea imagery of "Tempests". Mr Clay is hard and dry. He hates, he says, " 'the juices of the body. I do not like the sight of blood, I cannot drink milk, sweat is offensive to me, tears disgust me.' "

Mr Clay symbolizes, like Eliot's Gerontion, the old age of our culture. But the indictment made through him is even stronger than in "Gerontion". For Gerontion is a poetical man who knows what has been lost. But Mr Clay is not only without desire and faith; he is without imagination and, most striking of all, without memory. He is the object of a very powerful satire; his characterization might be called serious caricature. When at seventy he is almost paralyzed with gout (the last symptom of his rigidity) and cannot sleep, his only resource is to have his old account books read aloud to him through the night. When he exhausts these records of his past triumphs, he asks, "reluctantly and as if himself uneasy and doubtful", whether the clerk who has been reading to him "had not heard of other kinds of books". The contrast between imagination and double-entry bookkeeping can be carried no further.

This clerk, Elishama, is another very powerfully symbolic figure. He is a Polish Jew whose family were all killed in a pogrom. He endured "strange sufferings" all over Europe before being "lifted up and shifted eastward" by destiny to Mr Clay's office in Canton. He seems sinister. A genius at bookkeeping, he is "like a tool ground upon the grindstone of life to an exceedingly sharp edge, with eyes and ears like a lynx, and without any illusions whatever of the world or of humanity". But then we are told that though Elishama might with such equipment have been a highly dangerous person, it was not so; for he totally lacked ambition. "Desire, in any form, had been washed, bleached and burnt out of him before he had learnt to read."

The comparison of Elishama to something cast up by the sea suggests that his lack of desire is different from Mr Clay's. In Mr Clay, desire has turned into will, into the personal force that resists desire. But Elishama floats without hope on the stream of universal desire. He has the innocence of one who *started* at rock bottom—the innocence and indestructibility of the fish who, as we are told in "The Diver", did not and cannot fall, for where would they fall to. The same thing is said here in an image that corresponds to the world's opinion of Elishama. "Outwardly and inwardly he was like some kind of insect, an ant hard to crush even to the heel of a boot."

Elishama—whose Hebrew name means "hearken to the Lord" —is in fact the Ariel of this story, the Ariel who in Isaiah's prophecy speaks out of the dust with a devilish voice. As a satire, "Immortal Story" takes off from the Ariel force in its lowest manifestations. Like Shakespeare's Ariel, Elishama, without feeling desire himself, fulfills other people's desires. Only here, Elishama, who despises the goods of the world, serves the greed for money that is the perversion of biological and spiritual desire.

He begins, however, to serve the Ariel force when, in response to Mr Clay's question about other kinds of books, he remembers a scrap of Hebrew writing that he once had translated. The words are Isaiah's (35: 1-7), prophesying that "the desert shall rejoice, and blossom as the rose". The sublime Ariel of "Tempests" reads in Isaiah of her degradation; the degraded Ariel of this story reads in Isaiah of his redemption.

When Elishama says he thinks Isaiah lived " 'about a thousand years ago' ", Mr Clay answers angrily:

"It is a foolish thing to foretell things which do not begin to take place within a thousand years. . . . People can record things which have already happened, outside of account books. I know what such a record is called. A story. I once heard a story myself. Do not disturb me, and I shall remember it."

The improbability of such ignorance as is displayed by Mr Clay, and even by Elishama, makes the scene poignantly ironic. For the thing symbolized—the loss of cultural memory—is real enough.

Mr Clay proceeds to tell this one story, which he heard a sailor tell one moonlit night at sea long ago. The sailor told how as he came ashore one night in a big town, he was approached by a splendid carriage from which emerged an old gentleman who asked him whether he wanted to earn five guineas. The sailor of course did, and the old gentleman took him home to his splendid house where he sat him down to a sumptuous meal and explained what he wanted him to do. This rich old man needed an heir in order to foil the people who expected to inherit his fortune. He had married a young wife, but she was no good to him. At this point, Elishama interrupts and finishes the story. He tells how, after leading the sailor into a luxurious bedroom where a beautiful lady waited in bed, the old gentleman gave the sailor a piece of gold—" 'a five-guinea piece, Mr Clay" '—before leaving him with the lady for the night.

Amazed, Mr Clay asks whether Elishama can have met the sailor to whom this happened. Elishama says he has heard many sailors tell this story on many ships. " 'It is the story of all sailors in the world. . . . But all sailors are pleased when, once more, one of them begins to tell it.' " To Mr Clay's question why they tell it if it is not true, Elishama says they tell it because it is the reverse of the truth—because in reality sailors pay for the love of unattractive old prostitutes. They would not tell it, he says, if they thought it could happen; and if by chance it did happen to one sailor, that sailor would not tell it. The sign it is a story is that, whatever the other variations, the price is always the same —five guineas, which is, considering the number of sailors ready to undertake the job, " 'contrary to the law of demand and supply' ".

The last observation is important. It is probably based on Kierkegaard's speculation that all that has come down, from the folk tradition, about Don Juan is the comically precise 1,003, the number of women he seduced in Spain.[1] The idea explains the meaning of number here and in the stories, generally, starting with *Last Tales*. The fact that it is so conspicuously in place of literature that the account books are read to Mr Clay suggests that number is the only certainty remaining when cultural incoherence renders us speechless. Elishama, the degraded agent of the Biblical tradition, who keeps the accounts and reads them,

[1] "Musical Erotic", *Either/Or*, Vol. 1, New York, p. 90; London, p. 74.

is the poet and prophet at an absolute minimum. We are told that all he wants in life is to shut himself at the end of day in his womblike room and repeat the numeral series, drawing comfort from the idea that its figures are all there. This is poetry and prayer at a minimum.

We are also told of Mr Clay and Elishama that, unknowingly, they behave toward each other like father and son. If we take this idea and the idea of number back to "Converse", we see that Mr Clay and Elishama are the king and poet of that story, fallen into the bookkeeping approach to life that the king, by his madness, and the poet, by his drunkenness, resisted. Mr Clay is the degraded symbol of Logos, to whom the poet and son can only give back as mythos an epic of commercial triumphs written in numbers.

To complete the trinity of "Converse", a woman is required, and Mr Clay sends Elishama in search of her. Unconsciously, Mr Clay reasserts pattern; he serves the Ariel force, though he intends to do the opposite. His unconscious connection with the Ariel force is suggested by the unheeded meanings that run round the dry land of his life. He trades across the sea in an exotic commodity. He lives in exotic Canton in a house that speaks, if he could hear it, of a life of esthetic and sensual gratification. He remembers a story of the sea and desire, which he himself overheard on a moonlit sea in that Southern Hemisphere where—if we remember *Winter's Tales*—imagination and reality are one.

Mr Clay intends to reassert against the Ariel force his own omnipotence. Since he cannot control a world in which fiction has more currency than fact, he decides that this one story at least " 'shall become reality' ", that " 'one sailor in the world shall tell it . . . as it has actually, from beginning to end, happened to him' ". If Elishama supplies the lady for the bed and Mr Clay himself plays the old gentleman, the sailor should be easy to find. Mr Clay is a degraded Prospero, who uses his Ariel as a procurer in order to realize a degraded version of an imaginative pattern. Yet he is dealing, even at this low level, with magical forces of which he is not, as Prospero is, aware. Elishama, who knows the difference between life and art, sees that Mr Clay "is going mad, and nearing his end". His madness will be, like the king's in "Converse", a saving madness.

For the part of the lady, Elishama chooses a high-class French courtesan with imagination. He does not know that this Virginie is the daughter of a tea-trader whom Mr Clay, at a time when the Frenchman owed him 300 guineas, ruined and drove to eventual suicide. The number is significant, for it contains the 3 which is the paradigm of all stories and the 30 of the Judas story. The house Mr Clay now owns and lives in was the Frenchman's. The Frenchman made his wife and children promise they would never again set eyes on Mr Clay.

The Frenchman, a bourgeois who has the charm and taste of the aristocracy without the hardness of either class, seems to represent the moment in history that is symbolized for Isak Dinesen by the Second Empire. The Second Empire dominates Virginie's imagination. Her father brought her up on the accounts that reached him of its gaudy splendor, and it remained her symbol of the ideal.

It is a sign of his corruption that he quoted to her as a moral precept the Empress Eugénie's remark to the Emperor Napoleon when he was courting her—"that the only way to her bedroom ran through the Cathedral of Notre Dame". This courtesan's morality became Virginie's code; only she lives the code in reverse, since the path to her bedroom runs from the offices of the town. There is an ironic echo here of the Dean's remark in "Babette" about God's paths. And, indeed, Virginie was raised by her father to understand that the real may be an ironical reversal of the ideal. He used to say of her: " 'Ah, Virginie is subtle! She is a connoisseur of irony!' " These two quotations from her father are the *leitmotifs* of her imaginative life.

Virginie's father is, as the source of her ideals, a degraded version of Malli's. He is also—with his easygoing motto of " *'Pourquoi pas?'* " of mere nonresistance to temptation—a degraded symbol of desire. Just as Malli remains a virgin out of loyalty to her father; so Virginie pays tribute in reverse to the ideal of virginity. In giving herself to all men, she gives herself to none. Her lovers, we are told, are too puny to make any impression on her imagination. Only her first made an impression. He took her to Japan where on their very first night together an earthquake made the whole earth shake and tremble, as she saw it, over the loss of her innocence. Like Malli, Virginie wants to be an actress as a way of acting out her vision of the ideal. Elishama offers her the chance to play a part in a story.

When Elishama makes his proposal, she projects upon him her guilt over her own desire to comply. She speaks French, as Herr Soerensen speaks in verse, when she speaks in her ideal aspect as a heroine. When she learns she is to play her part in the house where she was once an innocent young girl, she strikes Elishama, scratching him and drawing blood. She makes the Jew atone for what she knows she is going to do; and to impress upon him the enormity of her sin, she quotes the remark of Empress Eugénie.

" 'That way of which you spoke,' " says Elishama, " 'which ran through the Cathedral of Notre Dame—it is in this pattern. Only in this pattern it is reversed.' " Caught by "the strange sweetness of his voice", she asks how he knows that the pattern of which he speaks, the pattern of giving in, runs in her family. Quoting her father's motto, " '*Pourquoi pas?*' " she assents, on the condition that she be paid the three hundred guineas over which Mr Clay ruined her father. " 'That, if you like, is a pattern,' " she says.

Her father's motto means at this point something more than mere compliance. We realize this when we learn that *Pourquoi pas?* became Isak Dinesen's own motto after she had lost everything in Africa and started life anew as a writer. She cannot, she says in her speech "On Mottoes of My Life", account for the meaning of the motto. "But it worked. It was encouraging and inspiring. 'Why?' by itself is a wail or lament, a cry from the heart; it seems to ring in the desert and to be in itself negative, the voice of a lost cause. But when another negative, the *pas*, the 'not', is added, the pathetic question is turned into an answer, a directive, a call of wild hope."[1]

It is because Virginie can project her guilt on to Elishama, by calling him Judas and Wandering Jew, that she is able to fulfill her desire and step into the story through which she regains innocence. With Elishama, Isak Dinesen completes the study, begun with Marcus Cocoza, of the Jew in the European imagination. Marcus seems satanic because he is fabulously rich, intelligent and cultured; Elishama, because he is the lowest of the low. Both turn out angelic. The Christian attitude toward them runs to extremes of fear and admiration, because the Jews are the fallen

[1] Proceedings of *The American Academy of Arts and Letters and The National Institute of Arts and Letters*, Second Series, Number Ten (New York, 1960), p. 355. The speech was delivered at a dinner meeting in New York on January 28, 1959.

Ariel of Isaiah's prophecy, who speak out of the dust with the voice of memory. They bring before Christian eyes, most disturbingly—here Ariel and the Wandering Jew come together—the image of Christ. Elishama feels a shame that is Christlike. We are told that he changed his name to Ellis Lewis, "not—like some other people in those days emigrating to China—in order to cover up any trespass or crime of his own, he had done it to obliterate crimes committed against himself."

When on the appointed evening Mr Clay and Elishama drive to the waterfront to find the sailor, the first two sailors they approach run away as soon as it becomes apparent that the immortal story has become real. The third says yes, because he is an innocent young boy who expects dreams to come true. His first voyage ended in shipwreck, and he has just been rescued from a marvelous island, like Prospero's, where he spent a year with no one to speak to. " 'There were many sounds on my island, but no one ever spoke. I myself sang a song there some-times—you may sing to yourself. But I never spoke.' " We have here again the theme of speechlessness. The song signifies, like the numbers of Mr Clay and Elishama, a direct connection with Logos. The numbers, however, are all that remain after speech has been lost; the song precedes speech. The three men are waiting to step into the story that will give them speech.

At supper, Mr Clay does something not called for by his role as the old gentleman of the story. It is the second sign that the story that will come to pass will not be the one the sailors tell. (The first is the sailor's innocence, since the comic effect depends on his knowing that the events of the story are opposite to reality.) Setting himself up in opposition to the boy and, as he dimly apprehends, to the Prophet Isaiah, Mr Clay offers a defense of his life that is really a self-accusation. Elishama, surprised, realizes the value of a comedy, "in which a man may at last speak the truth".

Mr Clay makes clear that his love of gold is a substitute for sexuality and experience—that it is an attempt to make himself into pure spirit, in the puritan way, through will and abstraction, rather than, in the Ariel way, through desire. Making clear the connection in capitalist culture between economic and psycho-logical vicariousness, he says he would like to beget the heir to his fortune in the way he begot the fortune. For you who live only in the moment, he says, the only reality tonight will be " 'the pleasure of your body and the five guineas in your pocket' ". You will not know you are effecting my purpose. Just as, he says in a moving passage,

"The starving coolies in the tea-fields, the dog-tired seamen on the middle watch, never knew that they were contributing to the making of a million pounds. To them the minutes only, the pain in their hands, the hail-showers in their faces, and the poor copper coins of their wages had real existence. It was in my brain and by my will that this multitude of little things were combined and set to co-operate to make up one single thing: a million pounds."

We are reminded of Prince Potenziani, who wants to beget an heir vicariously and says that only the man who conceives an act can be said to have done it. Prince Potenziani is talking about an imaginative conception in which, like the artist and God, you experience what you conceive. Mr Clay is talking about a managerial function that depends for its effectiveness on not experiencing what you conceive. Prince Potenziani is wrong but not as far wrong as Mr Clay, who thinks the same kind of vicariousness will get him his heir as got him his fortune. The fact that, in this passage, Mr Clay participates for the first time in the human experience that got him his fortune is a sign that his imagination has been awakened by some faint kindling in him of desire.

When Mr Clay leads the sailor into the bedroom where Virginie is waiting, he is impressed for the first time in his life by a woman's beauty and has a fleeting memory of childhood. The Prophet Isaiah, the Ariel force, whom he thought he would defeat, has, we are told, played a trick on him by turning him into a child; so that he now begins "to play with his story". He evokes his envious sense of what will occur that night by describing the young people as two " 'strong and lusty jumping-jacks within this old hand of mine' ". You are mere puppets, he says, in " 'nothing but a story turned, at my word, into reality' ". By calling the story a story, he has turned it into reality in a way he never intended. A genuine emotion of his own has taken over and turned the old gentleman of the story into the real Mr Clay.

At supper, Mr Clay remarks that this sumptuous house must seem very different from the sailor's island. We see, however, that since the house is for the sailor the materialization of a dream, it is to be the island where this Prince Ferdinand will meet his

Miranda. The house has been an island for Mr Clay, too, but an island opposite to the sailor's. For the sailor's island connected him with the Ariel force and Mr Clay's isolates him from it. The sailor has come back from the island for only one reason, to satisfy his desire to own a boat—a desire associated in the pattern of Isak Dinesen's imagery with desire for a woman.

When the sailor tells Virginie that his name is Paul, we are reminded of another island, the tropical island of Bernardin de Saint-Pierre's eighteenth-century romance, *Paul et Virginie*. The idyllic love affair of Bernardin de Saint-Pierre's couple comes to an end when Virginie leaves the island for civilization. On her return to the island, her ship is caught in a storm offshore, and she drowns because she is too modest to undress before trying to swim back to shore. The sea that washes her body on to the island reunites the lovers; for Paul, when he learns she died clutching his picture to her heart, dies of grief soon afterward. Bernardin de Saint-Pierre's Virginie has betrayed nature; Isak Dinesen's has betrayed her own nature. Elishama has, as the Ariel force, returned her to Paul on the tropical island Paul carries inside him.

Their night together is a remarkable idyl, for Isak Dinesen has managed to make it both erotic and innocent. It is Paul's first time with a woman, and he takes Virginie to be seventeen like himself. At the moment of consummation, she screams, " 'There is an earthquake.' " Her innocence lost in one earthquake has been regained in another. The way to Notre Dame has run for her through the bedroom.

At dawn, Virginie's only thought is to send Paul away before he can see upon her the face of a wicked old woman. When he insists on taking her along, she reminds him he has been paid. The reminder is his fall, teaching him the difference between the ideal and the real. " 'You will have your boat,' " she says. The boat will be for him what the gold coin was for Malli's mother.

By the same dawn light, Elishama finds Mr Clay sitting, dead, at the dining-room table. We are not explicitly told he is dead, and it is difficult for Elishama to make out that he is. It is the appropriately done death of a man who never lived. Yet the death is a fulfillment; for it came of the one time he did live, did feel a surge of genuine desire. He sat up "to drink off at sunrise the cup of his triumph. But the cup of his triumph had been too strong for him." We are told that he looks this morning "like a jumping-jack when the hand which has pulled the strings has suddenly let them go". This is a sign that he, who called the lovers his jumping-jacks and intended to be the puppet master, had himself, because of his emotional involvement, stepped into a puppet show the strings of which were pulled by God.

Elishama recognizes that Mr Clay has fulfilled a destiny. For he quotes, in regard to him, one verse of Isaiah, and another, in regard to the lovers whose weeping he can hear. We understand both verses to refer to death and rebirth. Elishama classes Mr Clay with the lovers, as the three people who played roles in Mr Clay's story. He differentiates them from himself as people for whom "it was very hard" because they "wanted things so badly that they could not do without them. If they could not get these things it was hard, and when they did get them, surely it was very hard". In saying that every story of desire is tragic, Elishama is apparently contradicting General Loewenhielm's statement in "Babette" that we are given both what we have chosen and what we have refused. But Isaiah's verses reconcile the two statements by suggesting the sense in which every destiny is tragic and comic. Elishama arrives at this reconciliation in the last lines of the story.

As Paul is about to leave, Elishama, who finds him not so young as he had thought, suggests, out of loyalty to his master, that the boy will now be the one sailor who will be able to tell the sailors' story truthfully. The boy, who cannot even remember what story Elishama means, says, when it is recalled to him, " 'But that story is not in the least like what happened to me.' " And after a while, " 'I would not tell it for a hundred times five guineas.' " Having been exposed through Elishama's retelling of the story, to the "truth" about last night—that Virginie was probably like himself paid to act out the story—Paul nevertheless salvages his ideal sense of the night. He thus regains the innocence he lost when Virginie first exposed him to the "truth". The garden to which he steps out looks in the morning light as if it "had just this hour been created", and Elishama sees that the boy is after all very young.

Paul takes out of a bag he had left on the verandah a "big shining pink shell" from his island, which he asks Elishama to give to Virginie from him. " 'Will you tell her to hold it to her ear?' " Before giving the shell to Elishama, Paul holds it to his own ear, and his face takes on "an attentive, peaceful look". After he has left, Elishama lifts the shell to his ear and his face takes on the same expression as the boy's. For there is "a deep, low surge in it, like the distant roar of great breakers", and he has "a strange, gentle, profound shock, from the sound of a new voice in the house, and in the story. 'I have heard it before,' he thought, 'long ago. Long, long ago. But where?' "

The sound in the shell is the immortal story, of which the sailors' story, Isaiah's prophecy and the numbers of Mr Clay and Elishama are versions. It is the music of the Logos, out of which speech, numbers and stories arise and to which they return. It is the Ariel force, as Elishama, in his gradual recovery of memory, finally recognizes. The happy ending lies in his recognition that all that has happened belongs to this force and is therefore well.

In dealing once again with a man who tries to make a story in life, "Immortal Story" sets forth the essential situation of all Isak Dinesen's stories. For life is in her view a repetition. We live by projecting out of memory—personal memory that shades off into cultural memory—patterns through which we hope to accomplish our purposes. We accomplish our purposes but not in the sense we intended; for somewhere, in acting out our own stories, we step into God's and serve His purpose. We step into God's story when we are carried by a genuine emotion to that depth where our desire meets His—when, as happened to Mr Clay's story, the pattern experienced from inside seems as though it had never happened before.

All Isak Dinesen's stories are anecdotes of destiny. That she should finally have arrived at this title shows how she constantly clarifies her theme by clarifying her vision of the absolute. She is increasingly detailed in depicting the line of force along which our lives connect with God; she is also increasingly schematic, as though she were constantly finding the pattern of her pattern. Looking back, we can see that "Poet", for example, deals with the trinity of father, son and woman of which we are made aware in "Cloak", "Converse" and "Immortal Story". The fourth figure in "Poet", Count Schimmelmann, does not, however, bring us any closer to absolute vision; the Councilor must himself both die like Mr Clay and arrive at Elishama's happy recognition.

Pino, in "The Cloak" stories, does bring us closer to the absolute, but he stands outside the triangle.

In Elishama, who is both in and out of Mr Clay's triangular story, Isak Dinesen has finally done with complete success the fourth figure. Elishama is so involved in the triangle as to share with Paul the role of son. Paul takes the woman over from the father sexually; but Elishama takes over her imagination, predisposing her to act out the father's intention. Yet Elishama, who does not participate in the desire that binds the other three, remains the outsider, a shadowy figure who reminds us that the triangular story of desire, while complete in itself, is also part of a mystical rectangle that transcends desire. He represents—as he himself recognizes in the end—the "new voice in the house, and in the story", that makes the story, whatever the events, a comedy. It is because the paradigm introduced in *Last Tales* is completely realized in *Anecdotes* that *Anecdotes* is the supremely comic volume. Its schematic clarity is achieved at the expense of immediacy, of the unfinished human wildness that attracts empathy. But then *Anecdotes* does not call for empathy. It calls for serene contemplation.

The few brief notes sounded in "The Ring" make an interesting epilogue to the volume. For if as prologue "The Diver" sounds the theme of Ariel, of the man who either soars or dives, the epilogue reminds us of the contrary theme that has been dealt with for the most part negatively in *Anecdotes*—the theme of the richly ambiguous human way. Like Eve when she meets Satan, the newly married, inhumanly innocent wife encounters a young thief and murderer. To buy him off, she offers him her wedding ring, which he spurns so that it falls to the ground and he kicks it away. He picks up, instead, the handkerchief she has also let fall, wraps it around the blade of his knife and puts the knife back in its sheath before disappearing. The sexual symbolism suggests that there has been a union between them, that he has taken her spiritual, as her husband took her physical, virginity. When, lying to her husband, she tells him she has lost her wedding ring, she realizes that she has now married two men—that "with this lost ring she had wedded herself to . . . poverty, persecution, total loneliness. To the sorrows and the sinfulness of this earth." Only now, we are to understand, when she has this secret from her husband, is her marriage to him fully consummated.

The wife's fate shows how Ariel, when he falls into humanity, becomes a tragic figure. In ending *Anecdotes* on a tragic note, Isak Dinesen shows the artist's instinct for a complex symmetry. Looking back from a vision that transcends tragedy, she says what she has implied throughout, that tragedy is our distinctively human glory. But she praises tragedy from a point of view that makes it a part of comedy. From the currents that run below the book's serene surface, she stirs up a final, momentary ripple that in subsiding makes even more comprehensive and substantial the book's comic vision.

It is *Ehrengard* (1963), however, that makes the really appropriate climax to *Anecdotes of Destiny*. Indeed, *Ehrengard* brings all Isak Dinesen's work to a triumphant conclusion. For Isak Dinesen's talent always was essentially comic and pastoral, and *Ehrengard* is the lightest, the most purely comic and pastoral story she ever wrote. It is not as profound or emotionally rich as some of her other stories, but it is unsurpassed for sheer loveliness. The Ariel of *Ehrengard* does not have to reject life for art, or pay the price of tragedy; art and life combine to give her fulfillment. In *Ehrengard*, there is complete reconciliation between heaven and earth.

Ehrengard takes off from the novel, "Diary of the Seducer", with which Kierkegaard concludes his account of the esthetic life in *Either/Or*. Isak Dinesen actually proposed Kierkegaard's title for her story, when the *Ladies' Home Journal* suggested a change in title for its abbreviated version which came out in December 1962 as "The Secret of Rosenbad".[1] Kierkegaard's seducer is an esthete whose interest is in the way the seduction is managed. He wants to possess not so much the girl's body as her imagination—to awaken in her the idea of the erotic so that her "only desire is to give herself freely". Only in this, he says, is there "true enjoyment, but this always requires spiritual influence".[2]

The passage is the germ of *Ehrengard*. Yet *Ehrengard* is like "Babette" an answer to Kierkegaard, in that Isak Dinesen accepts Kierkegaard's analysis of the esthetic life but not his

---

[1] "You might call it," she wrote to the *Ladies' Home Journal* on June 25, 1962, " 'The Seducer's Diary' "—which is, of course, a quotation from Kierkegaard, but which is here to be taken ironically and might from the beginning give the reader an idea of the nature of the story."

[2] *Either/Or*, Vol. I, New York, p. 337; London, p. 283.

evaluation of it. Kierkegaard apparently wants us to consider the seducer a scoundrel or at least to see the esthetic life as a dead end. But Isak Dinesen sees in the seducer's desire to bring the girl to fulfillment—to bring her womanhood to birth, in Kierkegaard's metaphor—an emblem of the artist's desire at just the point where it meets with God's. Far from being a dead end then, the esthetic life is for Isak Dinesen continuous with that spiritual or religious life which Kierkegaard is at such pains to distinguish from it.

Her point requires, however, that the seduction be given a different setting than the squalidly bourgeois world of Kierkegaard's novel, in which there are none of the symbols that help us see the erotic principle in its ideal aspect. She requires a setting made and defined by art. Thus, she sets her story in a storybook world; divides it like a musical composition into a prelude, a pastorale and a rondo; makes her seducer a painter; and uses, as one of the symbols that awaken the girl to the erotic idea, a statue of Leda and the swan.

Ehrengard takes place in the storybook world of the little German principalities—in the Grand Duchy of Babenhausen. The name seems made up; yet there really was such a principality, ruled over by the family of Fugger-Babenhausen. The old regime really had—it is Isak Dinesen's whole point about it—a storybook quality. Although the story takes place only one hundred and twenty years ago, the world of the little principalities seems far more remote than that.

We have the story from an old lady who knows it from the letters that the famous painter and Don Juan of his time, Wolfgang Cazotte, wrote to her great-grandmother. The events follow a mythical pattern in that the Grand Duke and Grand Duchess of Babenhausen, having grieved a long time because they were childless, are finally vouchsafed a perfect son of ethereal beauty and aloofness. The Grand Duchess in fact worries because Prince Lothar, when he reaches marriageable age, shows no susceptibility to that *belle passion* which is necessary to the perpetuation of the house of Fugger-Babenhausen and the foiling of the dynasty's wicked lateral branch. In the hope of awakening her son to the erotic idea, the Grand Duchess encourages his friendship with Cazotte. She is not disappointed. After a visit with Cazotte to the court of Leuchtenstein, Prince Lothar announces his desire to marry the beautiful Princess Ludmilla. Cazotte's influence went a little farther than the Grand Duchess had planned, however; for sometime after the happy nuptials, Prince Lothar informed his mother "that the Ducal heir, on whom her mind and heart had for so long been concentrating, was about to make his entry in the world a full two months before law and decency permitted".[1]

Cazotte advises the horrified Duchess to get out of the predicament by taking another view of it, by turning it into a work of art—into the idyl she instinctively knows it to be. The Prince and Princess, together with a small trustworthy court, are—according to Cazotte's plan—to retire in April to a secluded residence in the country, where the baby will be born in May. For two months the small court will form "a stone wall of loyal hearts round an exalted secret". Then in July a cannonade will announce the birth of the child. There will be a great baptism ("it was a lucky thing that the old Archbishop was extremely short-sighted"), after which the princely couple will retire to their regular summer residence. "About the end of September the proud Babenhauseners would be pluming themselves on their lusty and clever little Prince."[2]

The idyl will take place during those spring months when a circle of secrecy will protect the erotic miracle from Christian and conventional judgments. It will take place during the two months when the baby will be entirely justified as a child of love, without additional sanction of law or baptism. Cazotte chooses for the place of seclusion the chateau of Rosenbad, a charming rococo hermitage which he decorates as a rococo Venusberg in order that the baby, when it is born, will be seen to be, not an illegitimate child, but an amorino, a chubby little rococo Cupid. That is what happens. Cazotte creates a softly elegant idyl devoted to the beauty of women and children.

It is important to find the right maid of honor for the Princess during her seclusion, and Cazotte names for this post the daughter of General von Schreckenstein—Ehrengard. " 'A young Walkyrie,' " he calls her. " 'Brought up in the sternest military virtues, in the vast and grim castle of Schreckenstein, the only daughter of a warrior clan. An almost unbelievably fitting white-

---

[1] New York: Random House, 1963, p. 18; London: Michael Joseph, 1963, p. 14.
[2] New York, pp. 23-24; London, p. 18.

hot young angel with a flaming sword to stand sentinel before our young lovers' paradise!' "[1] She is of course the most inappropriate possible choice for so voluptuous a place. That is as much of the joke as we get in the "prelude".

The joke goes farther when we learn in the "pastorale" that Cazotte has been planning to seduce Ehrengard, that the first time he saw her he cried with Michelangelo: " ' "My greatest triumph hides within that block of marble." ' " Cazotte may even have arranged the whole idyl as a setting for this seduction. The possibility parodies the extravagant measures taken by Kierkegaard's seducer to accomplish his purpose. We learn of Cazotte's intention through his letters to the narrator's great-grandmother. These letters contain the reflections that are the whole substance of Kierkegaard's novel and that show our seducers as interested in reflection rather than existence. Isak Dinesen uses the letters superbly as a lyrical accompaniment to the action, an accompaniment in which she turns Kierkegaard's turbulent poetry and wit into her own serene combination of the two.

Cazotte does not even want the single act of physical consummation required by Kierkegaard's seducer as a token of success. He wants only to bring forth the hidden flower of Ehrengard's being. After asking in a letter where this flower might "give forth itself most exhaustively", he himself answers: "In the blush." The answer completes his image of Ehrengard as a block of marble. He will not only bring forth the statue, he will bring it to life. "You will not, I know, for a moment," he writes,

be thinking of the blush of offended modesty which might be called forth, from the outside, by a coarse and blunt assailant. . . . To the mind of the artist the very idea is blasphemy. . . . What is really to happen to this admirable, this unique nature is to happen within herself. So I shall in time be drawing my young Amazon's blood . . . from the deepest, most secret and sacred wells of her being, making it cover her all over like a transparent crimson veil and making it burn her up in one single exquisite gasp of flame.[2]

This is Isak Dinesen's erotic and spiritual intensification of Kierkegaard's: "There are different kinds of feminine blushes. There is the coarse brick-red blush. . . . There is the delicate blush; it is the blush of the spirit's dawn. In a young girl it is

---

[1] New York, pp. 27-28; London, p. 20.
[2] New York, pp. 34-36; London, pp. 25-26.

priceless."[1] Isak Dinesen goes on in this letter to connect the blush with the inner fire, the force of desire, that animates and spiritualizes all nature.

In high mountains, as you will know, there exists a phenomenon of nature called *Alpen-Glühen*. . . . After the sun has set, and as the whole majestic mountain landscape is already withdrawing into itself, suddenly the row of summits, all on their own, radiate a divine fire, a celestial, deep rose flame, as if they were giving up a long kept secret. After that they disappear, nothing more dramatic can be imagined: they have betrayed their inmost substance and can now only annihilate themselves. Black night follows.

Tall white-clad mountains will naturally be a little slow in the uptake, but when at last they do realize and conceive, what glow, you heavens, and what glorification. And what void afterwards. I have seen the *Alpen-Glühen* once, the moment is among the greatest of my existence. . . . And yet after all it has been but a presage of my adventure with Ehrengard.[2]

The more coldly virginal the girl is, the more complete is her awakening to passion and her annihilation as a virgin.

The idea fits the myths of Ehrengard's archetype, the maiden-goddess—the myth of Persephone, for example, whose maidenhood comes to flower in the story of her rape. There is the most delicate exploitation here of the two related cycles of myths treated by Jung and Kerényi in their book on the Divine Child and the Kore or Divine Maiden. Eros or Cupid is one manifestation of the Divine Child, and the erotic mystery of virginity is expressed in the union of the Divine Maiden with the Divine Mother—Persephone and Demeter are aspects of a single figure.

The baby, says Kerényi, reminds us of the love that begot him.[3] It is the birth of the Princess's baby that first awakens in Ehrengard the erotic idea. She does not know, Cazotte writes, that she has fallen "in love with the God of Love himself . . . the first step towards a deeper, final fall".[4] Kerényi connects the maiden goddess with water; and sure enough, one very early July morning, Cazotte comes upon Ehrengard bathing nude in a lake, assisted only by her maid. He receives the vision gravely,

---

[1] "Diary of the Seducer", New York, p. 359; London, p. 302.

[2] New York, pp. 37-38; London, pp. 26-27. The passage brings to a climax the theme of the blush that begins in "Roads Round Pisa", where Prince Potenziani shows his erotic imagination by blushing, just before he dies of love, at the thought of how Rosina's "whole body blushed like an oleander flower".

[3] *Science of Mythology*, p. 76.

[4] New York, pp. 49-50; London, p. 34.

for he has been proven right in his valuation of the girl's beauty and has been granted a motif for a painting—"The bath of Diana"—which will be the crowning glory of his career.

An artist possesses his beloved by painting her, says Kierkegaard's seducer.[1] Cazotte plans to seduce Ehrengard by secretly painting her at her early morning baths. He imagines the scene in which the painting is unveiled to the world, and "no one but he and she"—the bather's face being turned away—"would know the truth. . . . She would be, in the midst of the brilliant crowd, alone with him." They would be bound together by that erotic idea of the secret, that Isak Dinesen takes from Kierkegaard; and Cazotte imagines how under her clothes Ehrengard's body "would slowly become all aglow".[2] This is the moment when he would possess her. She would see herself in the picture as beautiful and naked, and this self-consciousness would constitute her fall.

He paints her every morning for a week, until one morning she disappears suddenly after a short cry from her maid. He fears he has been apprehended and that there will be no more baths of Diana. But later in the day, the Princess comes unwittingly to his aid by asking him to admire the little Prince in company with Ehrengard. " 'Surely you will be needing a model for an amorino in a scene of love,' " says the Princess when he enters her pale-blue boudoir. " 'I lend him to you for the purpose.' " The boudoir is atwitter, like an aviary, with court ladies; the scene is a charmingly rococo adoration of the child.

The Princess bids Ehrengard lift up, for Cazotte's inspection, the basket full of white stocks in which the baby has been laid. Cazotte and Ehrengard stand a minute "quite still, his face like hers bowed over the fairy cradle". The scent of stocks, "an invisible cloud of Venusberg incense, encompassed their two heads".

Cazotte and Ehrengard stop afterward before the fountain out of whose clear water rises the statue of Leda and the swan. " 'My maid tells me,' " she says, " 'that you want to paint a picture. Out by the east of the house. I wish to tell you that I shall be there every morning, at six o'clock.' " Cazotte's response is expressed in a one-sentence letter: "The damnable, the dynamic,

[1] "Diary of the Seducer", New York, p. 384; London, p. 323.
[2] New York, pp. 67-68; London, pp. 45-46.

the demonic loyalty of this girl!"[1] This is not the seduction as he imagined it; nor would it be, under these terms, a seduction at all. Besides, the force which brought Ehrengard to this point is not the one he had in mind. It is the force of feudal loyalty. He had counted on it when he chose her for the post at Rosenbad. He did not, however, expect that she would accede to him because as a good courtier she had adopted the conventions established by the Princess.

As always happens when someone in Isak Dinesen tries to play the artist in life, the chain of events set in motion by Cazotte has now got out of hand. By achieving an apotheosis of virginity as a warrior maiden, Ehrengard comes alive erotically and proves Cazotte to have been right about her in a way he hadn't expected. This is both a charming jest and a sublime tribute to the erotic fire hidden in virginity. Ehrengard is Miss Nat-og-Dag, Athena Hopballehus, Lady Flora—all Isak Dinesen's fierce, highborn and potentially passionate virgins, brought finally to perfect fulfillment.

So far Ehrengard has, like Kierkegaard's girl, existed only in the reflections of the seducer. Kierkegaard's girl is a mere shadow; but it is amazing how vivid Ehrengard is, though we know nothing more about her than that she is a highborn chivalric virgin. When in the "rondo", she steps forward as the heroine of a feudal romance to which Cazotte is merely a spectator, she grows in stature by surprising us, as she surprises Cazotte, into a deeper understanding of what we already know about her. We remember of this story the quality of Cazotte's mind, but we *see* the image of Ehrengard as a stance straighter and nobler than that of the other characters. Again, Isak Dinesen shows how we have to revise current notions of what constitutes successful character-making in fiction.

In the "rondo", agents of the dynasty's wicked lateral branch bribe the husband of the little Prince's wet nurse to kidnap his wife with her mysterious charge.[2] Rosenbad is in despair, the baby's birth is to be announced the very next day. Cazotte and Ehrengard ride separately to the rescue. Cazotte imagines a charming scene in which he regains the initiative lost at the Leda fountain by presenting the regained baby to Ehrengard to hand

---

[1] New York, pp. 74-77; London, pp. 51-52.
[2] Another echo of the Kaspar Hauser story.

over to the Princess. "Would the girl not feel then for a verti-
ginous moment this particular amorino to be, spiritually and
emotionally, her own child—and his!"

Ehrengard is happy; for she is at last playing out her Walkyrie
nature as, astride her fiery black steed Wotan, she runs the
fugitives to earth at an inn. To the guilty peasant she looks, as she
bursts into their room, like "a young destroying angel". "The
old feudal consciousness of the right to punish seized and held
the daughter of the Schreckensteins."[1] She grips the man by his
long hair and knocks his head against the wall three times. The
chase is a merry rustic chase through a beautiful landscape; the
inn is picturesque; the punishment clownish; and Ehrengard is
touchingly feminine in her masculinity.

Ehrengard is engaged to a cousin, Kurt von Blittersdorff; since
they grew up together, the erotic idea has not yet awakened
between them. Cazotte plans to use the engagement as Kierkegaard's seducer uses the engagement of his girl—to make Ehrengard aware of the erotic idea by contrast to the merely social
convention of engagement. Now it so happens—as it should
happen in comedy—that Kurt, who is an army officer, is
celebrating downstairs with his fellow officers. Hearing the
peasant's screams upstairs, he rushes into the room where Ehrengard is knocking the man's head against the wall. There follows
a most amusing little recognition scene.

" 'Let them tell you whose child it is,' " says the peasant to
the officer. At this point Cazotte enters (the scene is staged as in
a theater so that the three swiftly successive entrances are
increasingly funny). He takes his place quietly on the bed, like
the spectator at a drama. He is to watch the woman who started
as an idea in his head become the reality that confronts him.
" 'It is my child,' " she announces. She says Kurt must promise
to leave her forever, " 'for it is my child. . . . You will have to
believe me,' " she says. " 'I have never in my life lied to you.' "

This first time she lies to Kurt is the moment of her fall and
the apotheosis of her feudal loyalty. She sacrifices everything,
her reputation for virginity and her engagement, to protect her
sovereign's secret. Now that she has fallen and broken their
engagement, the erotic idea awakens between them. Kurt asks,
" 'Who is the father of the child?' " He speaks as though they

[1] New York, pp. 94-97; London, pp. 63-64.

were alone. For to ask that question of the woman you love is to ask who was there in place of me; it is to participate vicariously in the act of begetting the child.

Ehrengard points at Cazotte, lifting her arm "like a young officer at his baptism of fire indicating to his men the entrenchment to be taken". (The image maintains the comedy at the poetic climax.) " 'It is he,' " she says. " 'Herr Cazotte is the father of my child.' " She is right. Cazotte has, like the Holy Ghost, impregnated her with the erotic idea that materialized in the baby.

Once more, Ehrengard has turned the tables on Cazotte. For she has handed him the baby that he planned to hand her. So it is he, consequently, who blushes. "His brow and cheeks, all on their own, radiated a divine fire, a celestial, deep rose flame, as if they were giving away a long kept secret."[1] The secret is his desire to be not only a spiritual seducer but the father of Ehrengard's baby.

Cazotte had planned for Kurt to be the "spiritual cuckold"[2] who would have external possession of Ehrengard while he himself had internal possession. But in naming her spiritual seducer, Ehrengard exorcises him and prepares the way for a union with Kurt of body and soul. By exorcising, as Malli cannot, what we may understand to be a combination of father image and disembodied ideal, Ehrengard is enabled to love two men in Kurt—the ideal and the mortal man. She can therefore step out of the realm of reflection, where Kierkegaard's lovers remain, into the realm of existence. Because she can name both men, she does not, like the lady in "The Ring", pay for existence the price of tragic ambiguity. Ehrengard gets heaven on earth.

The Prince and Princess make the necessary explanations to Kurt; and the betrothed couple attend the baptism of "the newborn Prince"[3] (his second birth parallels the second birth of their engagement), at which Ehrengard wears an Order given to noble ladies for service to the house of Fugger-Babenhausen. Cazotte, who is left in the frustration he planned for Ehrengard, retires to Rome from whence we learn that he has given up spiritual seductions for the orthodox kind. In making the girl turn the tables on her seducer, Isak Dinesen wittily rebukes Kierkegaard and the other men who write tales of seduction in

---

[1] New York, pp. 103-109; London, pp. 68-71.
[2] New York, p. 58; London, p. 39.   [3] New York, p. 111; London, p. 72.

which the woman is a mere passive victim. She bears out Cazotte's remark in his first letter that "to be seduced is the privilege of woman, the which man may well envy her"[1]; and she shows how, in preparing Ehrengard for so perfect a marriage, Cazotte wrought better than he knew. As an artist, Cazotte has been successful; but as an artist, he could not expect to achieve consummation in life as well.

The feudal motif shows the way through the dead end to which Kierkegaard brings the esthetic life. Kierkegaard sets his esthetic seduction in a bourgeois world without pattern. But to win your way to existence you must step, Isak Dinesen suggests, from a reflective or artistic pattern to a pattern in life. The old aristocratic order offers such a pattern in life, which, since it is based on memory, connects with art, desire and spirit. The old aristocratic order shows how—in life as in a story—the ideal in your head can be also the reality that confronts you; it shows how heroic action—which by definition belongs to a patterned reality—can be the counterpart of artistic conception. Isak Dinesen seems to be saying of Kierkegaard that he has, in driving a wedge between the esthetic and the religious life, overlooked the connection of spirit with the Ariel force—the connection that is the subject of all her work.

Isak Dinesen offers through that connection an answer to the split, bequeathed us by the Enlightenment, between fact and value. She accounts for the split by reminding us that if our pre-Enlightenment ancestors saw in people immortality where we see only mortality, it is because they were talking about a different order of person than we have in mind. They were talking about a self that is as much outside as us inside—a self that merges, like smaller Chinese boxes out of larger, from social roles that themselves emerge from archetypal identities. They were talking about a self that draws on enduring powers outside the individual body.

Like other writers of our time, Isak Dinesen has used the modern idea of the unconscious to dissolve the rigid outlines of the self bequeathed us by the Enlightenment. We hear a great deal nowadays about the loss of the self. But the self that has been lost is the autonomous and magically potent self that the nine-

[1] New York, p. 12; London, p. 10.

teenth-century romanticists identified as the one remaining source of value in a world where value was no longer objective. Such high claims for the self could not be long sustained, however, because the self the nineteenth-century romanticists had in mind was still the locked-up self that they had inherited from the Enlightenment. Isak Dinesen salvages the romantic idea of the self by showing that the self is not simply autonomous, but that it emerges—through the connection of consciousness with living, and even with nonliving, unconsciousness—from social roles and archetypal identities that themselves emerge from internal instincts that have their external origin in those earliest tremors of earthly life that were themselves transformations of sunlight, air and water.

Isak Dinesen has devised a way of projecting at once all these phases of the self and the different orders of judgment that may appropriately be turned on each. She shows that when all phases of the self are operative, then the self must be judged as, like nature, innocent. But she also shows—and this is what makes her, along with Yeats, Mann, Joyce and Eliot, distinctively twentieth-century—that it is through symbols that all phases of the self are made operative. By enabling us to recognize other phases of the self in ourselves and others, symbols enable us to pass from one phase of the self to the other and thus achieve fulfillment.

That is what happens to Ehrengard, who moves from feudal to erotic symbols to combine the two "ideas" in a heroic "action" that shows her what she desires and who she is. Ehrengard can do this because Rosenbad is, in its architecture, décor, gardens and statuary, the house of Europe. As maker of the story through which she moves, Cazotte has made available to her the community of symbols we call our culture. He has brought her to fulfillment by making it possible for her to pass from his mind into an external reality that is the mind of Europe and, beyond that, the mind of God. We fulfill ourselves by a movement analogous to the structure of Isak Dinesen's stories. We step into ever intenser realities, which is to say into an ever larger mind that is both inside us and outside.

This is Isak Dinesen's answer to the question raised by her theme of vicariousness—the question, bequeathed us by the Enlightenment, whether values exist only in the mind or are really out there. Her answer is (and she is saying in her terms what other writers of our time say in theirs) that to the extent that life is like a story—to the extent that it makes us fulfill ourselves in ways we did not consciously intend—we are living at the point where our desires meet with external forces. And at that point, inside and outside are two aspects, forever exchanging places, of the same reality. To the extent, in other words, that life is like a story in having any value at all, there could be no value inside if there were none outside, and vice versa.

It is remarkable, in an age which is on the surface growing ever more chaotic, how many writers are quietly reorganizing our idea of the world by reorganizing our idea of the self. I say quietly, because we have been so absorbed by the negative things our modern writers have been saying, that we have hardly caught up as yet with what they have been telling us in a positive way. If, as Isak Dinesen tells us, the white race has since the Industrial Revolution taken a path that separates it from the rest of the world and from the past, then the work of Freud and Jung is leading us, through its implications, back to union with at least the past (since the rest of the world are now following in our tracks). We are being led back, I think, to a mood of acceptance like the old tragic fatalism; but an acceptance which, because it will be based on knowledge rather than ignorance, should result not in the fear in which the world was anciently bound, but in confidence. The lessons of our modern writers, when we have learned them, cannot help but affect our view of the world; and Isak Dinesen's stories suggest what that view may be. They suggest that science, when it has finally been understood, when it has been absorbed into our culture and turned back into the poetry from which it originally sprang, will lead to a comic view of life and will manifest itself in an art which will be, in its final effect, comic.

Isak Dinesen recapitulates in her stories—in the evolution of Lady Flora after she kisses the statue, in the evolving aspects of Babette's dinner and in the evolution of Babette herself into a marble monument, in the evolution of a cynical story like *Ehrengard* into a pastoral comedy—Isak Dinesen recapitulates the change in European perceptions of reality during the last three or four centuries. By imposing upon each other, in the same story, at least three different judgments of the same events, she shows how we lost unity of perception and how we may regain it.

For when we look at life with single vision, with the one analytic eye that cuts facts off from value, then life is meaningless and depressing. When we look at it with both eyes, with the understanding and sympathy that enables us to project ourselves into events and other people, then life is beautiful and sad. But when, using more than our eyes, using also the resources of cultural and biological memory, we look through life, seeing it in a transforming vision that collapses the single person and event into a pattern of recurrence and our highest aspiration into our most primitive instinct, then we see how every part of life is necessary, how we could not have what we call the highest without what we call the lowest. Then we see life as the storyteller does, as we may imagine God does. We see it as beautiful and sad—and gay.

PUBLICATIONS BY AND ABOUT
ISAK DINESEN

With only a few exceptions, this list is limited to publications in English and Danish. For all the foreign editions of Isak Dinesen's books, see the catalogue of the Royal Library of Copenhagen. Unpublished material at Rungstedlund includes 41 handwritten notebooks.

Books by Isak Dinesen

Isak Dinesen, *Seven Gothic Tales* (New York: Harrison Smith and Robert Haas; London: Putnam, 1934).

Isak Dinesen, *Syv fantastiske Fortællinger* (Copenhagen: Reitzels, 1935).

Isak Dinesen, *Out of Africa* (London: Putnam, 1937; New York: Random House, 1938).

Karen Blixen, *Den afrikanske Farm* (Copenhagen: Gyldendal, 1937).

Isak Dinesen, *Winter's Tales* (New York: Random House; London: Putnam, 1942).

Karen Blixen, *Vinter-Eventyr* (Copenhagen: Gyldendal, 1942).

Pierre Andrézel, *Gengældelsens Veje*, "translated into Danish by Clara Svendsen [sic]" (Copenhagen: Gyldendal, 1944).

Pierre Andrézel, *The Angelic Avengers* (London: Putnam, 1946; New York: Random House, 1947).

Isak Dinesen, *Last Tales* (New York: Random House; London: Putnam, 1957).

Karen Blixen, *Sidste Fortællinger* (Copenhagen: Gyldendal, 1957).

Isak Dinesen, *Anecdotes of Destiny* (New York: Random House; London: Michael Joseph, 1958).

Karen Blixen, *Skæbne-Anekdoter* (Copenhagen: Gyldendal, 1958).

Karen Blixen, *Skygger paa Græsset* (Copenhagen: Gyldendal, 1960).

Isak Dinesen, *Shadows on the Grass* (New York: Random House; London: Michael Joseph, 1961).

——, *Osceola* [posthumous collection of her early Danish stories and poems], ed. Clara Svendsen (Copenhagen: Gyldendal, 1962).

BIBLIOGRAPHY

Isak Dinesen, *Ehrengard* (New York: Random House;   London: Michael Joseph, 1963).

Karen Blixen, *Ehrengard*, translated from English into Danish by Clara Svendsen (Copenhagen: Gyldendal, 1963).

Karen Blixen, Memorial edition of the mature fiction and *Den afrikanske Farm*, 7 vols. (Copenhagen: Gyldendal, 1964). *Skygger paa Græsset* already in this format; a volume of essays to come out later.

Booklets, Essays, Magazine Publications by Isak Dinesen

Osceola, "Eneboerne", *Tilskueren*, August 1907, pp. 609-35. Reprinted in *Osceola*.

Osceola, "Pløjeren", *Gads Danske Magasin*, October 1907, pp. 50-59. Reprinted in *Osceola*.

Osceola, "Familien de Cats", *Tilskueren*, January 1909, pp. 1-19. Reprinted in *Osceola*.

——, "En Stjerne" [poem], quoted in Thomas Dinesen, *No Man's Land* (Copenhagen: Reitzels, 1929), pp. 199-200. Reprinted in *Osceola*.

K. Blixen-Finecke, "Ex-Africa" [poem], *Tilskueren*, April 1925, pp. 244-46; *Berlingske Søndags Magasin*, December 6, 1942, pp. 1-2. Reprinted in *Osceola*.

Karen Blixen-Finecke, "Sandhedens Hævn: En Marionet-komedie", *Tilskueren*, May 1926, pp. 329-44; (Copenhagen: Gyldendal, 1960) under the name Karen Blixen.

Isak Dinesen, "Karyatiderne: En ufuldendt fantastisk Fortæl-ling", *Bonniers litterära Magasin* [Swedish], March 1938, pp. 166-93; *Tilskueren*, April 1938, pp. 269-308; "The Caryatids: An Unfinished Gothic Tale", *Ladies' Home Journal*, November 1957, pp. 64 ff. Reprinted in *Last Tales*.

Karen Blixen, "Om Retskrivn'ng" ["On Spelling"], *Politiken*, March 23-24, 1938 (Copenhagen: Gyldendal, 1949).

Isak Dinesen, "Sorrow-acre", *Ladies' Home Journal*, May 1943, pp. 22 ff. From *Winter's Tales*.

Karen Blixen, "Breve fra et Land i Krig", *Heretica* 1, 1948, No. 4, pp. 264-87; No. 5, pp. 332-55. Reprinted in *Dansk Skrivekunst*, ed. Erling Nielsen (Oslo: Cappelens, 1955), pp. 1-34.

Isak Dinesen, "The Uncertain Heiress", *Saturday Evening Post*, December 10, 1949, pp. 35 ff.

Karen Blixen, *Farah* (Copenhagen: Wivel, 1950). Reprinted in *Shadows on the Grass*.

288

Isak Dinesen, "Babette's Feast", *Ladies' Home Journal*, June 1950, pp. 34 ff; *Babettes Gæstebud* (Copenhagen: Fremad, 1955). Reprinted in *Anecdotes of Destiny*.

Isak Dinesen, "The Ring", *Ladies' Home Journal*, July 1950, pp. 36 ff; *Harper's Bazaar*, October 1958, pp. 159 ff. Reprinted in *Anecdotes of Destiny*.

Karen Blixen, "Hartvig Frisch som Nabo" [essay], in *Hartvig Frisch* (Copenhagen: Fremad, 1950), pp. 26-32.

Karen Blixen, *Daguerreotypier* (Copenhagen: Gyldendal, 1951).

Isak Dinesen, "The Ghost Horses", *Ladies' Home Journal*, October 1951, pp. 56 ff; *Spøgelseshestene* (Copenhagen: Fremad, 1955).

Karen Blixen, *Kardinalens Tredie Historie*, illus. Erik Clemmesen (Copenhagen: Gyldendal, 1952). Reprinted in *Last Tales*.

Karen Blixen, *Omkring den nye Lov om Dyreforsøg* (Copenhagen: Politiken, 1952).

Karen Blixen, "Samtale om Natten i København", *Heretica* VI, 1953, No. 5, pp. 465-94. Reprinted in *Last Tales*.

Isak Dinesen, "The Immortal Story", *Ladies' Home Journal*, February 1953, pp. 34 ff. Reprinted in *Anecdotes of Destiny*.

Karen Blixen, *En Baaltale med 14 Aars Forsinkelse* (Copenhagen: Berlingske Forlag, 1953); *Det danske Magasin* I, 1953, No. 2, pp. 65-82.

Karen Blixen, "Dykkeren", *Vindrosen* I, November 1954, pp. 400-414. Reprinted in *Anecdotes of Destiny*.

Isak Dinesen, "The Cloak", *Ladies' Home Journal*, May 1955, pp. 52 ff. Reprinted in *Last Tales* as "The Cloak", "Night Walk", "Of Secret Thoughts and of Heaven".

Karen Blixen, review of Sacheverell Sitwell's *Denmark*, *Sunday Times* of London, May 6, 1956, p. 5.

Isak Dinesen, "A Country Tale", *Botteghe Oscure* [international magazine published in Rome], XIX, 1957, pp. 367-417; *Ladies' Home Journal*, March 1960, pp. 52 ff. Reprinted in *Last Tales*.

Isak Dinesen, "Echoes", *Atlantic Monthly*, November 1957, pp. 96-100. Reprinted in *Last Tales*.

Isak Dinesen, "The Nobleman's Wife", *Harper's Bazaar*, November 1957, pp. 139 ff. From "Tales of Two Old Gentlemen", *Last Tales*.

Karen Blixen, "Den store Gestus", *Alt for Damerne* 1957, No. 51, pp. 10-14. Reprinted in *Anecdotes of Destiny*.

Karen Blixen, "H. C. Branner: Rytteren" [literary criticism], *Bazar*, April 1958, pp. 50-63; May, pp. 71-94.

Isak Dinesen, "The Wine of the Tetrarch", *Atlantic Monthly*, December 1959, pp. 125-30. From "Deluge at Norderney", *Seven Gothic Tales*; as told in American recitals.

Isak Dinesen, "The Blue Eyes", *Ladies' Home Journal*, January 1960, p. 38. From "Peter and Rosa", *Winter's Tales*; expanded version used in final American recital.

Isak Dinesen, "Alexander and the Sybil", in Glenway Wescott, "Isak Dinesen Tells a Tale", *Harper's*, March 1960, pp. 69-70. From "Tales of Two Old Gentlemen", *Last Tales*.

Isak Dinesen, "On Mottoes of My Life", *Proceedings of the American Academy of Arts and Letters and the National Institute of Arts and Letters*, Second Series, Number Ten (New York, 1960), pp. 345-58. Reprinted as booklet by the Danish Ministry of Foreign Affairs, 1962.

Karen Blixen, Introduction to Truman Capote, *Holly* (Copenhagen: Gyldendal, 1960).

Isak Dinesen, Introduction to Olive Schreiner, *The Story of an African Farm* (New York: Limited Editions Club, 1961).

Karen Blixen, Introduction to Basil Davidson, *Det genfundne Afrika* (Copenhagen: Gyldendal, 1962).

Isak Dinesen, Introduction to Hans Christian Andersen, *Thumbelina and Other Fairy Tales* (New York and London: Macmillan, 1962).

Karen Blixen, "Rungstedlund: En radiotale" [essay], in *Hilsen til Otto Gelsted* (Aarhus: Sirius, 1958), pp. 18-41. Condensed as Isak Dinesen, "Tale of Rungstedlund", *Vogue*, November 1962, pp. 132 ff.

Isak Dinesen, "The Secret of Rosenbad", *Ladies' Home Journal*, December 1962, pp. 51 ff. Condensation of *Ehrengard*.

Books and Selected Articles on Isak Dinesen

Bror von Blixen-Finecke, *African Hunter*, translated from the Swedish by F. H. Lyon (London: Cassell, 1937; New York: Knopf, 1938).

BIBLIOGRAPHY

Mark Van Doren, "The Eighth Gothic Tale [on *Out of Africa*]", *The Private Reader* (New York: Holt, 1942), pp. 277-81.

Per Vogt, "Tilfellet Karen Blixen", *Tendenser Mot Tiden: Kulturessays og Portretter* (Oslo: Tanum, 1946), pp. 123-39.

Tom Kristensen, "Syv fantastiske Fortællinger", *Mellem Krigene* (Copenhagen: Gyldendal, 1946), pp. 134-40.

Hans Brix, *Karen Blixens Eventyr* (Copenhagen: Gyldendal, 1949).

Hans Brix, "*Sandhedens Hævn* Til Isak Dinesen: 'Vejene omkring Pisa' ", "Et Eventyr af Karen Blixen", *Analyser og Problemer* vi (Copenhagen: Gyldendal, 1950), pp. 286-306.

Christian Elling, "Karen Blixen", *Danske Digtere i det Tyvende Aarhundrede*, ed. Ernst Frandsen and Niels Kaas Johansen (Copenhagen: Gads, 1951), pp. 521-55.

Ernst Frandsen, "Udsigt over et halvt Aarhundrede", in above book, pp. 5-32.

Aage Henriksen, *Karen Blixen og Marionetterne* (Copenhagen: Wivel, 1952).

Vagn Riisager, *Karen Blixen* (Copenhagen: Gyldendal, 1952).

Jørgen Claudi, *Contemporary Danish Authors* ([Copenhagen]: Det Danske Selskab, 1952), pp. 109-14.

Børge G. Madsen, "Isak Dinesen, a Modern Aristocrat", *American-Scandinavian Review*, Winter 1953, pp. 328-32.

Jørgen Gustava Brandt, "Et Essay om Karen Blixen", *Heretica* vi, 1953, No. 2, pp. 200-23; No. 3, pp. 300-20.

Louise Bogan, "Isak Dinesen", *Selected Criticism* (New York: Noonday, 1955), pp. 231-34.

Aage Henriksen, *Guder og galgefugle* (Oslo: N-S-K, 1956).

Harald Nielsen, *Karen Blixen: Studie i litterær Mystik* (Copenhagen: Borgens, 1956).

John Davenport, "A Noble Pride: The Art of Karen Blixen", *The Twentieth Century*, March 1956, pp. 264-74.

Eugene Walter, "Isak Dinesen" [interview], *Paris Review*, Autumn 1956, pp. 43-59.

Johannes Rosendahl, *Karen Blixen: Fire Foredrag* (Copenhagen: Gyldendal, 1957).

Louis E. Grandjean, *Blixens Animus* (Copenhagen: Grandjeans Publications Fond, 1957).

P. M. Mitchell, *A History of Danish Literature* (Copenhagen: Gyldendal, 1957), pp. 275-78.

BIBLIOGRAPHY

Giacomo Antonini, "I Racconti Bizzarri di Isak Dinesen", *La Fiera Letteraria* [Italian magazine], June 22, 1958, pp. 7-8.

Ole Vinding, "Karen Blixen og det gyldne snit", *Ord Och Bild* [Swedish magazine], 1958, No. 1, pp. 47-52.

Erik Sönderholm, "Karen Blixen", *Helgafell* [Icelandic magazine] IV, 1959, No. 2, pp. 122-26; Nos. 3-4, pp. 191-98.

Jean Stafford, "Isak Dinesen: Master Teller of Tales" [interview], *Horizon*, September 1959, pp. 111-12.

Curtis Cate, "Isak Dinesen: The Scheherezade of Our Times", *Cornhill*, Winter 1959-60, pp. 120-37; "Isak Dinesen", *Atlantic Monthly*, December 1959, pp. 151-55.

Eric O. Johannesson, *The World of Isak Dinesen* (Seattle: University of Washington Press, 1961).

Glenway Wescott, "Isak Dinesen, the Storyteller", *Images of Truth* (New York and Evanston: Harper and Row, 1962), Chapter 6.

Kuno Poulsen, "Karen Blixens gamle og nye testamente", *Vindrosen X*, 1963, No. 5, pp. 364-80.

Karen Blixen [memorial anthology, with prose and verse by European, American and African contributors], translated into Danish and edited by Clara Svendsen and Ole Wivel (Copenhagen: Gyldendal, 1962).

Isak Dinesen [memorial anthology] (New York: Random House, 1964). Prints contributions in English, French and German, but omits Danish contributions except for articles in English by Thomas Dinesen and Clara Svendsen.

Hanne Marie and Werner Svendsen, *Geschichte der dänischen Literatur* (Copenhagen: Gyldendal, 1964), pp. 478-80.

INDEX

Robert Langbaum was born in New York City in 1924. He entered Cornell University in 1940, taking a leave of absence in 1942 to enlist in the Army, where he learned Japanese and was assigned to translate Japanese documents in Japan and the United States for Military Intelligence. He returned to Cornell for his A.B., and in 1949 received his M.A. in English from Columbia University. He began teaching English at Cornell in 1950, and received his doctorate from Columbia in 1954. His doctoral dissertation, *The Poetry of Experience*, was published in England and the United States in 1957, and was reissued in paperback in 1963. His edition of Shakespeare's *The Tempest* was published in 1964.

Mr. Langbaum married Francesca Levi Vidale in 1950; their daughter was born in 1956. In 1960, Mr. Langbaum moved to the University of Virginia, where he is now Professor of English. In writing about Isak Dinesen, he traveled to Denmark in the summers of 1959 and 1961, and the project won for him a Ford Fellowship for 1961-62. Among the many journals that have published Professor Langbaum's articles and reviews on literary and political subjects are *The American Scholar*, *Commentary*, *Virginia Quarterly Review*, *New York Herald Tribune Book Review*, *Saturday Review* and *PMLA*.